ALSO BY DANIEL SMITH

Monkey Mind: A Memoir of Anxiety

Muses, Madmen, and Prophets: Hearing Voices and the Borders of Sanity

HARD FEELINGS

*Finding the Wisdom
in Our Darkest Emotions*

DANIEL SMITH

SIMON & SCHUSTER
New York Amsterdam/Antwerp London
Toronto Sydney/Melbourne New Delhi

Simon & Schuster
1230 Avenue of the Americas
New York, NY 10020

For more than 100 years, Simon & Schuster has championed authors and the stories they create. By respecting the copyright of an author's intellectual property, you enable Simon & Schuster and the author to continue publishing exceptional books for years to come. We thank you for supporting the author's copyright by purchasing an authorized edition of this book.

No amount of this book may be reproduced or stored in any format, nor may it be uploaded to any website, database, language-learning model, or other repository, retrieval, or artificial intelligence system without express permission. All rights reserved. Inquiries may be directed to Simon & Schuster, 1230 Avenue of the Americas, New York, NY 10020 or permissions@simonandschuster.com.

Copyright © 2026 by Daniel Smith

All rights reserved, including the right to reproduce this book or portions thereof in any form whatsoever. For information, address Simon & Schuster Subsidiary Rights Department, 1230 Avenue of the Americas, New York, NY 10020.

First Simon & Schuster hardcover edition March 2026

SIMON & SCHUSTER and colophon are registered trademarks of Simon & Schuster, LLC

"Every Single Night." Written by Fiona Apple Maggart (ASCAP). ℗ 2012 by FHW Music (ASCAP). © 2012 Sony Music Entertainment Inc.
Used by permission. All rights reserved.

Simon & Schuster strongly believes in freedom of expression and stands against censorship in all its forms. For more information, visit BooksBelong.com.

For information about special discounts for bulk purchases, please contact Simon & Schuster Special Sales at 1-866-506-1949 or business@simonandschuster.com.

The Simon & Schuster Speakers Bureau can bring authors to your live event. For more information or to book an event, contact the Simon & Schuster Speakers Bureau at 1-866-248-3049 or visit our website at www.simonspeakers.com.

Interior design by Carly Loman

Manufactured in the United States of America

1 3 5 7 9 10 8 6 4 2

ISBN 978-1-9821-0390-3
ISBN 978-1-9821-0392-7 (ebook)

Let's stay in touch! Scan here to get book recommendations, exclusive offers, and more delivered to your inbox.

*For Emily Bobrow
and for Marilyn Smith*

Every involuntary repulsion that arises in your mind, give heed unto. It is the surface of a central truth.

—EMERSON

... emotion is biography.

—DONALD NATHANSON,
Shame and Pride: Affect, Sex, and the Birth of the Self

CONTENTS

PART ONE

chapter one **THE GIFTS**   3
chapter two **THE MORALITY OF EMOTIONS (A BRIEF HISTORY)**   22
chapter three **WHAT IS AN EMOTION?**   30

PART TWO

chapter four **ANNOYANCE**   57
chapter five **SHAME**   82
chapter six **ENVY**   105

PART THREE

chapter seven **BOREDOM**   137
chapter eight **REGRET**   161
chapter nine **DESPAIR**   187

ACKNOWLEDGMENTS 215
SELECTED BIBLIOGRAPHY 219
INDEX 231

PART ONE

chapter one

THE GIFTS

Six months before my second child was born, I turned forty, and my wife threw me a party at a local beer garden. It was one of the great events of my life. The garden, lush and dim, with wrought-iron lampposts along its border, was filled with smiling people I adored. My friend Peter made chocolate chip cookies with sea salt crystals on top. Emily, my wife, made a chocolate layer cake. There were steak fries and warm Bavarian pretzels and dry red wine and pitchers of good beer. My mother tumbled backward off a low fence and was caught just in time by a nimble cousin. Everyone talked to one another; everyone got along. At midnight, Emily and I carried the gifts home in sturdy shopping bags, breathless and grateful. I couldn't stop kissing her. We had been married for just three months.

The next morning, I woke up and walked downstairs to make coffee. I filled the kettle, set it on the stove, and turned the burner to high. Then I sat down at the kitchen table and began to unpack my gifts.

I had unwrapped the gifts at the party, but only in a ceremonial way, to show my appreciation. Now I looked them over more carefully, and my attention immediately fixed on two in particular. These gifts were books. The first, from Stephen and Franny, two of my dearest friends, was a leather-bound, two-volume set, published in London during the reign of King George III, of Robert Burton's 1621 treatise, *The Anatomy of Melancholy*. The second, from my two older brothers, was an immense coffee-table book, as heavy as a large newborn baby, of the complete paintings and drawings of Hieronymus Bosch.

I laid these books in front of me on the table and, in a state of pre-caffeine haziness, I thumbed through them. I already had some idea of what they would contain. I had never read Burton, but I knew of his enormous influence and his reputation for strangeness and complexity. As for Bosch, I had stood in front of two of his paintings during a long-ago trip to Venice with my ex-wife, and I had seen reproductions of many more. Still, the books startled and troubled me. They teemed with lurid, exquisite horrors: rage, terror, grief, self-hatred, despair, torture, suicide. They were, each in their own odd and obsessive ways, vast catalogs of human suffering, encyclopedias of misery. And they were my birthday presents, offerings at the delicate entryway to middle age—and to a new life, a new configuration of family and meaning—from four of the people who knew and loved me best in the world.

On the flyleaf of the first Burton volume I found an engraving of a man in the grip of a depressive panic. The man stares past the frame, locked into his private torment. His eyes are wild. His hair is wild. His wife and young child clamor helplessly at his knee. Beneath the image lay an epigraph, a snippet of verse from a minor eighteenth-century poet.

> *...forgotten quite*
> *All former scenes of dear delight,*
> *Connubial love — parental joy —*
> *No sympathies like these his soul employ;*
> *But all is dark within...*

The title page of the Bosch had wings that opened into a minutely rendered vision of Hell. Wretched souls, pale and thin as worms, hang from gibbets, or are mocked and persecuted by leering demons, or writhe together in a thick, dark muck. One man is being driven at the head of a wooden cart, like an ox. Others drown in a black lake. The only light in the painting is the light of flames, from hellfire and ruins and the roasting corpses of the damned.

The kettle screamed. I turned off the burner. For a minute or two, I stood above these gifts, trying to decide in what spirit—with what level of irony or self-awareness—I should receive them. Then I switched off the kitchen light, climbed the stairs, and crawled back into bed.

•

In the weeks that followed, I tried not to think about the books. I stowed them high atop a living room bookcase, like contraband, between a boxed set of Graham Greene novels and an illustrated history of *Saturday Night Live*, and I went about my business. This was a heady time, a period of energetic fussing. We had a lot to do to prepare for our son's arrival: onesies and blankets to wash and fold; hand-me-downs to unpack and organize; diapers, creams, moisturizers, and wipes to order. But the main thing was just to wait and try to enjoy the temporary calm. Emily and I took many long, rambling walks during which we could not stop marveling at our luck: that we had met each other after experiences of intense heartbreak and loneliness, that we were well-matched and in love, and that we had conceived, at our ages, immediately, with no difficulty at all. We understood our good fortune and we acknowledged it as one might offer thanks to God, with the humility of having known the alternatives. I was happier, I think, than I had ever been.

Still, those books wouldn't quite leave my mind. I would be loading the dishwasher or fetching a package from the stoop or trimming my beard in the mirror and I would remember them, and my heart would jump a little. I didn't know why they had this effect. I only knew that it felt like an intrusion, an unpleasant insistence from the shadows, and I didn't like it.

The fall went by quickly. So did the winter. Emily grew. She would look at her body in the bureau mirror and burst out laughing, tickled by its oddness. We were tickled, also, by the ultrasound images of our child inside her, all head and budding limbs, somehow already boyish in profile, I thought, and serene.

In February, just after Valentine's Day, we decided to leave the city for the weekend. I booked us a room at a bed-and-breakfast in the Hudson Valley. We wanted to lie around and read, and be served in a nice restaurant, and go to see art at Dia Beacon, the modern art museum. We didn't know when we might have the chance to do these things again.

We arrived at the museum on a Sunday afternoon. It had snowed heavily the night before, and the museum entrance was crowded with couples and families. A group of children in wool hats and colorful boots chased each other around the bright hall, squealing. Two of them, towheaded twins in matching green jackets with epaulets, wielded rolled-up floor plans like billy clubs. I became annoyed and impatient. I had hoped to arrive at the museum earlier, to avoid any crowds, but Emily had wanted to walk and I hadn't wanted to disappoint her. I regretted not disappointing her. Now we would have to thread our way through throngs of people with their outstretched iPhones to see the art. We would have to dodge and scheme for the best angle, the clear view. It would be an ordeal just to enjoy ourselves. It would hardly be worth the effort.

I glowered at the children, willing them to shut up. For a moment, I imagined them muzzled and bolted to the wall in some dank medieval dungeon. Then I became annoyed with myself, and ashamed, for I noticed that I was on vacation with my pregnant wife and mentally imprisoning children. It was pathetic. It was a sign of my intolerance and sense of entitlement. It was absurd to feel that I had any greater right to the museum than anyone else there. Emily stood slightly ahead of me on the ticket line. I tried to pull myself together. I didn't want her turning around, noticing my mood, and becoming irritated in turn. I didn't want to spoil a rare trip away for us, and likely the last for a while.

As it happened, I had gotten worked up for no reason. Dia Beacon is a sprawling, cavernous place, and it easily accommodated and diluted the crowds. The space seemed even to dilute sound, drawing it up to the vaulted ceiling and dispersing it. A cool, diffuse light, almost colorless, ideal, filled the museum.

Yet I couldn't shake my foul mood. The anger, frustration, resentment, impatience, and shame stuck to me like burrs. Or, more accurately, they were like tablets, salts, that had plopped into the pool of my mind and dissolved, and were now inseparable from it. It couldn't have helped matters that the art on display was so demanding and austere: a large square canvas painted uniformly white; a single plywood panel bisecting an empty room; a long gray beam on a bare floor. In my state, I had more trouble than usual communing with these abstractions, and the more trouble I had the worse I felt. As we passed from gallery to gallery, I pressed a thin smile onto my face. I tried to achieve an expression of intelligent consideration. *Ah yes, I see. How remarkable.* Emily, a walking, curly-haired bullshit detector, wasn't buying it. She read me perfectly, and, out of admirable self-preservation, she drifted farther and farther away. After twenty minutes, we were in separate galleries.

This didn't help either. But what could I do? She was right to distance herself. She was wise to safeguard her own experience and leave me to mine. I walked around, hoping for the natural return of equanimity. I walked past Robert Smithson's shattered glass, past Gerhard Richter's tall gray mirrors, past Maren Hassinger's field of wire rope—works of jaggedness and dread that affected me exactly as they were meant to. Then I came to a far corner of the museum and a sculpture by Michael Heizer titled *North, East, South, West*.

I call it a sculpture. It is in fact the inverse of a sculpture. It is a monument in negative space. Across the full length of the gallery Heizer had cut or inserted into the metal floor four enormous geometric shapes: a partial cone, a cone, a wedge, and two stacked cubes, one large and one small. In other words, holes in the ground. Very large holes. The goal, according to the wall text, was to create "an atmosphere of awe" so that the viewer would feel that "something has been transcended."

Looking at *North, East, South, West* from behind a glass barrier, from a distance, I did not feel awe, and I did not feel that anything in myself had been transcended. On the contrary, what I felt was the pull and power of everything in myself, in my character and mind, that was not transcended and probably never would be. What I felt, with a mounting nausea, was that I was not rising above anything at all. I was sinking deeper into myself.

From where I stood I couldn't tell how deep the holes went. I could see no bottoms to them at all. I could see only the gradual dissipation of the light, which suggested movement downward, downward without discernible end. The longer I stared—and I must have stared for a long time—the more dismaying the experience became. How to explain it? It was like collapsing and falling into my own shadow.

That night, back home, I had trouble sleeping. When I finally did sleep, I dreamed of my son, born and standing and conscious—frightfully conscious. He was watching me, absorbing me like radiation. He was swelling, gorging on forces that he took from me, or that I gave to him. I could see them through his pale skin, swirling like strands of chocolate in a glass of milk. They looked like puffs of smoke in a balloon. I awoke holding my breath.

In the morning, I retrieved those books from the living room and carried them into my office, where I have had them with me ever since. Year after year, through disappointments and delights; through my son's birth and early childhood; through the birth, two years later, of a daughter; through my return to school and the beginning of a second career as a psychotherapist; through the ebb and flow of friendships; through the long, tumultuous illness of my oldest child; through deaths, creative blocks, conflicts, crises, anniversaries, celebrations, and a multitude of uncertainties—through all the flux and confusion of this, my deepening middle age, I have kept those two books on a shelf beside my desk, at the border of my vision. They serve as a kind of symbol. They are a reminder, whenever I need one, of those parts of myself that I cannot and should not allow myself to forget. They are the voice that says, "Here we are. Here you are, in all your stubborn, varied, fractious, ever-recurring darkness.

"Now, what are you going to do about it?"

•

The most constant thing I can detect in myself is the turbulence of my emotions. The most reliable thing about me is that I am buffeted, often moment to moment, by forces that feel out of control. My mother, who is an experienced and skilled psychotherapist, has said that I am "emotionally labile," a clinical term that suggests that my emotions are subject to rapid, unexpected change. A therapist of my own once observed that I am prone to "emotional escalation." A girlfriend once accused me, more (I think) in fondness than in criticism, of being "melodramatic." My ex-wife would say, and has said, justifiably, that I am grouchy and cranky. So, as it happens, has Emily. My friend Kate says that we are alike and members of a club: the club of the overwrought.

What would I say? I don't exactly know. I don't yet have the language, if any organizing language exists, to describe the clutter, complexity, and inhospitality of my emotional constitution. After nearly a half century of life, there are aspects of my personality and experience I like to think I understand well enough. I like to think I could say clear, useful things about writing and loss and humor and what happens when you rely a little too much on your intellect to get you through. But about those forces that routinely take hold of me and pull me under, that alter and distort me and sometimes make me hard to live with and be around—that make it hard for me to live with and be around myself . . . about these "negative emotions," as we tend to refer to them, I often feel as ignorant as a child.

When my friends and brothers bought me those books for my birthday, they weren't trying to alert me to my ignorance. They weren't making a commentary at all. They were appealing to my interests—in art, in literature, in religion, and above all in mental health and mental illness. They were being generous. "Jesus, we didn't mean to make you rethink your entire life," my brother David said. "They were just gifts." But we receive gifts, as we receive most things, within a context that isn't necessarily clear to the giver, or to us. The conditions of our lives endow objects with resonances they were never meant to carry.

In this case, there were three conditions, three contexts that conspired to pique my self-consciousness and provoke this book-length reckoning with these feelings.

The first context was an emotional explosion, a kind of Krakatoa of the mind. Five years before that birthday party, during a summer that had been shaping up to be one of the most gratifying and significant of my life, my first marriage abruptly ended. I say "abruptly," but short of sudden or accidental death no marriage ends abruptly. Every divorce is overdetermined, the terminus of a hundred thousand insults, misunderstandings, and offenses, most of them studiously unclocked by the conscious mind.

There had been problems; I knew that. Serious conflicts about parenting, money, sex, and our incompatible aspirations for the future. We were in couples therapy. But we lived in New York—most couples we knew were in therapy—and through it all I had never doubted the permanence of our commitment to each other. Had I ever been so misguided? It was like suffering from a chest cold and then being told, "No. No, I'm sorry, it's Ebola. You have Ebola. Did you really not notice the blood pouring from your eyes?"

But it felt abrupt. It felt as abrupt and incongruous as a bomb at a feast. I had just published a book, a memoir, that was gaining wide and positive attention, and that seemed poised to provide us with a degree of financial security we had for too many anxious years been lacking. The book was both dedicated to and, in part, about my wife. It told the story of our courtship and marriage, a narrative of difficulties and reversals ending, like an Elizabethan comedy, in joyful union. It was an appealing, hopeful story—I intended it to be—and its success seemed a good omen. In July, the *Today* show called. A producer came to our apartment to interview my wife and me. They shot B-roll of us walking hand in hand down the sidewalk outside our building, smiling. Good omens. Then, in August, hours before we were to leave on vacation, as our daughter played in the next room, my wife sat on the edge of our bed and informed me in a tone that blended grief, anger, and relief that she did not want me. Probably she never had.

In an instant, everything changed. My understanding of myself as a husband, someone devoted fully and sacramentally to my marriage, without conditions, collapsed. My understanding of myself as a father, as a daily, sustained force in my daughter's life, collapsed. My understanding of my wisdom, my sexual desirability, my ability to apprehend reality as it presented itself to me—my understanding, not least, of where on earth I was going to sleep from that night on—collapsed, and I was left swaying on the floorboards like a boxer in late rounds. A couple of hours later, not knowing what else to do, we left for the ferry to take us to the beach. For the next forty-eight hours I drank Negra Modelos and glowered at the Atlantic as though, if only I stared intently enough, a solution would rise out of the ocean like Venus to set things back to right.

But there was no solution. There wasn't even a satisfyingly cogent explanation I could recite. There was only the sensation of one life ending and another not yet discovered. There was only the strain and vertigo of tremendous loss.

It didn't escape my notice, after the initial shock, that one of the salient causes of my impending divorce was my propensity for darkness and my wife's distaste for that propensity. It wasn't any single offensive emotion but a complex of morbid feeling. A spirit of pessimism, of sharpness, negativity, and doubt. I've always been too easily irritated, a little curmudgeonly, a tad misanthropic.

When I was younger, I would have defended this tragic view of the world on grounds of ice-cold granite realism. Life, all the available evidence suggested, was shot through with loss, pain, ignorance, confusion, cruelty, and injustice, and while it was crucial to laugh your way through the mortal darkness, to discount or deny the darkness was to stake out an unforgivably stupid position. Otherwise you were a dupe, a Pangloss, a Forrest Gump. When my wife and I started dating, she lived with two friends from high school. One of them, T., would often smile broadly and say, "Never had a bad day in my life!" I liked T. He worked with disadvantaged youth. He was considering joining the seminary. He was kind, welcoming, generous, and fun. I was sincerely grateful for his existence. Yet I could not for the life of me abide this buoyant, shiny exclamation. Every time he said it I wanted to sit him down and show him a high-res photo of a tumor, or his mother in childbirth, or his own grave.

In short, I was young. I was young, callow, and I read too much. Social critics no longer accuse literature of corrupting the young—

other forces now do that work more efficiently and at a greater scale—but that doesn't mean literature is no longer up to the job. Take a sheltered, oversensitive, suburban American male with no athletic prowess and a mild social phobia, train him from a young age to idealize poetry and novels—particularly "serious" poetry and novels written after, say, 1918—throw in a dead father for good measure, and you will more than likely end up with someone who derives maybe just a touch more of his worldview from *The Waste Land* than is good for him. Some children dream of being astronauts or firefighters; I dreamed of being paid to complain on TV, like Andy Rooney.

But the negativity I embraced as a sign of my astute intelligence in my twenties had curdled into something unmanageable in my post-divorce thirties. My friend Stephen has referred to this time as my "period of disorientation." It was a kind of madness, and it lasted years. In a way, it lasts still. What had once felt cohesive and holistic—a mental tapestry—became frustrated, wild, restless, and loud. Loud thoughts. Loud perceptions. Loud emotions. My petty irritation, my listless boredom, my destabilizing envy, my pointless regrets, my abject pessimism, my pitiless and self-mocking shame: Everything got amplified. The worst parts of me, the parts that sap me of vigor, momentum, and compassion, the parts that my education and good sense have led me to disdain, rose up, snapped through their handcuffs, and started trashing the joint. They turned the place into a frat house, or an asylum. These guests were unwelcome, and they haven't left.

The good fortune of meeting Emily a few years after the divorce had quelled the riotousness of these emotions, tamed them for the time being, but they remained, latent and roiling, and so did my animosity toward them. These were the thoughts that returned to me when I received those birthday gifts. I knew that I had done little to reckon with these dark parts of myself, these old and indelible parts, for which I had cultivated a stern, godlike contempt. Which I knew and worried was, by definition, a contempt for myself.

•

The second context was a powerful sense of emotional responsibility. In a word: fatherhood.

One of the injuries from which my first marriage grew septic and died was my ambivalence about having a second child, and that same ambivalence almost made my marriage to Emily never happen. For reasons spanning from the financial to the creative to the ecological, I just wasn't sure I wanted to go through all that again. Perhaps the most significant reason, though the hardest to admit and articulate, was that I couldn't tolerate the excessive scrutiny that comes with being a parent. Not the scrutiny of peers, relatives, teachers, or "society," but the scrutiny of the child, which is constant, formative, and oppressive.

When she was ten, my oldest niece, Isabella, said to her parents, ominously, "Remember: I'm always watching. I'm always listening." She was being clever, but it's true, and it's terrifying. There is no escape from the attention of one's children. To become a parent is willingly to place oneself under daily surveillance, and surveillance of a special kind, in which one's attitudes and actions are not only observed but recorded, coded, assimilated, and emulated. What monkey sees, monkey does not always do. But what monkey sees again and again, day after day, year after year until she leaves for college, inevitably shapes monkey's mind and soul.

What you tell a child about how to live is of course much less important than what you show. And emotions always show. They betray themselves in the minutest expressions and movements. In the clench of your jaw behind the wheel. In the distant cast of your eyes over dinner. In a wrinkled brow, a bouncing knee, the clearing of a throat, the slumping of shoulders, a slack expression, a distracted bearing, an unmet gaze, a shrug. A silence. You can keep your fantasies, your memories, and your thoughts secret, but in the context of family your emotions are about as private as a freeway billboard. From what you feel—not what you want to feel, but what you do feel—your child will learn what emotions are appropriate to have in which situations and at what level of intensity.

During the years I was staggering from the collapse of my marriage, I resolved that I would not inflict myself on a child, or a child on me—on my freedom to be erratic and selfish—ever again. The stakes were too high, and I was too unsteady. Then I met Emily, who longed for a child (if not necessarily, at first, by me), and my resolve softened. I willed it to soften, for I loved Emily, and I both wanted her and wanted her to have what she wanted. The love itself was a bracing force, an emotional antidote. With Emily I was, I generally am, more positive, more cheerful and forthright. Sturdier. Emily possesses a strength and resilience I do not, and these qualities, it seemed reasonable to hope, could be the dominant influences in any child's development, as they could be, I hoped, the dominant influences in my own further development. Love! The eternal cure! The great crisis, it appeared, had passed. All that remained was to go forth and multiply.

So I reasoned. So I hoped. But now the child was imminent, only weeks away, its smooth, spongy brain primed to absorb its daily lessons in How to Be. And I could hear the old inmates again, stomping through the dusty halls, saying, "Here we are. We're still here. Don't forget about us."

•

The third context was nothing more—but it was a lot—than the passing of time. I had simply reached a point in my life when, thank goodness, I could no longer sustain the delusion that I was anything more refined or attractive than I actually am. Experience had revealed to me, as often happens in midlife, the full unadulterated pattern of myself.

Throughout my twenties and well into my thirties I managed to cling to the absurd notion that I possessed not just a changeable but a fixable self. I believed firmly, with a conviction I must have known was disreputable and a little crazy, since I told no one about it, that my personality was composed of two different kinds of attributes: those that were true and permanent, and those that were false and temporary. It was as basic and neurotically harebrained as that. The first, respectable class of attributes, which included courage, conviction, confidence, devotion, wit, and imagination, constituted the real me. The firm, foundational me. They coalesced into a kind of core self or eternal soul. They defined me. The members of the second class of attributes—timidity, envy, misanthropy, impatience, laziness, and so on—were not easily dismissed. They were formidable actors on the psychological scene, in some cases cultivated as signs of my cleverness and superiority. But they didn't define me. They often harassed me. They obscured me. They sometimes embarrassed and distressed me, like badly behaved children. But they weren't of me, not really. They were so ancillary to my true self, in fact, that I could afford to be cavalier about them. I could be passive. Time itself would do the work, scouring them from my mind and life like barnacles from the hull of a ship, leaving me, I supposed, pure.

I don't know what a midlife crisis feels like for others. But for me it felt like the realization that this scheme was fantasy. Worse, it was the realization that the fantasy had duped me into inaction. Instead of working hard to shape my soul, I told myself that my soul was already well-shaped, and that whatever ailed and oppressed me were foreign bodies, the passing pathologies of youth. They would fade in time.

But they didn't fade. Possibly they never would have. In any case, if growing older meant anything to me it meant accumulating ample and incontrovertible evidence that I was lastingly marbled with all of those elements I dismissed and reviled—the dark, the shadowy, the knotty, the cynical, and the negative. It meant understanding what I needed to accept and what I needed to more mindfully reject. It meant finding the wisdom to change what I could and endure what I couldn't. It meant better understanding this darkness, which meant better understanding myself. It meant seeing and accepting not the monochrome dream but the spotted, parti-colored totality, like it or not. It meant trying to like it.

"Thank goodness," I say, because the truth is always a gift. The opportunity to understand and come to terms with the truth is a gift. It is a disquieting and demanding gift, to be sure. But self-delusion, too, is disquieting and demanding. And I want to be whole. What is life for if not to discover the wholeness of ourselves, to discover and to love it all—every last gnarled, negative bit?

•

Of course, this is all a lot easier to say than to do. *Accept the negative. Love the darkness. Embrace the whole.* These are lovely phrases—rousing imperatives. But they are inadequate. Like all slogans and summaries in the service of self-improvement, they are too broad, too sweeping and insistent, to serve as anything more useful than starting points. Beneath their blunt surfaces lies a profuse, unwieldy, stubborn complexity.

In my first months as a therapist, I sometimes found myself making a mistake to which many new therapists are prone. This was the mistake of overeagerness, and therefore of overactivity. I would greet a new patient in my office, or on the screen, and the pain that person expressed, in word or manner, would spark in me a restless hunger to help. The trouble was not so much the hunger—though that too with experience would morph into a more measured, sustainable impulse—as it was the restlessness. Everywhere I looked I saw an opportunity to contribute, to soothe and heal, and I would rush in headlong with comments, prompts, suggestions, shrewd techniques, clever interpretations that, in my enthusiasm, I believed would break the psychic case wide open. At times it seemed that my intervention had caused a significant change in someone—there would be a resonant pause, or a promising tonal swerve—but this was almost always a mirage, or an effect as temporary and superficial as a shot of lidocaine. I soon metabolized the fundamental and indelible lesson that there is no rushing the work of change, no trapdoor to self-understanding or relative equanimity. There was only the determined, persistent, attentive devotion to—

Well, to what? Here is where the difficulty begins, and not just for the scrupulous therapist. What is the right stance to take toward emotional unrest? What is the best, wisest approach when contending with our unruly and offensive emotional selves, those aspects of ourselves we least like and most want to cast off? In the thick of these emotions, patience seems hardly appropriate, or even possible. Distress demands relief. Anguish is defined by its urgency. When I myself am beset and befuddled by despair, shame, envy, regret, rage, or any of the other emotions and mood states that often storm the cockpit of my mind, I am not looking for forbearance, compassion, elucidation, or even love, fine as these may be. I am looking for a way out. A lamp to brighten the corners and erase the shadows. A vacuum to clear away the debris. I am looking, like everyone, for help. Help! And *now*.

But wanting something desperately doesn't make it any more salutary, or any more available. When it comes to our negative emotions, enduring help—help that deserves to be called help—is rarely available in any tidy or direct way. What we are talking about are not tires to be replaced or tumors to be cut out. Even to call an emotion "negative," in fact, is to submit to a dangerously false view of the situation. To call something negative is, in essence, to condemn it in advance. It is to brand it as lacking value, usefulness, progressive purpose, and moral dignity. It is to place it in a kind of exiled opposition to the worthwhile and the true. More often than not, it is a license to stop listening—an excuse. For what would be the point of listening to something whose only goal is to harm you?

This, as I see it, is the great danger: to stop listening. And this, as I see it, is the work, the hard and abiding work: to listen to everything, including—especially—everything in you that you would rather ignore.

No emotion is inherently bad. No emotion is bad, full stop. Trust no one who tells you otherwise, for they are trying to sell you, and usually themselves, something. They are trying to evade the primary responsibility we have toward our emotions, which is nothing more or less than to try to understand them, to meet them as emissaries with messages to convey, if only we would learn their languages and hear them out. Emissaries from every precinct of our lives: our cultures, our families, our pasts, our hopes for the future, our needs and confusions, our conflicts and concerns, our desires.

Do you want a prescription for your woes? Here is one as simple as it is challenging: Neutralize your judgment. Banish it to the hills. Treat every emotion as articulate, freighted with meaning and intent. Of every difficult emotion you feel ask, "Why have you emerged? What are you trying, in your barbed and brutish way, to tell me? What do you *want*?" Reject nothing. Receive everything. See what you learn.

•

In the year after my first marriage fell apart, when I was at my most tenuous, I had to travel a lot for work. Every three or four weeks I found myself in an airport terminal with the usual expanse of time to fill before boarding. I would try to read and inevitably I would fail, too distraught to get through more than a paragraph and too restless to sit still. Instead, I took to wandering the terminals while listening to music. At this time, I was listening compulsively to a single album: *The Idler Wheel* . . . , by Fiona Apple. In particular, I was listening compulsively to a single song on that album. The song is called "Every Single Night."

"Every Single Night" is about self-consciousness, feeling, and pain. Every night, the song begins, awful thoughts occur to the singer. Worries. Doubts. Regrets. Self-recriminations. Should'ves. Shouldn't-haves. All the stuff of the brain chugging away in the dark. But this isn't "where the pain comes in." The pain only comes when the stuff of the brain filters down into the body, where it swells into a "blaze," and where the emotions become unmanageably large, larger even than the body they fill. Now the singer feels that her "breast's gonna bust open." She will lose control. She will lose herself. These are the stakes, and so the experience is a clash with something that is both her and not her, an enemy at the wheel: "Every single night's a fight with my brain."

But that's not the end of the story. If that were the end of the story, the song would be little more than a complaint—a bad poem. And this is a song that grows. A minute and a half into "Every Single Night," after many beautiful descriptions of anguish and anxiety, a new refrain emerges. "I just want to feel everything," Apple sings tentatively, and then again: "I just want to feel everything." And the song shifts like a sonnet between stanzas, not away from pain but toward it, into it, headlong, into a kind of active acquiescence, a Zen-like anti-effort, and in a way a celebration. The singer comes to recognize that her capacity for turmoil is a moral good: "My heart's made of parts of all that surround me. / And that's why the devil just can't get around me." The last thirty seconds of the song belong to the refrain, the singer's hard-won, hard-retained credo:

> *I just want to feel everything*
> *I just want to feel everything*
> *I just want to feel everything*
> *I just want to feel everything*

This line has become my credo, too. During periods of strain I repeat it in my head, or play the song itself. I chant it like a mantra. A mantra, for that is what I think it is. It is a compressed piece of wisdom. It is a clarifying, recentering principle. It is a point to return to when we are in turmoil.

Feel everything. Don't look away.

The name of the game, now and forever, is curiosity.

chapter two

THE MORALITY OF EMOTIONS
(A BRIEF HISTORY)

The tendency to divide our emotions into those that are "positive" and those that are "negative" is in the superficial sense a fairly new one. Psychology lifted the terms themselves from chemistry, from the study of ions, radicals, and electrical charges. It was Benjamin Franklin who first used the terms scientifically, in a 1751 treatise. But the underlying tendency to evaluate emotions as either good or bad—the habit of looking at our emotional lives through the lenses of ethics and morality—predates modern psychology by centuries. It is a habit that is deeply entrenched in our thinking on the subject, so much so that it happens almost automatically, as a kind of genetic legacy—and one that needs to be dug up and examined if we are going to have any chance of avoiding it.

It is a heavy lift. We have been morally implicated by our emotions through much of human history. Philosophy, it is fair to say, has its origins in these judgments. In his *Nicomachean Ethics*, written 2,300 years ago, Aristotle goes to great lengths to establish the role that our emotions play in the formation of our moral characters. To be a good person, Aristotle argues, means not just having the right emotions, but having the right emotions at the right times and in the right amounts. Some emotions, such as spite and envy, are flat-out bad. Don't have them. As for the more appropriate emotions, virtue means getting the levels just so, titrating them like some psychic anesthesiologist.

The Greek Stoics, writing not long after Aristotle, were even more severe about the emotions. Aside from a few rarefied exceptions—reverence, awe, some types of love—no emotions were legitimate to the Stoic. All betrayed the weakness, immaturity, and irrationality of the person having them.

To the Stoic, an emotion is strictly voluntary. If you get angry because you're trying to write and your son is downstairs screaming because he wants his Pokémon underwear and his Pokémon underwear are all in a basket of dirty clothes (to conjure an example out of thin air), it isn't his fault for making you angry—it's yours. You have allowed yourself to fall prey to two false and pernicious beliefs: first, that it's a bad thing for a kid to scream while you're trying to work, and second, that anger is an appropriate response to your kid screaming while you're trying to work. A wise father, one with a virtuous, ethically refined disposition, wouldn't allow himself to get angry—even if he knew, say, that the reason the Pokémon underwear were all dirty was because his son refused to learn to wipe his ass properly. A virtuous father would refuse to permit the anger entry into his mind. He would be . . . stoical. As Marcus Aurelius admonished himself about four hundred years later: "Realize at long last that you have within you something stronger and more numinous than those agents of emotion which make you mere puppets on their strings."

Aurelius was writing at the dawn of Christianity. As that religion developed and spread over the coming centuries, it would seriously ramp up the moral stakes of our emotional lives. The Greeks and Romans were principally concerned with virtue, tranquility, and human excellence. The Church Fathers were concerned with sin, purity, and the fate of the eternal soul. With Christianity, negative emotions took on a darker cast. They became obstacles to being welcomed into the Kingdom of God—signs of demonic influence. Emotions could defile you.

It was a fourth-century monk and spiritual teacher in the Egyptian desert who first codified this tradition. In a treatise directed toward the ascetics under his guidance, Evagrius Ponticus enumerated eight experiences that might tempt, divert, and disturb his wards. Evagrius called these experiences "evil thoughts," but most were what we would today call emotions, including greed, sadness, anger, pride, and a form of restless boredom called *acedia*. All were "capital" sins, meaning that they were the primary routes to damnation. They were the "gateway drugs to countless [other] sins," as one recent account has it.

This moralizing approach caught on. Another monk, John Cassian, visited the desert, then returned to Europe to write up and broadcast his own list of "evil" emotions—still eight in number but now known as "principal faults." In the late sixth century, Pope Gregory the Great, the sixty-fourth head of the Catholic Church, reconfigured the list again (envy now made the roster, and pride was elevated to a kind of super sin), trimmed it down by one, and introduced notes of militarism, terror, and zealotry that help to explain why the list would forever after be popularly known as the seven deadly sins. Example: "For whoever is exalted with pride, whoever is tortured by the longings of covetousness, whoever is relaxed with the pleasures of lust, whoever is kindled by the burnings of unjust and immoderate anger, what else is he but a testicle of Antichrist?"

Gregory's classification and rhetoric would, with a late alley-oop by the preeminent medieval theologian Thomas Aquinas, hold sway in the West until at least the Renaissance, inspiring Bosch, Dante, Geoffrey Chaucer, Edmund Spenser, and innumerable other artists, and scaring the piss, the historical record suggests, out of Europeans for a millennium or so. How could they not have? The message was clear: Feel the wrong thing without adequate repentance and you may not burn in hellfire for eternity, but your punishment will hardly be a stroll around the market square. In Dante's telling, the envious were forced to languish in Purgatory, their eyes sewn shut with iron wire.

It bears mentioning that the seven deadly sins are alive and well. The *Catechism of the Catholic Church*—a church that has 1.4 billion members worldwide—still includes and endorses Pope Gregory's 1,400-year-old list, noting that sins such as greed, envy, and *acedia* are "contrary to divine law" and "give rise to social situations and institutions that are contrary to the divine goodness." The rhetoric remains cosmic and dire. "How ugly envy is!" Pope Francis declared during a 2016 mass. "[It] grows in the heart like a weed. . . . It is a tormented heart, it is an ugly heart! . . . Scripture says clearly: Through the envy of the devil, death entered the world."

•

In and around the seventeenth century, more naturalistic accounts of the emotions began to compete with such forbidding moralistic theology. A new detached, scientific way of thinking about the emotions emerged. The Dutch philosopher Baruch Spinoza, for example, in his *Ethics* (1677), defined emotions dryly as "the modifications of the body, whereby the active power of the said body is increased or diminished, aided or constrained, and also the ideas of such modifications." In his book *A Treatise of Human Nature* (1739–40), David Hume's primary concern was with how emotions work, and in particular with what causes emotions, not with what influences they have on the soul.

By the nineteenth century, the most influential accounts of the emotions concerned themselves squarely with biology and physiology. Charles Darwin collected countless minute observations of how humans and animals express emotions through behavior and attempted to track back the origins and purposes of that behavior, some of which—baring one's teeth while angry, for example—likely had survival value for the species. Today, in the age of the genome and the PET scan, we would seem to have put even more daylight between our emotional lives and any sense of moral risk. Scientists now typically conceptualize our emotions in terms of brain anatomy, neural pathways, chromosomes, developmental stages, physiological markers, microexpressions, attachment styles, and mental disorders. These rationalist ideas about the emotions seem to leave little room for concepts such as virtue, vice, evil, or sin.

As it happens, the very fact that I am using the word "emotion" in this book suggests a transcendence of the old value-laden ways. Until the nineteenth century, no single, overarching term existed to describe what we now call the emotions. Instead, there were a range of words: "passions," "affections," "desires," even "lusts." As the historian Thomas Dixon has noted, these terms all share a "biblical pedigree." The word "passion" in particular has a religious resonance, as in the Passion, or redemptive suffering, of Jesus Christ. The words "emotion" and "emotional" carry no such religious baggage. That is why scientists and philosophers of the modern era began to use them. To say "emotion" instead of "passion" is to say, essentially, *Okay, folks, we're moving on. Our concern is to study and explain, not to judge.*

But we have not moved on. Explaining does not preclude judging. On the contrary, the two seem to be inevitable partners.

Consider how psychologists and mental health experts smuggle ethical and moral precepts into their own presumably more enlightened discourse. The philosopher Robert Solomon and the psychologist Lori Stone argue that our very use of the categories "positive" and "negative" is a form of "medieval thinking" masquerading in "scientific guise." Why, they ask, are we still sorting experiences as multifaceted and complex as our emotions into neatly opposing groups? Is "positive vs. negative" any different from "virtue vs. vice"?

The psychologist Jerome Kagan has argued that all that has really changed is what we think of as virtuous and worthy of pursuit. Today when we call an emotion "negative" what we invariably mean is that it "interferes with happiness and health." Emotions like fear and anger get in the way of our achieving our optimal state of being. But what we consider optimal varies according to time and culture; it is inherently subjective. Hence, Kagan concludes, "it is not obvious that [positive and negative] are any more useful as scientific concepts than the notions 'pretty' and 'plain.'"

No matter how dubious as scientific concepts, however, they clearly work well as selling points. If the objects are now happiness and health rather than holiness and purity, and the presiding authority clinical rather than religious, the pitch is the same as ever: deliverance from a kind of dark bondage.

Consider, for example, the book *Emotional Freedom* (2009), by the psychiatrist Judith Orloff, the former chief resident of UCLA's Affective Disorders Clinic. This book, which carries the subtitle "Liberate Yourself from Negative Emotions and Transform Your Life," invites the reader to "take a remarkable journey, one that leads to . . . a mastery over negativity that pervades daily life." Orloff offers her work as a "lifelong guide to release you from the compulsive tyranny of negative emotions such as worry and anger," to help you cope with "emotional vampires" who sap your positive energy, and to learn the "secret to serenity." The language here is the language of imprisonment and release, shadow and light, good and bad. It is the moralism of the church recast in therapeutic terms.

For the past twenty-five years or so, this bipolar way of speaking about the emotions has been most prominently embodied in Positive Psychology, a movement dedicated to fostering those emotions and states that enable us to flourish and diminishing those that cramp our spirit, health, and opportunities. Founded in the late 1990s to counter psychology's long-standing emphasis on dysfunction and disorder, Positive Psychology quickly developed into not only an academic orientation but an influential popular philosophy—an engine of inspiration and personal improvement. It has generated countless peer-reviewed studies examining how positive people lead longer, more resilient, more productive lives, and it has spawned countless self-help books, online courses, corporate training programs, podcasts, workshops, and TED talks—a veritable happiness industry exhorting us to throw off the yoke of our negative feelings and to embrace joy, hope, and equanimity.

At their best, the proponents of Positive Psychology can be cautious and circumspect, as in the disclaimer by the movement's founder, the psychologist Martin Seligman, that pessimism plays a vital role in our lives, offering us a "keen sense of reality when we need it." At their zealous worst, as critics both inside and outside the movement have argued, they uphold a facile dichotomy between good and bad emotions, wildly overstate ambiguous empirical results, and pathologize a whole set of universal emotions in the name of a dubious "science of happiness."

Something odd seems to happen when the scientists of positivity leave their laboratories and venture into the public sphere. Their prudence evaporates and they begin to make sweeping promises about increased creativity, productivity, sexual satisfaction, health, social engagement, career achievement, and so on. They begin to sound like motivational speakers—as some have in fact lucratively become—or like preachers. Seligman himself has summed up his movement's work with this simple question: "What is the word in your heart? Is it 'yes' or is it 'no'?" The resonance is not scientific; it is biblical: "I treasure your word in my heart, so that I may not sin against you" (Psalm 119:11).

This kind of odd spiritualism crops up even within the staid precincts of scientific literature. While researching this book, I came across an unusual illustration in an otherwise saltine-dry textbook called the *Handbook of Emotion Regulation* (2015). It is a flow chart, meant to outline the way in which negative emotions make it harder for people to "resist temptations [and] suppress unwanted impulses." We get sad and hoover up a pound of chocolate-covered almonds. We feel mad and curse at our children. What exactly is going on here? The flow chart contains big boxes, small boxes, arrows, labels—standard-issue illustrative equipment. Then, at the bottom of the chart, a flourish: Instead of giving the negative emotions their own tidy box, the authors depict them as feral, grasping vines, à la *Little Shop of Horrors*, that reach into and corrupt the different faculties of the mind. The vines—"poison tendrils," the authors, both distinguished researchers, call them—emerge from a hole in the ground. The hole is black and fissured all along its circumference, as if the earth has been violently pried open by some demonic subterranean power. As if our negative emotions have their origins not in our minds themselves but rather in some profane, perfidious, yawning underworld—the place of nightmares.

chapter three

WHAT IS AN EMOTION?

Consider the Utku. Consider their poise, so much greater than yours.

The Utku—the Utkuhikhalingmuit, "the people of the place where there is soapstone"—are an Inuit people, a small, nomadic band who for generations lived at the northern edge of the American continent, near the mouth of the Back River, in what is now the Canadian territory of Nunavut, one of the most sparsely populated regions of the world. The Utku subsisted on salmon, trout, char, whitefish, seal, birds' eggs, and caribou. They trapped foxes for fur and carved caribou bones into toys to trade for tea, tobacco, kerosene, and guns. In the winter they cut ice for igloos, using slush for mortar. When the weather improved, the igloos melted over their heads and they moved into tents. The Utku never, or hardly ever, got angry.

They didn't get angry. Before we examine this claim in any detail, a question: Is it even within the scope of your imagination to entertain it? Is it within the scope of your experience? Can you yourself conceive of a life, *your* life, without anger? Not a life, mind you, in which you control your anger—bank it, suppress it, sublimate it into work, exercise, politics, whatever—but a life in which you don't even *feel* it, in which anger isn't even an issue, or is so little of an issue, so minute a portion of your emotional repertoire, that only an outsider, perplexed by your easy equanimity, unsettled by the blunt contrast with her own tempestuousness, would think to make it an issue. I know I can hardly imagine it, anger is so regular a part of my life. Anger at politicians. Anger at zealots. Anger at corporations. Anger at cancer. Anger at a pickle jar with an ill-fitting lid. Anger at a succulent that falls off a window ledge. Anger anger anger, from the opening of the bedroom blinds to the closing of the bedroom blinds. I might as well ask whether one can imagine life without consciousness.

Much of what we know of the Utku comes from an anthropologist named Jean Briggs. In the summer of 1963, Briggs, a thirty-four-year-old graduate student from New England, traveled to the Back River with the goal of researching a dissertation on "the social relationships of shamans" among the Utku. She arrived in a single-engine government plane, knowing only a handful of native words and terrified that she might freeze to death when winter came. It took weeks for her to discover that the Utku had no shamans; they were all devout Anglicans, having been converted by missionaries decades before, and believed that any shamans that did exist were "either in hell or in hiding." She stuck it out anyway, learning the language as best she could and living for seventeen months as the "*kapluna* [white] daughter" of an Utku family. The eventual result was the lively and compelling book *Never in Anger* (1970).

Briggs's time among the Utku was often confusing—for her but also, she came to understand, for her hosts. The Utku were unfailingly gracious and obliging toward Briggs. They shared their home and their food with her. They helped her to navigate and survive the extreme environmental conditions of the tundra. They protected her as they would a child. This was in part because they saw her as something of a child, especially in emotional terms.

A cardinal virtue among the Utku, Briggs wrote, is self-control, and a central concept is *ihuma*, which means something like reason, or good sense. "The Utku expect little children to be easily angered and frightened and to cry easily when disturbed, because they have no *ihuma*. . . . In the Utku view, growing up is very largely a process of acquiring *ihuma*, since it is primarily the use of *ihuma* that distinguishes mature, adult behavior from that of a child, an idiot, a very sick or an insane person."

Briggs, from an Utku perspective, had very little *ihuma*. She could be gloomy, nervous, and demanding. She asked too many questions. She had bouts of anxiety and sadness that caused her to isolate herself. ("In the past month my tent had become my refuge, into which I withdrew every evening after the rest of the camp was in bed, to repair ravages to my spirit with the help of bannock and peanut butter, boiled rice, frozen dates, and Henry James.") Worst of all, she was prone to losing her temper. When interrupted in her work, she stormed off into the wild. When a hunk of slush dropped from the dome of the igloo and landed in her typewriter (a regular occurrence), she let loose a string of profanities, or threw something. Struggling to cut apart a frozen whitefish to boil a chowder, she screamed, "I HATE fish! And I hope when I go home I never see another fish."

The most significant incident occurred during Briggs's second summer with the Utku, when a group of white sportsmen came to the river to fish. These men borrowed a canoe from the Utku and damaged it. They then asked to borrow another canoe, the only one remaining. Briggs was indignant. She coldly informed the men of the impertinence of their request. This incident, Briggs wrote, brought to a climax the Utku's long-standing discomfort with her "un-Eskimo volatility; and as a result of my unseemly and frightening wrath at the fishermen I was ostracized, very subtly, for about three months." The Utku simply stopped dealing with her. They withdrew their warmth.

Briggs was well aware, as is the reader of her book, that in American terms she is hardly an outlier. She was an ordinary person in extraordinary circumstances, giving vent to her sincere, spontaneous feelings, so that a phrase such as "frightening wrath" seems ironic, a winking appropriation of an impossible Utku standard according to which such behavior is not only inappropriate but dangerous—an unassimilable threat to a long-standing and precious emotional ecosystem. "Wrath"? Briggs delivered a lecture to the fishermen, a scolding at the worst, and by the way one motivated by concern for the well-being of her hosts. To the Utku, however, it was a reaction that they couldn't abide in a grown woman, and they resolved to put distance between themselves and her. As Briggs's Utku father, Inuttiaq, had already warned her, "We don't get angry here."

•

What does this statement mean: "We don't get angry here"? What do we mean, exactly, when we say that someone "gets" angry? This is one of the questions about her time in Nunavut that preoccupies Briggs and makes her book an invaluable document for anyone trying to understand the emotions and how they work. Does to "get" angry mean to "act" angry, or does it mean to "feel" angry? Does it mean that you have "expressed" the emotion—that you have shown it outwardly, in a way that is clear and public? You have shouted, or stomped your foot, or punched a hole in the drywall, or gone flush and silent and trembling? Or does getting angry mean, less concretely, that you have experienced an inward sensation or apprehension regarding the world that others, if clued in, would recognize as anger? In the rich privacy of yourself you have felt this particular phenomenon, distinct from other particular phenomena, that Aristotle defined as "a distressed desire for conspicuous vengeance in return for a conspicuous and unjustifiable contempt of one's person or friends." In what area of human experience, Briggs wanted to know, are the Utku so preternaturally gifted: emotional control or emotion itself? And what, if anything, is the difference?

This question is fundamental, since to ask it is basically to ask what an emotion even is in the first place. What is this essential, vibrant, shape-shifting, rock-bottom part of each and every one of our lives? If we are to have hope of living well with our negative emotions, we have to have some sense of what an emotion is. Is an emotion something visceral, something in the pulse of our hearts and the pace of our breathing? Is it something cognitive, something self-aware and full of content? Do emotions arise spontaneously in response to circumstance, like a reflex? Or do we conjure them willfully into existence? Do they contain elements of rationality and reason? Are emotions a species of belief, a way of interpreting and giving order to existence? Does an emotion always have a target, or can it be diffuse and directionless? We use the word "emotion" constantly, without hesitation. What does it mean?

As it turns out, this has proven to be a uniquely difficult question to answer. It is also, therefore, highly contentious. Ask a roomful of philosophers and psychologists today to define "emotion" and they will coalesce into packs and tear into each other like hyenas. Cognitivist will attack phenomenologist, phenomenologist will attack social constructionist, social constructionist will attack neo-Darwinian, and in the end everyone will be equally bruised and frustrated. Over the course of the twentieth century, according to one estimate, experts proposed more than ninety distinct definitions of emotion. When the psychologist Carroll Izard surveyed leaders in the field, in 2010, he found no consensus—though a sizable share of his respondents were inclined to believe that the term should be abandoned altogether. "The only thing certain in the emotion field," the psychologist Alan Fridlund told a journalist in 2015, "is that no one agrees on how to define emotion."

There is something comforting about this, I think, and even beautiful. Our emotions are an abiding mystery. Their meaning is as complex, protean, and elusive as the meaning of love, truth, knowledge, or God. To read the great thinkers on emotion, from the ancient Greeks to the present day, is to witness a procession of exquisite minds develop insights of extraordinary breadth and brilliance—and little solidity. There seems to be no end to it, no conclusion. There are only ingenious theories in conversation with one another, and these theories are often intricate and deeply confusing.

René Descartes, for example, had both a mechanical and a spiritual view of the subject. An emotion, in Descartes's view, is caused by changes in the brain and circulated around the body by way of tiny particles in the blood he called "animal spirits." These animal spirits then cycle back to the brain, strengthening and maintaining the emotion. This all happens automatically, without thought. Emotion for Descartes is a type of perception, like smelling dinner cooking on the stove or feeling hungry. Yet it is a perception that "refers" to our immaterial souls—who we are at our core. The result of our emotions is to "dispose the soul to will the things which Nature dictates are profitable to it, and to persist in this will; as also the very agitation of the spirits, accustomed to cause them, dispose the body to the motions that further the execution of those things. Wherefore to calculate them, we are only to examine in order, after how many considerable manners our senses may be moved by their objects."

It was writing like this that made the psychologist and philosopher William James, in the late nineteenth century, say that he would as soon "read verbal descriptions of the shapes of the rocks on a New Hampshire farm" as be forced to struggle again through the classic works on the emotions. His own writing on the subject was far sharper, bolder, and more cogent. In a classic 1884 paper titled "What Is an Emotion?" James presented a revolutionary theory of the emotions about which psychologists are still arguing today.

Most of us assume, James wrote, that emotions serve as a kind of bridge between what we perceive out in the world and what our bodies do in response to external reality. A stranger lunges at us in the street, for example, we feel the emotion known as "fear," and we recoil, our heart pounding and our muscles tensed. We see someone vomit, we feel the emotion known as "disgust," and we become dizzy and nauseated. Common sense tells us that this is the order of things. James believed, however, that common sense has it wrong. What actually happens, he argued, is something like the reverse of what we assume. A stranger lunges at us in the street, we recoil, our heart pounding and our muscles tensed, and then we experience ourselves recoiling, our heart pounding, etc. We see someone vomit, we become dizzy and nauseated, and then we experience dizziness and nausea.

And that's it. The experience of the bodily sensations is the emotion. There is no abstract "there" there, no conundrum. What else could an emotion be, James asked, but the awareness of brute physical changes? Imagine that you were a brain in a jar. Could you feel joy? Could you feel sadness? How would you know you were having these emotions? What would signal to you that you were joyful or sad? What would the emotion consist of? "If we fancy some strong emotion," James wrote, "and then try to abstract from our consciousness of it all the feelings of its characteristic bodily symptoms, we find we have nothing left behind, no 'mind-stuff' out of which the emotion can be constituted, and that a cold and neutral state of intellectual perception is all that remains."

> What kind of an emotion of fear would be left, if the feelings neither of quickened heart-beats nor of shallow breathing, neither of trembling lips nor of weakened limbs, neither of goose-flesh nor of visceral stirrings, were present, it is quite impossible to think. Can one fancy the state of rage and picture no ebullition of it in the chest, no flushing of the face, no dilatation of the nostrils, no clenching of the teeth, no impulse to vig-

orous action, but in their stead limp muscles, calm breathing, and a placid face? . . . A purely disembodied human emotion is a nonentity.

•

James's theory is one of the pillars of modern scientific interpretations of the emotions, and a starting point for many discussions of the subject. The other pillar is the work of Charles Darwin, though Darwin never tried to solve the deep riddle of emotion. He didn't concern himself with the mechanics, meaning, or experience of emotion. He didn't ask what an emotion *is*. What interested Darwin was how we "express" our emotions—how our bodies display, in our faces and our movements and in our physiological responses, what we are feeling—and how our emotional expressions reveal our intimate, unbreakable relationship to other, "lesser" animal species.

Darwin began collecting evidence on emotional expression early in his career. His first child, William Erasmus, was born in 1839, when Darwin was thirty years old. His voyage to the Galápagos was only three years behind him, and he saw his son's infancy (as he saw most things) as an opportunity to gather data in support of his theory of evolution. Darwin believed that emotional expression in humans developed as everything in nature develops: through the glacially slow, inexorable process of natural selection. William was his baby, but he was also an invaluable source. Darwin recorded everything: how William fell into a "violent passion" when a lemon slipped out of his tiny hands; how he "looked grave" and burst into tears when his father made an unusual snoring noise; how he uttered an "incipient laugh" when playing peekaboo. Darwin wanted to know precisely when each expression arose and how it related to the behavior of other creatures. When William was eleven months old, for example, he noted that "if a wrong plaything was given him, he would push it away and beat it; I presume that the beating was an instinctive sign of anger, like the snapping of the jaws of a young crocodile just out of the egg."

Darwin sustained his interest in emotional expression over the course of decades. William was only the first, and closest, of his sources. He observed orangutans, baboons, birds, rabbits, kangaroos, the children of friends, and his own dog. He solicited reports on the residents of mental hospitals, believing that "the insane ... are liable to the strongest passions" and therefore a fount of clear evidence. He sent questionnaires to scientists and missionaries in New Zealand, Borneo, Malaysia, and China asking for descriptions of the emotional expressions of indigenous peoples. He finally published his findings in *The Expression of the Emotions in Man and Animals* (1872). It is a dense and detailed work, the upshot of which is that the way we express our emotions is an undeniable part of our evolutionary inheritance. To Darwin, our expressions are the behavioral equivalent of wisdom teeth or the tailbone—vestigial structures that for our biological ancestors had served some purpose but that for us no longer do. The wolf snarls to signal that he is prepared to attack; when we are angry we sneer, lifting the corner of our mouths and showing our teeth. When cats are frightened they arch their backs and puff out their fur; when we are frightened our hair stands on end. Our expressions are reflexes, physiological leftovers, echoes from the distant past.

Darwin's book was improbably popular in its time, far outselling both the epochal *On the Origin of Species* (1859) and *The Descent of Man* (1871). Then for nearly a hundred years it was either ignored or rejected. For the first five or six decades of the twentieth century, the dominant paradigm in psychology was behaviorism, which maintained that anything associated with the "mind"—emotion, will, belief, desire, consciousness, etc.—was beyond the reach of experimental science. Subjectivity was a black box. All you could truly study were inputs and outputs: the things that happened to an organism and how that organism responded, physically and visibly. If it couldn't go on a clipboard, it wasn't real. One might think that this jibed well with Darwin's methods of studying expressions, which after all are behaviors. But there was a catch. Although Darwin restricted himself to emotional expressions, his approach led logically to a sweeping claim about the nature of emotions themselves. This claim was that our emotions, or at least a subset of them, are universal. The logic went like this: If our emotions trickled down to us from a common ancient ancestor, if they arrived at their present form through the process of evolution by natural selection, then those expressions, and therefore the emotions that underlie them, are biologically innate. We did not learn how to feel or how to express what we feel; we come as it were preprogrammed, our nervous systems calibrated and primed for certain fundamental emotions like fear, anger, and disgust. These emotions are inherited, fixed, and universal.

Behaviorists could not tolerate a theory like this. Neither could leading twentieth-century intellectuals like the anthropologist Margaret Mead, who insisted that human behavior, including emotional expression, was wholly flexible and therefore wholly determined by culture. Everyone everywhere was different. Full stop. Emotions simply could not be universal. This wall of resistance held firm until the 1960s, when it began to disintegrate due to the work of a dogged young American psychologist named Paul Ekman.

Ekman started as a behaviorist. But for him behaviorism was above all an experimental doctrine. It meant that you banished all preconceptions, you looked only for what was observable, and you followed the facts where they led you. His interest in emotional expression grew out of his early work as a psychotherapist. By studying expressions, Ekman hoped to discover a way to track the progress of patients that was clearer and more "scientific" than the traditional method of parsing patients' spoken words. As for Darwinian universalism, he assumed it was wrong, but he wasn't dogmatic on the subject. He just wanted to see what he could find.

Ekman's method of studying expression was almost the same as Darwin's: He took photographs of people displaying different emotions in exaggerated, caricatured ways—wide flared nostrils, big goofy grin—and he asked subjects to try to identify them. The crucial difference is that Darwin canvassed people only in his native England. Ekman took his show on the road—far on the road. In twenty-one countries, including Chile, Japan, Indonesia, Scotland, Estonia, Argentina, and Turkey, he showed people photographs of facial expressions, all carefully posed, and asked them to match those expressions up with a small selection of emotion words. The results were striking. Everywhere he went, his work suggested, a high percentage of people recognized one face as anger, another face as fear, another face as disgust. To make sure his findings weren't caused by the global popularity of Western popular culture (maybe the Estonians, Indonesians, and Chileans had all seen the same expressions in *Gone With the Wind* or *I Love Lucy*), he performed a version of the experiment in a remote area of Papua New Guinea. Same results. The members of an isolated Stone Age tribe in a jungle in the South Pacific were able to identify emotional expressions about as well as a random group of Argentinians.

Ekman's research was visually compelling and sharply defined. It completely transformed the field. He declared the work of "cultural relativists" like Mead to be obsolete, deposed and replaced by his new, elegant Basic Emotion Theory. That theory, which reigned for decades, is starkly Darwinian. It holds that there exists a discrete set of emotions—happiness, sadness, anger, fear, surprise, and disgust—common to every member of the species *Homo sapiens*, no matter how widely dispersed from its origins on the African plains. According to the theory's proponents, the fact that people everywhere are able to recognize certain facial expressions proves that there are innate and universal emotions underlying those expressions. Our basic emotions are in essence reflexes, hardened by long, successful use in the wrangle for physical survival. In the pure Basic Emotion view, every instance of an emotion is a kind of physiological cascade that starts in the brain, spreads outward into the rest of the body, causing changes in respiration, digestion, heart rate, glandular activity, and so on, and ends in some sort of expression. This expression might be dramatic, as in a temper tantrum, or it might be so subtle—a slight contraction, say, in a particular eye muscle—that only a highly trained observer could detect it, or a machine. But it is there. It is always there. Each of our brains contains the neurological equivalent of those quarrelsome, color-coded homunculi from Pixar's *Inside Out* films: separate, hardwired impulses that operate instinctively and, at least initially, beyond our control.

But only initially. For Ekman and his followers, culture does play a role in our emotional lives; it's just that culture's role is to mediate our emotions, not to dictate if and when we feel them. We would get into all sorts of mischief if we gave full animalistic vent to each and every emotion that circumstance triggers in us. We aren't gorillas. We can't bellow and beat our breasts whenever we feel challenged by a competitor. Every ride on the crosstown bus would be pandemonium. Every trip to the park would incite a riot. We have to get along. So we learn what Ekman calls "display rules." We learn how to be civil with each other. Tradition and upbringing, which do of course vary, teach us how to block, hide, adjust, and manipulate the pure, unadulterated forms of emotional expression so that we may exist peacefully among other people.

The sum of this is that Basic Emotion Theory sets up a kind of dualism: on the one hand the biological fact, the objective emotion etched into our brain structures and neurons; and on the other hand the interpretation of that fact, the culture-specific rules governing how an emotion emerges on our face and in our behavior. The emotion, and the *ex post facto* ascription of meaning to the emotion. How could it be otherwise? Everyone gets angry *sometimes*. Anger is baked into the central nervous system. It's just that some, like the Utku, tell themselves that anger is *verboten*, an unconscionable reversion to a childish pre-*ihuma* state—a thing always to suppress—while others, like Briggs, like me, like you, like pretty much everyone you've ever met in the industrialized West, tell themselves that anger is just something that happens, appropriate in some situations, inappropriate in others, a matter of context and degree and temperament—he an angrier person than you, you an angrier person than her—but anyway altogether normal and wholly undeniable. Under the hoods, we are the same. But different groups uphold different customs on how to operate the emotional machine.

•

An important point about Basic Emotion Theory is that it makes intuitive sense. It seems to describe accurately what happens when, say, someone cuts in front of you on line at the post office: the sudden, reflexive physicality of the experience followed closely by at least the opportunity for a less "hot," more willful response. Basic Emotion Theory has practical value, too. Parents use it all the time in order to teach their children self-control. You feel frustrated . . . scared . . . frightened . . . pissed off. Okay. Fine. Let's examine the appropriateness of that emotion. Let's explore, using our logical faculties, whether the emotion you feel is suitable to the situation. Let's more consciously assess the meaning of those visceral experiences, those deep and convincing phenomena, and in this way cultivate a greater degree of mindfulness, distance, and freedom. Let us learn to use our thinking, our cognitive skills, to harness and control our unruly emotional impulses.

Yet as clear and pragmatic as Basic Emotion Theory is, it harbors within its elegance a fairly serious flaw: It probably isn't true. In recent years, the empirical evidence has been mounting, reaching something of a critical mass, that the theory's central claims—that there exist fundamental emotions that are globally recognizable through standard facial expressions, and that these emotions have dedicated physical reactions in the body and brain—are, in a word, wrong. Our emotional lives seem to be far more complex, variable, and slippery than the prevailing scientific explanation for them has allowed.

The evidence against the first claim, about facial expressions, centers on the likely oversimplicity of Ekman's research methods. Matching an emotional face to an emotional label isn't necessarily that hard when the face is basically a cartoon and there are only five or six labels to choose from. The approach doesn't conform to real-world conditions. In fact, as the psychologist Lisa Feldman Barrett points out in her book *How Emotions Are Made* (2017), the poses used by Ekman and others were not based on expressions people actually make when feeling different emotions. They were based on images found in Darwin's century-old book. The researchers essentially decided by fiat that these were the classic, universal expressions of our most common emotions.

When later researchers introduced a little more nuance into the mix, the results became less impressive. In 2021, for example, psychologists in Barrett's laboratory, at Northeastern University, conducted a study using photos from the book *In Character: Actors Acting* (2006). In this book, distinguished actors react according to different emotionally laden scenarios. One of the scenarios reads: "He just witnessed a shooting on a quiet, tree-shaded block in Brooklyn." The featured actor here, Martin Landau, reacts with wide gaping eyes, an open mouth showing his bottom teeth, and a lined and tightened forehead. The researchers divided their subjects into three groups: One only read the scenarios, one only saw the actors' faces, and one was privy to both. In this case, two-thirds of subjects who either read the scenario alone or read it along with Landau's photo identified the situation as a fearful one. But in the group who saw Landau's picture alone, only thirty-eight percent identified his expression as fear. Significantly more, fifty-six percent, labeled it surprise. In another scenario—"She is trying to decide if she should tell her husband about a rumor going around that she is gay before he hears it from someone else"—with the actor Melissa Leo, seventy percent of those who both read the scenario and saw Leo's photo rated her expression as showing fear. Among those subjects who saw Leo's face alone, more than seventy percent identified her expression as one of sadness.

From these results, the researchers drew a commonsense conclusion: Context matters. Take context away from the identification of facial expressions, and ambiguity rushes right in. Similarly, the expressions themselves depend on context. There is no single face for an emotion like fear. Rather there are a wide variety of faces, each of them contingent upon circumstance. When afraid, you may close your eyes and scrunch up your face, or narrow your eyes to focus on a single point, or turn the corners of your mouth down as if you are about to cry, or open your eyes wide to take in the full visual scope, or any other of an unspecifiably large number of possibilities. With emotions, diversity is the norm. Uncertainty is to be expected.

Another route by which researchers have undermined Basic Emotion Theory's claim about facial expressions is studying babies. The logic here is that babies have yet to learn those "display rules" that bend and twist the purest expressions of emotion. In 2007, researchers in the U.S., China, and Japan tried to induce fear and anger in infants by, respectively, frightening them with a growling gorilla doll and holding them by the arm so they couldn't move. The babies made such varied facial expressions across the board that the results of the two situations were indistinguishable from one another. At the same time, when the researchers showed videotapes of the babies to adults, the viewers neatly identified the babies as scared in the first situation and angry in the second. They came to these conclusions even when the researchers blurred out the babies' faces. Again, context was everything.

The evidence against Basic Emotion Theory's second central claim, that each fundamental emotion has a physical analogue, or "fingerprint," in the body, has been if anything more damning. The scientific record here is like a scavenger hunt that comes up short, hands empty. Over the past thirty-five years, hundreds of studies have been conducted that induce emotional reactions in subjects while recording the physiological effects. These studies have used measures ranging from heart rate to blood pressure to respiration rate to body temperature. Dozens more studies have attempted to pinpoint the location of particular emotions in the brain, in regions including the amygdala, the orbitofrontal cortex, the anterior insula, and the anterior cingulate cortex. Meta-analyses of all of these studies, comprising more than twenty thousand test subjects, have failed to find a precise, statistically consistent physiological process for even a single emotion. Not one. Nowhere can we point with confidence to a discernible pattern of bodily responses, of contractions, dilations, secretions, accelerations, winces and blinks, neuronal flashes, and say, *There. That is anger, or surprise, or sadness, or disgust. That is what the emotion* is. The objective emotional essences that Basic Emotion Theory presumes turn out, in the final analysis, not to exist.

In a way, this failure should come as no surprise. At least, I find it difficult to muster surprise. In its characteristic way, psychological science here only confirms what, if we stop to think about it, we already know. None of us truly feels, over the course of a lifetime, or even over the course of a month, something called "Anger"—some typical, essential, singular thing. Rather, we feel a great assortment of angers. Angers large and small, slow and fast, immediate and retrospective, slack and directed, righteous and petulant, agitated and melancholic, confused and certain, fleeting and stubborn, florid and seething ... and on and on. Anger is not a monolith but a village, a complex warren of habitations to which we give a unifying name: "Anger." It is a grouping of meanings, sensations, and behaviors. And when we feel angry, our facial expressions and bodily responses will differ from one instance to the next. Our blood pressure may rise or fall. Our skin conductance may increase or decrease. Our brain will light up here and there, then in another place, then in another. All is variety. All is contingency. All is flux.

•

But this is no answer. It is only the refutation of an answer. It disputes Basic Emotion Theory, but it doesn't solve what Barrett—the most eloquent and thorough critic of that theory—has called the "emotion paradox." The paradox is as follows. We all talk about emotions as if they are individual entities. We tell our spouse we are "frustrated." We tell our friend we are "sad." We tell our therapist we are "jealous." We refer to our emotions, and in fact experience them, as if they are what philosophers call "natural kinds," which is to say, things in the world. But scientists have so far been unable to locate these things, or even, Barrett writes, to "produce a set of clear and consistent criteria for indicating when an emotion is present and when it is not." Emotions are tangible to us, often they are oppressively tangible, but they are empirically intangible. They are phantasms, will-o'-the-wisps. They are there but not there. What gives?

Over the past twenty years or so, in response to this conundrum, a new way of understanding emotions has gained sway. This new way is less intuitive, less graspably formulaic. But it is ultimately more convincing and better suited to the available evidence. It is known as the Theory of Constructed Emotion.

A key difference between this new theory and its rival and predecessor is in how each views the essential character and function of the brain. Basic Emotion Theory sees the brain as fundamentally passive and reactive. You see a tall shadow move in the alleyway, the sight triggers your fear module, and you hurry past, hands bunched into fists.

The Theory of Constructed Emotion, by contrast, understands the brain as active and predictive. Your brain isn't sitting lazily in your skull waiting for the world to call it into service. It is *already* in service. It is always receiving inputs, interpreting the incoming signals from your five senses as well as the signals from within your own body, trying to figure out what's coming next, using attention and personal memories and known facts to anticipate your next move—and then refining its best guesses according to what actually happens. It is an ever-learning, ever-adjusting simulation machine. Indeed, its primary job, many neuroscientists now believe, is to simulate and predict. You are walking down the street, approaching an alleyway. You have read books and seen movies in which criminals jump suddenly out from dark corners. You have read news reports of muggings in this neighborhood. Years ago, you yourself were once robbed at knifepoint—an indelible and traumatic experience. As you approach the alley, your blood pressure ticks up. Your rate of respiration increases. Your body temperature drops. Your brain redirects blood to the large muscles in your legs, in case you have to flee. Extra glucose is delivered to your visual cortex and to the auditory regions of your brain, to sharpen your perceptions. All of this happens, most of it out of conscious awareness, in preparation for an assault that likely, hopefully, never comes. And a good thing, too. If your brain were to wait until something bad happened to react, you'd be felled every time, separated easily from your wallet, and possibly your life.

This reconceptualization of the brain as a predictor of events rather than a responder to them has crucial implications for our understanding of emotion. It transforms emotions into events not externally triggered but built out of smaller, more basic parts: those memories and scraps of knowledge and physiological shifts mentioned in the previous paragraph as well as incoming sensory signals from the eyes, ears, and so on. It strips emotions of their status as static, universal entities and recasts them as the sum totals of the different combinations of experiential elements that flow into any given moment. If you were to draw a diagram of Basic Emotion Theory, the diagram would be linear. One thing leads to another, left to right: box to arrow to box to arrow to box. If you were to draw a diagram of the Theory of Constructed Emotion, the diagram would be circular: a wheel of components connected to a central hub by arrows, like flights streaming into O'Hare. Or, to use one of Barrett's metaphors, each emotion state is like a loaf of bread made of different ingredients, none of which are on their own quintessentially "emotional." Just as flour is just flour, and yeast is just yeast, a feeling of tightness in the sternum is just a feeling of tightness in the sternum, the memory of a lost love just the memory of a lost love. You must combine the ingredients in order to create the state, which is something more than the sum of its parts.

But still, the constructivists say, you do not yet experience an "emotion." After all, a tightness in the sternum and the memory of a lost love could combine to make any number of emotions: nostalgia, grief, resentment, delight, dread, regret, longing, envy, desire, anger. In order to create an instance of an emotion, something extra is needed—some sense of what all those components, when brought together in that particular moment, mean. You need a capstone to the experience.

For Barrett, that capstone is what she calls a "conceptual act." In order to have an emotion, she argues, you have to endow what you are sensing, feeling, and remembering with emotional significance. And that entails having an organized understanding of what an "Emotion" and specific emotions such as "Nostalgia," "Regret," "Envy," and "Anger" are. It entails possessing concepts for "Emotion,"

"Nostalgia," "Regret," "Envy," and "Anger." Again, the bits that we use to make an emotion are not in and of themselves emotional. Think of your experience of a diamond. On its own, the object in front of you is just a matrix of carbon atoms arranged in a crystal structure. The light reflects off the object and enters your eye. You can touch it and feel its hardness, the sharpness of its cut edges. You can pick it up and measure its heft and weight. But the object has no significance to you until you categorize it as "Diamond," with all the connotations that carries with it. In short, you have to label the experience. This labeling is not a magic trick: *Poof! These feelings make "Anger."* It is a matter of basic necessity. If you could not categorize your experiences, if you could not contextualize them, then you would have no clue as to what anything meant. You would have no ability to make conscious sense of all those elements that are constantly flowing into you from all directions. You would be totally lost.

Here a final analogy, to language, will be helpful. If you know nothing at all of, say, Maori, and are plopped down blindfolded among a group of people speaking that language, you will for a time experience it as merely a stream of meaningless sounds—intricate and overlapping vibrations of molecules impacting upon the membranes and bones of your ears, transmitted by the auditory nerves to your brain, and perceived as little more than noise. Or perhaps perceived as "spoken language," for you already have and use that concept. Beyond that you'll be adrift in sound, until you learn to find the seams in the sound, the joints at which you can carve the sound into units, and until you learn to attach those units to what they are meant to signify in the world, and in relation to one another, and in relation to what you already understand about the world and how it operates. Learning, by and large, is the establishment and delineation of concepts that we use as tools to make sense of, and to anticipate the significance of, a never-ending welter of experience.

And where do we get those concepts? We make them up. This, too, is a matter of necessity. People need to have ways of communicating with each other about what different sensations mean in different circumstances so that they are more predictable to one another. They have to find common ground in order to function as a society, to raise their children, to manage and distribute resources, to determine how to act and how not to act, to be able to influence others, and just generally to be able to structure the chaos of experience. Having an emotional life, writes the anthropologist Clifford Geertz, "is a matter of giving specific, explicit, determinate form to the general, diffuse, ongoing flow of bodily sensation; of imposing upon the continual shifts in sentience to which we are inherently subject a recognizable, meaningful order, so that we may not only feel but know what we feel and act accordingly."

Emotions, then, are created. This is not at all to say that they aren't real. They are real. But they are real in a social sense. They are real in the sense that "money" is real, or "freedom," or "literature." That is, they are real because we say and agree that they are real. We require these concepts. We require them in order to function. But they do not come predetermined.

Moreover, we don't all require the same concepts. As Barrett and others have documented extensively, different cultures get by with different emotion concepts. The experience of "sadness," for example, is a kind of physical agony in Russia, but is a kind of loss in the U.S., very different from anger. Meanwhile, in Turkey sadness and anger are attributes of a single emotion category called *kizginlik*.

The Portuguese have an emotion concept, *saudade*, meaning, in the words of the scholar Tiffany Watt Smith, "a melancholic yearning," powerful and spiritual in nature, "for someone, or something, that is far away or lost." Filipinos have a concept, *gigil*, that Barrett defines as the "urge to hug or squeeze something that is unbearably adorable." The Baining people of Papua New Guinea talk about *awumbuk*, an emptiness experienced after a visitor leaves. We think of an emotion as something individual and embodied. Other cultures, such as the Pintupi of Australia and the Ifaluk of Micronesia, conceptualize emotions as social experiences that require two or more people. Some cultures, Barrett reports, don't even have a coherent concept for "Emotion." They get by without one.

All is variety. All is contingency. All is flux.

•

Which brings us back to the Utku and the uncertain meaning of the word "get" in the phrase "get angry." The question was: Are the Utku virtuosos at controlling their feelings of anger, or do they simply not feel anger in the first place? Do they feel anger and then successfully manage, hide, or suppress it, so that it seems to others as if it wasn't there? Or is it truly not there? For the Utku, could anger be a nonentity?

Physically, of course, there are no notable differences between Jean Briggs and her Inuit hosts. All have the biological and physiological equipment needed to feel anger. All have cranial capacities of between around 1,300 and 1,500 cubic centimeters. All have brains and adrenal glands capable of producing adrenaline, noradrenaline, and cortisol. All have brain stems and frontal lobes. In this way, they are identical. But there are considerable environmental differences between Briggs and her hosts. There are serious differences in upbringing, language, interpretation, and understanding.

Briggs identifies herself as a "middle-class, urban, Protestant New Englander." She was born in 1929 in Washington, D.C., and grew up in Maine and in Newton, Massachusetts, the bookish daughter of a Swedenborgian minister. She studied at Vassar, Boston University, and Harvard. By all accounts she was stubborn, individualistic, and temperamental. This is Briggs's context, and much more could be said about it, the most relevant of which is that when she traveled to the Canadian tundra, Briggs carried with her a fully fledged concept that her culture labels "Anger," a lifetime of deploying that concept in a diverse array of circumstances, and a belief that anger is natural, normal, and in many cases inevitable.

By contrast, the Utku, an isolated, nomadic, collectivist tribe, had no such concept, no such history, and no such belief. Their context is radically different from Briggs's. In fact, Briggs elaborates at length as to whether the mainstream Western concept of anger corresponds in any meaningful way to related Utku concepts. She worries that it doesn't, and that in making her translations and conducting her analysis she is "doing violence to the Eskimo ways of conceptualizing feelings." The closest Utku equivalent to "anger" is *ningaq*, and that word most commonly expresses "the idea of physical aggression, fighting." Sometimes it seems closely linked to a concept, *qiquq*, that Briggs tentatively defines as "being clogged up." ("Whenever people are *ningaq*," one Utku unhelpfully explains, "they *qiquq*.") Other times, or simultaneously, it seems related to a concept, *uluru*, that Briggs defines as "annoyance." Except that when the Utku refer to a situation or themselves as *uluru*, they never give the impression of being irritated, thwarted, frustrated, or hostile, and when Briggs tries to extract a serviceable definition she is invariably told, "It means 'unsmiling.'"

It is hard to know exactly what to make of all this. It seems hasty to conclude that the Utku don't feel anger as we do, or to discount the importance of their powers of self-control and restraint. We can even sketch a plausible theory as to why they would need to cultivate those powers in the first place: A small, interdependent society with limited access to resources in an unforgivingly harsh climate has every reason to restrict a potentially destabilizing emotion like anger. And Briggs believes that she can read volatility and agitation—an anger-like emotional heat—in the faces and postures of some of the Utku. They don't act angry, but every now and then one of them seems to shimmer with the spirit of anger. Utku parents carefully train their children to be passive and unbothered by events, to take everything in stride. That said, the Utku judge Briggs severely and move to ostracize her from the group—behaviors that may occur as the result of a banked, unexpressed anger.

And yet, what does that even mean? Can someone be said to gain mastery over anger, or to feel it inwardly, if they don't even have a word for the emotion? In the English-speaking world, "anger" has deep philosophical and political roots. It attaches to a wide but finite range of feelings and experiences, and is itself part of a family of emotions that includes aggravation, indignation, rage, and frustration. This is our world; it isn't the Utku's. The Utku have their own world, made up of its own rules, structures, beliefs, myths, and rituals. These elements, I think, aren't separate from emotional life. They constitute the field on which emotions operate. They establish and maintain the range of emotional possibilities in a culture. Briggs and the Utku don't even have a common model for how the mind works. Inuit psychology focuses on behavior, not inward experiences of feeling or mood. They don't conceptualize or categorize emotions as we do. If an Inuit anthropologist observed you and wrote that you seem to struggle with *ihuma,* and that you are clearly *ningaq,* would you agree?

This isn't to say that the emotions of others are impossibly private and inaccessible, that we can't understand each other across cultures, languages, subcultures, families. It isn't to claim that we are hopelessly apart, segregated forever into our own little pockets of feeling. If that were true then you would have no hope of understanding me and I would stop right here, my work rendered useless.

But I don't believe it is useless. I believe, merely, that it isn't basic. I believe it is intricate and fluid, immensely particular at every level, from the capillary to the religious rite, the bead of sweat to the marital bond, the neuron to the nation-state. I believe, and try to act within this belief in what follows, that to understand any emotion you have to try to understand the complex structures and patterns that underlie it. You have to work to tease it apart, anatomize its workings, recognize and explain the stories and assumptions, the needs and desires, the contexts and concepts that make it what it is and give it its force. You have to struggle like a miner to find the meaning of the emotion, the irreducible meaning—even, or especially, if that emotion is your own.

PART TWO

chapter four

ANNOYANCE

In 2008, I tried to escape New York and almost succeeded. In the years since, I have continued to dream of fleeing the city for some sparser, more congenial place, and I've even made some other attempts, but I've never come so close again and have to admit now that I probably never will. I am moored here, as encumbered and out of my element as a ship in dry dock.

My near-escape took place just before the crisis that would bloom into the Great Recession, though we didn't know it yet. I lived then with my first wife and our daughter in an apartment halfway between the Brooklyn-Queens Expressway and a small Catholic college whose colors and crest I recognized from subway ads. The marriage wasn't yet three years old. The child wasn't yet one—a wee, blonde, shrieking thing who entered this world with a perplexing aversion to both sleeping and eating. Every baby is a shock. This baby was a greater shock than most. But I don't think I would have felt so desperate to leave the city if it hadn't been for the confounding apartment in which we fumbled to raise her.

It was like trying to start a family in a Skinner box. It was like living at the mercy of some unseen, ice-blooded behaviorist whose every move is designed to prod, tax, and fray the human nervous system. At every time of day, from every direction, we were besieged by stimuli, assaulted by claims on our senses, so that between the chaos of our baby and the chaos of our home, it was probably inevitable that in time we'd go a little nuts and start scrambling for the exit.

Here is a catalog of the insults we endured from our neighbors—decent people, I'm sure, only trying to live their lives, but their lives were a trial for us, and I daily wished them harm.

Above us lived a soft-spoken retired couple who spent their days watching television. This was the kind of television that doubles as a piece of furniture, in this case an immense wooden cabinet, tall as a man, with speakers built into its base. The unit stood squatly on the couple's uncarpeted living room floor. This had the effect, when the television was on, as it almost always was, of transforming our apartment into a natural amplifier, palpably vibrating with the sound of whatever our neighbors happened to be watching at the time. In this way, I heard a sizable percentage of the 127-episode run of the sitcom *Reba*, but treble-weak and distorted, as a fetus experiences the world outside.

Below us lived an ill-tempered working single mother. To smooth relations, I had put down area rugs and walked barefoot. But some unyielding resentment or finely tuned sensitivity placed her beyond the reach of accommodation, and she reacted to any heavy step or accidentally dropped book by whacking repeatedly at her ceiling with (I assume) a broom handle. She did this so quickly, with so little time between stimulus and response, that although I knew for a fact that she did leave the building, I imagined her standing permanent sentry in her apartment, broom in hand, a one-woman SWAT team waiting for the signal.

Adjacent to us lived a jazz bassist. There may be no need to elaborate beyond those two chilling words except to add that, due to the scarcity of affordable practice space in New York City, he frequently rehearsed with his band at home. I don't think you can say that you truly understand urban living until you have shared a poorly insulated wall with a contemporary jazz quintet hashing out original compositions for five hours straight. Something happens to a person under these conditions. I tried to be sympathetic. Music! It needs expression! But I must have complained one too many times, because one Sunday morning our neighbor's politeness broke and he said, "If you can't hack it maybe you should just, like, split, man." To this day I am disappointed that he didn't add, "Dig, daddy-o?"

At first I was indignant. But the more I thought about what my neighbor said, the more it seemed like sage advice, given at the right time. Before long, we put our apartment on the market and started looking for jobs across the country, in Oregon. My wife found work as a schoolteacher in the suburbs and I was offered a position as a feature writer at a glossy magazine. I bought a new digital voice recorder for interviews and started scanning listings for house rentals. And that was that.

Once we had decided to leave New York, a curious nausea assailed me—a wobbliness in my identity. On the one hand, I felt profound relief. To decide to move away was at last to declare, to myself and everyone else, that I wasn't temperamentally fit to live in New York. It was the straight dope, daddy-o. It wasn't just the neighbors. By then I had lived all over New York, from the Upper West Side to Chinatown to Prospect Heights. Had spent time in Astoria, Tribeca, the West Village, the Upper East Side, Chelsea, Murray Hill, SoHo, Fort Greene. Sometimes the neighbors were loud, sometimes quiet. But the city itself was a constant, and non-negotiable. Arguments, fires, arrests, fights, sirens, alarms, shouts, car horns. Music of every kind, every tempo. Cooking oil. Liquifying garbage. Cannabis. Gasoline. Cologne. Smoke. These were the elements that made the atmosphere as pervasive and ineluctable as, if you lived in the country, the wind in the trees and the crickets in the grass. No matter where you lived, between the sidewalk and your bedroom there was no fundamental difference. You could adjust the dials a little but you couldn't change the volume. I was ready to axe the stereo and torch the speakers. I'd had enough. No más. In finally admitting that I didn't have the nervous system to be a New Yorker, I felt the sinews of that system slacken and unknot.

On the other hand, shame. The racking hangover at the end of the delusion. The delusion, youthful and common, was the broad, almost radical pliability of the self. The belief that one's personality is mutable and unfixed, up for grabs. That you can train yourself with determination and desire, fathomless energy, invention and vaulting confidence, into any form, like a bonsai tree.

There had been nothing I'd wanted more since adolescence than to be a New Yorker. Where else in the world was there a place that bristled with even half the promise? Nowhere. A fool's question. From my youth on Long Island to my late teens and early twenties in Massachusetts I imagined, with absurd provinciality, that to build a life anywhere besides New York would be absurdly provincial of me. A *bildungsroman* hero in my own mind, I aimed myself at a single glorious target and launched at it the first chance I got, a few months before my twenty-fifth birthday, sure I'd never leave.

I wasn't fully delusional. I knew I was prone to annoyance. I'd been accused of being "oversensitive" since nursery school. I'd always been covetous of my solitude and impatient with interruptions. It was simply that I trusted New York, with its famous re-creative might and literary reputation, to make me otherwise. The goal was to transform myself into a bona fide New Yorker, and New Yorkers, as E. B. White wrote, "do not crave comfort and convenience—if they did they would live elsewhere." I was to enter the city as a length of hide enters a tanning drum, becoming by way of immersion constitutionally immune to the flux and discordance that addle the senses of mere tourists.

But I never leathered. I remained as tremulous and raw as a hatchling, year after year, while the city remained as noisome and indifferent as it always has been and always will be. I was now in fact worse off, since I no longer had the comfort of believing I might adapt. It turns out you can start out delicate as an orchid and stay that way, crib to coffin. In the weeks leading up to our move, as I made arrangements and organized a farewell party to say goodbye to the city, our friends, and local family, I took envious notice of the hundreds of London plane trees I passed on the street, their mottled trunks spreading 60, 90, 120 feet above my head, the branches heavy with globes of densely packed seeds. Plane trees are as hardy as weeds, able not only to tolerate but to flourish in inhospitable places, crowded in among concrete and asphalt, shoved up against galvanized steel fences, stolid and content even in the tiny, glass-strewn, pissed-on quarters the city allots to them.

In retrospect, that farewell party was the last time I felt within reach of a life in which my temperament and my environment would be in harmony, and the last time I enjoyed New York unreservedly, without hard feelings. Even the psychotic car horns sounded charming that night, bourbon in hand, surrounded by friends. Stepping outside for a cigarette, I saw a man defecate behind a Chrysler with a fan of parking tickets plastered to its windshield, and I thought, "New York, I may even miss you."

A week later, Lehman Brothers collapsed. Three weeks after the party, my new boss called to rescind her job offer. Ad revenue was plummeting. They could no longer afford a new hire.

"But I had a going-away party," I said. "I've started packing."

"Things are hard all around," she said. Though she was right, I couldn't eke much comfort out of so collective a truth. On the contrary, the letdown seemed to scour another layer from my tolerance, making me more susceptible, more helplessly annoyed, and resentful twice over, of New York and of my own inherent irritability. Just as the promise of food makes you more aware of your pangs of hunger, the nearness of escape made it that much more difficult to endure the contrast between who I was and where I was. From that point forward, as what could have been a short stint in the city was transformed—by family obligations, by professional necessity, and by New York State divorce law—into a life sentence, I settled, or unsettled, into an existence of more or less permanent annoyance. Held back by impersonal circumstances, I became more personally affronted. The result was that in time, without noticing or, until now, much questioning it, I turned into the very kind of person, the very grouch, I had hoped to avoid becoming.

•

Before I continue, I'd like to confess to an anxiety. This is a book about certain negative emotions that takes as its starting point my experiences with those emotions. As such, I have to take those experiences seriously. With the emotions to follow, this isn't difficult; despair and envy, for example, have a built-in gravity. I don't have to convince anyone that they're important. But in writing about annoyance, I can't help but feel a nagging concern that I'm coming across as melodramatic. I am concerned that it will seem as if I were confessing at length to something totally unremarkable, like disliking mosquitos and cold toilet seats, or preferring sunshine to rain. After all, no one likes the things about city living I find distasteful. No one is calling for louder neighbors, stinkier streets, or an increase in the volume of car horns. To go on then as I have about my tendency toward annoyance—to describe my life in New York as a kind of imprisonment and my temperament as a kind of curse—could make me sound not only oversensitive but ridiculous. An object of fun. I've tried to convey the seriousness of the problem for me, but I can't manage to dispel an odor of frivolity in the proceedings. No one died. No one's safety is at risk. I have home and food and family and work in a city of culture and excitement. Is it really worth the trouble to be so troubled by . . .

... I almost wrote "by petty annoyances," but it occurs to me that this is probably the exact point from which the odor is emanating. Annoyances are petty by definition. Literally. Every dictionary I consult emphasizes the smallness of the concept, equating it with things that bother us but that can't cause us real harm. In everyday speech, we do recognize gradations of annoyance. "This permit process is a major annoyance," a builder might complain. A driver forced to detour around a closed street might call it a "minor" annoyance. But all annoyances are meant to exist in the realm of the minor. They are experiences that we would prefer to be free of but that we can endure without much effort. Annoyances are small fry, no big deal, mere encumbrances.

This leads to a central question about the emotion: How are we to take annoyance seriously when we consider its objects to be inessential and ancillary? How are we to take the person who is feeling annoyed seriously? A lot of the time we don't. A lot of the time we laugh at the annoyed person. We turn him into a stock comic character: the curmudgeon, the sourpuss, the kvetch. The person incapable of play. The person who looks at a flea and sees a rhinoceros.

More to the point: How do we take annoyance seriously when it *is* funny? Because without question it is. It always has been. Irritability and oversensitivity have been touchstones of comedy since ancient Greece. There seems never to have been a time in human history when we did not enjoy watching a person flail in helpless exasperation, or grousing and whining and missing the fun, or being thwarted by the many mundane obstacles that life scatters in our way.

More than 2,400 years ago, Aristophanes portrayed a god, Dionysus, driven to distraction by a chorus of frogs. Looking back at the comedy I have loved since childhood, I see delightful annoyance at every turn: Bert's annoyance with Ernie, Daffy Duck's with Bugs Bunny, Abbott's with Costello, Jerry's with Newman, everyone's annoyance with Harpo Marx. Oscar the Grouch. Oscar Madison.

Archie Bunker. Bernie Mac. One of my fondest comedic memories is of a cartoon I watched sometime in the 1980s in which the main character is so annoyed by a fly buzzing in his bedroom that he ends up smashing his own house to the ground. I laughed so hard I almost aspirated my Rice Krispies. Even satire, by some lights a more sophisticated form of comedy, makes frequent use of annoyance, though in the opposite direction—by taking something that is legitimately threatening and shrinking it down. In Charlie Chaplin's *The Great Dictator*, Adolf Hitler becomes Adenoid Hynkel and Benito Mussolini becomes Benzino Napaloni, and instead of wrangling gravely over the conquest of Europe, they have a food fight. In satire, the bully becomes a fool, the jailer a clown, the autocrat a buffoon. We often make use of this maneuver in our own lives. "Oh, it's nothing," we say. "It's nothing to be too bothered about." And the more we say it, the more we hope to believe it, the less burdened we aim to feel.

The conception of annoyance as something light and unserious extends to the formal study of the emotions. Try to extract something useful about annoyance from psychology and philosophy and you will come up with only scraps, as if you'd gone to a theologian to learn about incense. It's a side subject, far from the heart of the matter. The emotions with which psychologists and philosophers have historically been most concerned are those that possess grandeur, significance, and force—and also those that they can plausibly argue are essential to human experience. People have been making lists of these basic emotions since at least Aristotle. Anger and fear appear on all the lists, and happiness usually makes the cut. The *Book of Rites*, a core text of Confucianism, includes love. The psychologist Paul Ekman's list includes surprise, disgust, and contempt.

In 1980, the psychologist Robert Plutchik proposed that there are eight basic human emotions and that these eight can be divided into four opposing pairs: joy versus sadness, acceptance versus disgust, fear versus anger, and surprise versus anticipation. Inspired by the kinds of color wheels you find in art supply stores, Plutchik designed a diagram he called the Wheel of Emotions. The idea is that, like colors, emotions come in different intensities and blend to form new, hybrid emotions. Annoyance does appear on Plutchik's wheel, but only as a diluted form of anger. On the Wheel of Emotions (using Crayola terms), annoyance is salmon to anger's brick red and rage's scarlet.

When psychologists who study emotions bother to think about annoyance at all, this is how they tend to think about it—as a bloodless subordinate to the real thing. I know of only one book dedicated exclusively to annoyance, *Annoying: The Science of What Bugs Us* (2011), by the journalists Joe Palca and Flora Lichtman. One psychologist told Palca and Lichtman that annoyance is a type of aversion. Another told them that it is a type of frustration. James Gross, an eminent Stanford psychologist, is a Plutchikian. "From my perspective, annoyance is mild anger," he said. "And there's a huge literature on anger." The Library of Congress lists more than 170 subject headings pertaining to anger, including "Anger—Cartoons and Comics," "Anger—Prevention—Study and Teaching—Activity Programs—Juvenile Literature," and "Anger—India—Kerala—Drama." It lists no subject headings pertaining to annoyance. (Palca's and Lichtman's book appears under the subject headings "Discontent" and "Aversion—Physiological Aspects.")

It is undeniably true, as Plutchik's wheel shows, that annoyance can swell and metastasize into anger. The way it does this is by aggregating its forces, like snowflakes. The irritations build. They amass and become a pattern, then an oppression. Two or three crows are a nuisance; thousands of them are a Hitchcock movie. As the frequency of annoyances increases, our tolerance decreases. We have tried to be patient. We have tried to be calm. Now we spill over.

I suppose I could defend the seriousness of my own annoyance on these grounds alone, by claiming that the feeling is a warning sign

I ignore at my peril, like an irregular mole. But something inside me balks at this concession. Why should my annoyance be forced to draw its respect from some allegedly greater emotion? For one thing, my annoyance rarely advances into anger. It typically stays just where it is, discrete and more or less stable. Also, my annoyance doesn't feel like anger. It differs not in quantity but in quality. A traditional definition of anger characterizes the emotion in terms of retribution: Aristotle's "distressed desire for conspicuous vengeance." It is true that annoyance is capable of taking on this air of serious injustice, and for some it can include the fantasy of inflicting harm on the perpetrator. But annoyance itself is never so grand or so wounded. It is never about abstract, capitalized ideals such as Honor, Virtue, or Dignity. It is about concrete, real-time behaviors. It is about infractions, infringements, manners, mores. Misdemeanors, not felonies.

Annoyance doesn't want retribution. All it wants is cessation. It just wants the signal to stop. Once the signal stops, the annoyance fades. If the patron saint of anger is Achilles, vengefully hacking apart every Trojan in sight, the patron saint of annoyance is Mr. Wilson, who just wants Dennis the Menace to leave him alone with his morning paper, thank you very much. That we tend to sympathize more with the carefree Dennis than with the dyspeptic Mr. Wilson—that we snicker at the prig—is further evidence that we regard the inclination toward annoyance as a flaw in character. Which it may very well be. But that doesn't diminish the reality or sincerity of Mr. Wilson's experience. It doesn't absolve us of the responsibility to look at things from his point of view. What does Mr. Wilson's annoyance feel like? What is it that he needs? How does his annoyance arrive and how does he understand it? How does he judge it? How does he feel about other people's judgment of it? And really, while we're at it, why don't Dennis's parents keep the little shit on a tighter leash?

•

If annoyance deserves respect because it is an independent emotion, it also deserves respect because it is a ubiquitous one. It is a universal fact of social life, and so of life itself. Anywhere two or more people rub up against each other—two or more people with their own desires, preferences, and needs, their own claims to authority and control—annoyance finds a breeding ground.

Homes are therefore petri dishes for annoyance. In families and couples, annoyance is endemic. He always forgets to turn the thermostat down at night. She never cleans her hair from the shower drain. He burps during meals. She takes too long leaving the house. He farts in bed. She farts in bed. She keeps touching my toys. He won't stay on his side of the room. Husband annoying wife. Wife annoying husband. Husband annoying husband. Kid annoying kid, which annoys parents. The prevalence of annoyance in families is almost a physical law. Just as pressure increases the rate of molecular collision, proximity increases the rate of annoyance.

Built into this system, though, is its own remedy. Togetherness increases the opportunity for annoyance but intimacy and shared custom—not to mention loyalty, love, and affection—provide a means of resolution. Intimate units devise intimate rules, tailor-made guidelines to accommodate idiosyncrasies and peccadilloes. Families have a way of improvising and sustaining salutary guidelines for behavior. Sunday morning is Mom's rest time; don't hassle her. Sister gets the bathroom from 8:00 to 8:30. Little brother is allowed to make an unholy mess but only on his side of the room. My own brother and sister-in-law cleverly diffuse annoyance simply by reminding one another that the feeling is inevitably mutual. When one complains about an annoyance, the other says, "You do things too!" And they both nod, smile, and go on their ways.

One of the difficulties of living in a city is that it is all but impossible to win even modest accommodations in one's environment. Those small but necessary and sanity-preserving adjustments we depend on in our private life are, in urban life, largely out of reach. Whom are we to negotiate with? Whom are we to call? To seek recourse even within the clearly established rules can seem churlish. One of my friends nervously asked me to edit an email he planned to send to his upstairs neighbors, whose toddler repeatedly knocks his toys against the floor. The building's bylaws state that all apartments must cover eighty percent of their floors with carpets, but the rule is unenforceable and he had to get the email's tone exactly right. Another friend wrote such an email and in response his upstairs neighbors took to dropping objects on the floor on purpose. He could hear them laughing above him, like cruel gods.

Scenes like these play out all over the city, in every neighborhood and on every block, probably in every building. And the subject of these scenes, more often than not, is sound: who makes it, when and where, and how to be free of it.

On the way to meet a friend for a drink, I spot a handmade sign taped to a subway wall.

SUBWAY ETIQUETTE
ALL TIMES

Nail clipping
Under no circumstances is the subway the right place for this. The sound is incredibly annoying and the little nail bits go flying all over the place. It's crazy that this even needs to be mentioned.

Note the tone: a pleading formality, the intimation of a taboo being broken, something domestic brought improperly into the public realm. Note too the complainant's emphasis on the *sound* of the practice. The little airborne bits are a problem, but it is the sound of the clipping, the *snip snip* of metal through nail, that is "incredibly annoying."

Philosophers have long posited a hierarchy of human senses, with sight almost always at the top of the pyramid. With annoyance, hearing is paramount. It is the sounds made by other people that most rankle. It is the vibrations they make in the communal air that we find hardest to bear—hardest to bear because hardest to elude. Sound waves violate. They enter and rattle the tiny bones deep in our ears, bang the tiny tympana, light up the auditory nerves. Clipping. Whistling. Humming. Honking. Coughing. Sneezing. Groaning. Singing. Muttering. Stomping. Slamming. Crying. Shouting. There isn't much to do in opposition to sound. Plug up the passageways and the vibrations will enter through your skull's quarter-inch of bone, through your boot sole's inch of rubber, through the muscles, sinews, and blood vessels in your neck. You will perceive it, like it or not. The name we give to unwanted sound is *noise*. Noise, from the Anglo-Norman *noice*, meaning disturbance, disquiet; before that from the Greek *nautia*, meaning seasickness, or nausea. Nausea: a highly unpleasant sensation brought on by conditions, external and internal, beyond one's control.

Sound—noise—is so effective and efficient an irritant that governments have often used it for military and intelligence purposes. In 1971, in Northern Ireland, British agents subjected fourteen suspected members of the IRA to "deep interrogation" techniques intended to disorient the suspects and deprive them of sleep. These techniques included, in the words of the European Court of Human Rights, "holding the detainees in a room where there was a continuous loud and hissing noise." An earlier human rights commission ruled that this practice amounted to torture.

Jonathan Pieslak, a scholar and composer, claims that this is the first well-documented offensive use of what he calls "sonic irritation." But the technique almost certainly predates the Troubles. By the mid-1950s, the U.S. Air Force had developed a training program, known as Survival, Evasion, Resistance, and Escape, or

SERE, to prepare servicemen for what they might have to endure if shot down and captured by the enemy—a program that soon came to include "prolonged exposure to loud noises and music." At one point, writes the critic Alex Ross, "the playlist reportedly included the industrial band Throbbing Gristle and the avant-garde vocalist Diamanda Galás." Although he was unable to find definitive evidence, Pieslak suspects that the Nazis used sonic irritation in their interrogations—a probability dramatized in the 1940 Hitchcock film *Foreign Correspondent*, in which Nazis break down a Dutch diplomat by repeatedly playing the big-band number "Harlem Congo," by Chick Webb and His Orchestra. In *One, Two, Three*, a 1961 film starring James Cagney, the interrogators and detainee are East German Communists, and the diabolical weapon is the pop hit "Itsy Bitsy Teenie Weenie Yellow Polkadot Bikini."

The Americans would appear to have been the real innovators in sonic irritation. In 1989, after U.S. forces toppled the Panamanian government, the ousted dictator, Manuel Noriega, found refuge in the papal embassy in Panama City. The U.S. Army mounted speakers on Humvees and blared hard rock and heavy metal at the building. At first, the intention was to limit Noriega's ability to communicate with his allies, as well as to prevent journalists from eavesdropping on the army's negotiations with Vatican authorities. Then the army received a report that the music annoyed Noriega. They cranked up the volume. They solicited requests through the local armed forces radio station. On YouTube, you can find a playlist of the songs used: Twisted Sister ("Stay Hungry"), Jethro Tull ("Too Old to Rock 'n' Roll: Too Young to Die!"), Styx ("Blue Collar Man"), Steppenwolf ("The Pusher"), Van Halen ("Panama," obviously).

Pieslak calls the Panama operation "perhaps the first battlefield employment of music as an instrument of irritation," and a defining moment for the practice. In 1993, in Waco, Texas, FBI agents pummeled the Branch Davidian compound with noise and music.

In 2002, Israeli forces played heavy metal as part of their attempt to flush Palestinian militants from the Church of the Nativity, in Bethlehem. Then came the War on Terror and the invasion of Iraq. The Bush administration advanced the notion that the infliction of psychological pain alone does not constitute torture. Since noise and music require no laying on of hands or fists and leave no physical marks, interrogators used them liberally. At Guantanamo Bay, at Abu Ghraib, and at CIA black sites, American soldiers and officers improvised playlists that would annoy and offend uncooperative detainees, causing, in the description of one U.S. Army sergeant, their "brain and body function [to] start to slide." Barney the purple dinosaur, Britney Spears, Metallica, crying babies: The purpose, another officer told Pieslak, was "to get on these people's nerves" and "break down their resistance." Interestingly, in the army at least, this meant taking both the interrogator's and the detainee's nervous systems into account. Regulations stipulated that, regarding psychological techniques of coercion, one must go through what the enemy goes through. "As long as they were listening to babies crying," Sergeant C. J. Grisham says, "I had to listen to babies crying."

In the examples above that involve music, one can detect two of the essential elements of annoyance: taste and control. Annoyance occurs—music or sound transforms into noise—when an annoyee has no affection for what he is compelled to hear. Where there is delight, there is no annoyance. For the lover of Italian opera, a passing car playing *Boléro* at full volume sparks recognition and pleasure. The same car playing Frank Zappa's "Who Are the Brain Police?" may spark an agitated disgust. Heavy metal worked well to degrade the will and spirit of Iraqi and Afghan prisoners, since that music conflicted with their experiences, their values, or their understanding. The music and poetry of the Peoria, Illinois, metal band Mudvayne ("I will crucify my own being / Satisfy selfish needs, fuck the deities") was not exactly what they were used to. On the other hand,

Sergeant Grisham found, Michael Jackson made no one talk; he was too familiar and too loved.

Yet even beloved sounds can become noise if they go on for too long, or if you're not the one controlling the dial. Conversely, noise can resolve back into sound if you know you can stop it with the press of a button. Annoyance is saturated with the dynamics and conflicts of power. To turn sound or music into noise can be an act of pure hegemony. Robert Duvall's helicopters blasting "Ride of the Valkyries" in *Apocalypse Now*, the Marines rolling into Fallujah blasting AC/DC, the NYPD pointing sound cannons at Occupy Wall Street protestors: What do these instances articulate but the message "I can force this upon you and you can't do anything about it. *I* have the strength. *I* have the power"? It is maybe notable that the most egregious offenders in ordinary life are now and long have been teenagers, who hover in an awkward liminal space between autonomy and external control. What better way to broadcast one's claim to and desire for independence than by loudly playing the music that the people with actual power over you find annoying and offensive? You literally get into their heads. For a short time, you redress the balance.

•

It is a source of wonder to me that New York City runs as well as it does, in the sense that its residents, 8.4 million people with radically disparate habits, preferences, and desires, do not as a rule lose their sanity or throttle each other over their annoyances. There are exceptions, terrible ones, but these exceptions only highlight the city's remarkable emotional stability. Tolerance is the virtue for which New Yorkers routinely congratulate themselves. Tolerance for difference, tolerance for all the anarchic stimuli and fractally boundless heterogeneity crammed into a mere three hundred square miles—indeed, a sustaining love and appreciation for difference—is the virtue the city's boosters celebrate as central to its character. Where else in the country, the commercials and campaign ads ask, do so many hues of citizenship cohere into a functioning whole? Where else in the *world*? The Black cop, the Sikh cabbie, the Hispanic schoolteacher, the Italian construction worker, the Slavic jeweler, the garbage collector, the bond trader, the falafel peddler, the street performer, the dancer, the banker, the punk: All appear on screen in service of the ideal of civic harmony. It is a city that works. Miraculously, it works.

Yes. But civic harmony tells us little about individual strain. New York is held together by asphalt and goodwill, but it is also held together by a billion solitary and heroic feats of emotional repression. I'm sure I am far from the only person who several times a day has the *impulse* to admonish one of my fellow New Yorkers, but who holds back out of some shifting combination of self-preservation, resignation, and fear. Fear above all. Fear the great adhesive. Fear the rumble strip that stops us from steering our car into a ditch. The assurance we can count on with our intimates doesn't apply to strangers. I am reasonably sure how my wife will react when I ask her again to please, for the love of all that is holy, rinse and squeeze the sponge when she's done using it. I have no idea how the man flossing his teeth on the crowded R train will react if I ask him to stop, and I'm not willing to find out. It is much safer in these situations to choke down your annoyance than to say anything. Better to seethe than risk a conflict.

But it is important to note that this seething is not evenly distributed. Tolerance may be a teachable skill, but the ability to develop tolerance is likely as inborn and immutable as height or hair color. What and how we feel—our capacities for joy, sadness, awe, anger, excitement, disgust—are as susceptible to genetics as the shapes of our mouths and the curves of our spines. Why shouldn't they be? Why should our emotional nature be any different from our physical one? Why should we blame ourselves when we are stretched beyond the bounds of what is possible for us?

Psychology makes a distinction between temperament and personality. The former is to the latter as a block of marble is to a sculpture in progress. The root of the word "temperament" means "to blend." What blend are you? If you lived roughly between the death of Socrates and the birth of Albert Einstein, you would probably answer this question by referring to the fluids sloshing around inside you. Are you carrying around an excess of blood? Congratulations. You have a sanguine temperament. You are brave, hopeful, and receptive to life's surprises. Too much yellow bile? You are choleric. You are ambitious, short-tempered, controlling, and moody. Too much black bile? You are melancholy, doubtful, cold. Too much phlegm? Calm, reasonable, agreeable.

In the 1940s, the psychologist Hans Eysenck proposed that humans be classified along the dimensions of extroversion and neuroticism. Highly neurotic people are those who have trouble adjusting to their surroundings. They become agitated more easily. They experience more than the usual share of negative emotions, and recover from them slowly. In the late 1970s, the psychiatrists Stella Chess and Alexander Thomas reported the results of a two-decade-long study of the temperaments of infants. According to Chess and Thomas, forty percent of children are "easy." They are regular in their habits and unafraid of new situations and people. Another fifteen percent are "slow to warm up"—not as stable as their easy counterparts, perhaps, but manageable enough. Around thirty-five percent of children can't yet be classified, while one in ten are officially "difficult." These poor, erratic babies respond to the world with turbulence and irritation, and recoil fearfully from the unknown and unfamiliar. They are more likely than others to develop psychiatric problems later on. "Although they may laugh loudly," one psychological text says of these children, "they also have extreme and negative reactions to frustrations."

When I moved to New York, in 2002, my brother David lived

squarely within one of the city's many webs of ceaseless activity, in a two-bedroom apartment in the West Village, a block from Washington Square Park. Every day, ambulances, police cruisers, and fire engines would scream hysterically north along the wide corridor of Sixth Avenue. Screaming, too, would come from souped-up motorcycles, their mufflers altered or stripped clean so that each cylinder blast ricocheted off the high-rises lining his street. Late at night, streaming from the dive bars on MacDougal Street, NYU students staggered home raucously drunk. Later still came the police again, spinning their lights and barking through loudspeakers. "All right, no one's buying drugs tonight! Everyone go home! Nobody's smoking crack here tonight!" Then the sound of scampering feet, curses, crushed vials.

If you asked David how he managed to cope with these disturbances, he would give you a typical New Yorker's answer: "Oh, you get used to it. You learn to be a deep sleeper." And he did. I knew David then to sleep as soundly as a bear in winter. On those rare occasions when the disturbances were too great even for David to tolerate, he would simply turn up the volume on his stereo. In this casual, uncomplaining way, he found that he could match and almost neutralize the decibels pouring in.

Several years later, when my oldest child was not yet in grade school, we moved to an apartment across the street from a supermarket loading dock. All day long, refrigerated tractor trailers would roll up, stop with the piercing shriek of air brakes, then remain idling, belching black diesel exhaust, for as long as it took to offload their cargo. This drove me to the heights of distraction. Section 24-163 of the New York City Administrative Code stipulates that no vehicle shall be permitted to idle its engine for longer than three consecutive minutes, or one minute in a school zone. I knew this. I'd looked it up and memorized the relevant language. I also knew that a trucker was unlikely to feel generously disposed toward a pale, bearded figure reciting the city's environmental regulations. I thought they might feel differently, however, if they were to learn that just thirty feet from where they sat there played an innocent four-year-old girl with a case of bronchial asthma so severe that the spike in atmospheric particulates caused by the eighteen-ton truck at their command could send her gasping to the emergency room, or to the grave. "I'm very sorry to bother you," is how I always began these appeals, which I tried to deliver in a tone of hat-in-hand humility—and which were total fabrications. For their part, the truckers invariably wore an expression of half-bewildered impatience. I imagine that to them I represented yet another in a long line of workaday inconveniences, along with gridlock and potholes. But they almost always did as I asked. They turned their keys and shut down their engines. Why? Because dead children. Because you can't argue with dead children.

On the other hand, you also can't argue with a grocery store's supply chain. If I were to confront every truck driver who drove onto my street I would be doing nothing all day but running up and down stairs, lying about my daughter, and I would produce work at an even slower pace than I do now. "Just ignore it," my wife at the time said. This advice was equally as practicable for me as the suggestion to "calm down" is for someone in the throes of a panic attack. I envy those who can choose what to attend to and what to ignore, who can adjust their mental filters at will. Increasingly, I see this ability as the core of genius, and a prerequisite for any truly significant worldly achievement. Napoleon said of himself: "Different subjects and different affairs are arranged in my head as in a cupboard. When I wish to interrupt one train of thought, I shut that drawer and open another. Do I wish to sleep? I simply close all the drawers and there I am—asleep." I feel that my own head has only one drawer, crammed with junk and perpetually open to the world. And all I want to do is to write a few good books before I die, not conquer Europe.

What was to be done? Annoyance is the father of invention. I saw no other solution than to wall myself off even further. I mean this literally. One irritated afternoon, I took exact measurements of the single window in my office. At Lowe's I bought a sheet of plywood, two sheets of Styrofoam, four lengths of two-by-fours, and two metal handles. I built a large rectangular plug that I could insert snugly into the window, blocking out the trucks for good. That in doing so I would also be blocking out all natural light was a fact that I accepted as a reasonable price to pay. I could tolerate the absence of light but not the presence of sound. To get on with it, I needed to be hermetically sealed off from what I found offensive.

Today, I am struck both by the immaturity and the wisdom of this solution. It seems to me the equivalent of a child's delusion that the world vanishes when she shuts her little eyes. Out of sight, out of mind: for most of us, not a sustainable way to live a life. Not sustainable and not possible. Our exposure to annoyances matches the inequities of the economy at large. The more wealth you possess, the more you can insulate yourself from annoyance: by square footage, by acreage, by employees, by sycophants, by lawyers, by the thickness of walls and the quality of building materials. This kind of peace can be purchased like a luxury good. It is perhaps the ultimate luxury good: the willful specification of one's environment to fit one's temperament. For most of us, however, the imperative is to learn how to accommodate ourselves to the world as it exists and to teach our children to do the same.

First you adjust the world to the baby, as the saying goes, then you adjust the baby to the world.

•

If my life were a Hollywood movie, my annoyance would fade. The gap between the ways of the city and the demands of the self would shrink and in the end I would find a quantum of peace in my surroundings. I would bellyache and grouse. I would lose things dear to me. Then I would reform. I would shift my taste, loosen my grip, and

I would come to experience a new spaciousness. *Here is New York. I take it as it is. I resign myself.*

Maybe this will still happen. It hasn't yet. The city annoys me in middle age as greatly as it did in my twenties and thirties. The city annoys me so often that I no longer register the comedy of being routinely interrupted in the writing of a chapter about annoyance by my annoyance. "It's all material," a friend said, laughing, when I described some instances: the construction noise across the street, the scampering and scraping of squirrels on the roof, the tear of a motorcycle down the block. "Put it in," he advised. "Put all of it in." But there is too damn much of it to put in, and I don't experience it as funny. I experience it, still, as distress.

In the Atrahasis Epic, written about a thousand years before Genesis, the Mesopotamian god Enlil floods the earth and destroys humanity. He does this not, unlike the Hebrew God, because humans are irredeemably wicked. He does it because they are irredeemably irritating.

The land was bellowing like a bull.
The gods were disturbed with their uproar.
Enlil heard their noise
and addressed the great gods.
"The noise of mankind has become too intense for me
with their uproar I am deprived of sleep."

So he wipes them out.

I am still often an Enlil in my own mind, disturbed from my rest by the clamor of the city and entertaining thoughts of smiting with a cool, godlike certainty. But I am not a god, and the control I exert is useless fantasy. I strip the alarms from the cars, pluck the squirrels from the roof, drape the construction site in an enormous blanket, but I do it all, as it were, with eyes closed. And the world goes on bellowing, as it always has and has every right to do.

At times, I confess, I slip into something like despair over the imperishability of my annoyance. Despair and also shame. We aren't supposed to acquiesce to our negative emotions. We aren't supposed to grant them permanent residence. We are meant to disempower them, perhaps by learning from the disturbances they cause. We are meant to see through these disturbances to our root desires and needs, and by doing so to grow. The greatest honor we accord to our negative emotions is the acknowledgement that they have been invaluable teachers. They have taught us how we respond to the world and, ideally, how we no longer have to. The more we understand them, the more we can contain them. Isn't that the goal? To rise above what is worst in us? To prevail over those parts of us that are petty, foolish, wasteful, mean, distracting, malignant?

Yet not all of our negative emotions wish to play the mentor. Not all are willing to be used as instruments of self-improvement. Some insist on remaining exactly what they are. Some are just facts, inflexible as math. Such, I conclude, is my annoyance. A hundred times a day it sends up its flares. It refuses to be dislodged or reduced, not by therapy, not by medication, not by meditation, not even by changes in location. Recently, my family and I moved to a more spacious house on a leafy, quiet street. Deprived of its usual supply of car alarms and construction noise, my annoyance now feeds on other stimuli: barking dogs, drafty windows, a persistent ache in my left knee. It is a brute and omnivorous beast. It just wants to be fed.

This poses something of a problem, since I am not content to be discontent. Another way of saying this is: I am not content to be myself. Not in this respect. It is an uncomfortable position to be in. I am desperate to change an aspect of myself that, all experience has shown, is unchangeable. I am desperate to reduce the distress of an emotion that is persistently distressful.

What is a temperamentally irritable person to do?

The only answer I can find is, modestly, to submit to the emotion but contain the damage it causes. Annoyance has a permanent seat at the table. I admit that. I give in. It is like some infernal sibling I wish would pipe down, but what can you do? Blood is blood. It will grumble and twitch over the dim lighting, the heavy seasoning, the small portion sizes, etc. I will let it do its compulsive thing. I will admit, even, that it has a point. These conditions are not ideal. I take annoyance's complaints seriously, for I am its host and bound to it.

But I will go no further. After that, I will turn away. I'll neither fight nor agree with my annoyance. I'll neither denounce it nor take up its cause, neither run toward it nor run away from it. I will simply remind myself, repeatedly, that it can never be satisfied. And it will never leave. Annoyance may join the party but its spirit must not be allowed to take hold. It has a seat; it does not have the floor.

In short, I will be bothered, as it seems I have no choice but to be bothered, but I will not allow myself to be bothered by being bothered. I will feel annoyed, as my temperament insists, but I will not collude with the annoyance by believing it to be right, appropriate, actionable, or true. I will withhold my conscious consent and place some distance between myself and my inherited nature.

This is, I realize, a somewhat cryptic answer. But it's a venerable one. Twenty-two hundred years ago, when the founders of the Stoic school of philosophy were working out their theory of the emotions, this is the approach they landed on. When we say "stoical" today, we mean resolute and free from destabilizing emotion—a kind of granite impassiveness, like Washington crossing the Delaware. But the original Stoics never claimed that we could escape our emotional responses to the world. They understood the power of temperament. The world throws things at us and we respond as if by reflex.

But the Stoics also claimed that we can choose how we react to our emotional responses. In fact, they believed that our first responses are not emotions at all. They are just impressions—the world pushing its thumb into us, quickening our heartbeat, constricting our blood vessels, activating our nerves. This part is involuntary. It just happens. The voluntary part, the emotion itself, is a decision. It is a belief that the impression is correct. To a Stoic, a negative emotion doesn't immediately follow a triggering event. A negative emotion follows a person's judgment that the triggering event calls for a negative emotion. This judgment happens quickly—so quickly that most people don't realize they are making a judgment. But they are. We are. Each and every time we feel distress, it is because we believe that, under the circumstances, we should feel distressed. Each and every time I get annoyed, it is because I believe that the situation is annoying.

"Remember that what insults you isn't the person who abuses you or hits you, but your judgment that such people are insulting you," taught the Stoic Epictetus. "So whenever anyone irritates you, recognize that it is your opinion that has irritated you. Try above all, then, not to allow yourself to be carried away by the impression; for if you delay things and gain time to think, you'll find it easier to gain control of yourself."

"Who is not himself the cause of his own unrest?" asked Marcus Aurelius.

And so it happens. The car horn is blaring. The dog is barking. The children are screaming. The old pattern starts. The feeling intrudes. It is then that I will try. It is then that I will pause and ask myself: Are you someone who gets upset over a mere annoyance? Do you need to be? Just what are you made of?

chapter five

SHAME

To you your father should be as a god;
One that compos'd your beauties; yea, and one
To whom you are but as a form in wax,
By him imprinted, and within his power,
To leave the figure, or disfigure it.

—*A Midsummer Night's Dream*, Act 1, Scene 1

When my father was sick with cancer, I asked him how it felt to be dying. I was nineteen years old and scared. We were in my father's home office. He sat behind his desk in his worn leather swivel chair. The chemo, or the radiation, or the stress, or his own fear—something had caused his auburn hair and beard to thin and turn a snowy white. It was as if the disease was offering us, as a consolation prize, the chance to see my father as the old man and grandfather he would now, it was perfectly clear to all, never become.

My father did not like the question. Who would? He tried to evade it with a taut little chuckle and a rapping of his wedding band on the desk. Indelicately, I persisted. I was home from college for the summer and pursuing with a desperate single-mindedness my one and only extracurricular activity: trying to connect with my father before he was lowered into the ground. His reticence was an obstacle.

I asked him what went through his mind as he sat tethered to the IV bag, the cocktail of poisons draining into his arm. I asked him what he was glad for and what he regretted. I asked him if he had any notion of an afterlife, and if so if it was a comfort. He was fifty-one, just a couple of years older than I am now. Before long, his patience ran out.

"What is it you want to know?" he asked. "What do you want to hear? That I'm scared shitless? That I hate that my hair is falling out of my head? That I'm sick of puking and having diarrhea every morning?" He was shouting now. He never shouted. "That all of this sucks and I fucking hate it? That I feel robbed? Would that make you happy? Hm? Would *that* satisfy you?"

These were, of course, rhetorical questions. He was only trying to shut me up. But the straightforward answer was: Yes. Yes, indeed, it would satisfy me. Even this rare display of temper, though it proved effective in ending the conversation, satisfied me to a certain extent, since it provided a glimpse into my father's inner life, and it was my father's inner life to which I wanted access. I wanted, as I put it then, to be his "friend." I wanted a depth of intimacy greater than the one I had known. Given decades to age alongside my father, I could pursue this goal at a leisurely pace. There would be one-on-one meals in dim restaurants, long walks in leaf-shadowed parks, heart-to-hearts about love, sex, marriage, work, responsibility, devotion, money, aging, death. But there were probably only months left, so I would take what scraps I could get.

I never did get more than that. My father was warm, empathic, compassionate, and affectionate. He could have taught a graduate seminar on how to give hugs. My friends would come over to our house to hang out with me and wind up in the living room with my father, pouring out their problems and anxieties, and leaving with wise, sensitive advice. My father, all agreed, was a man you could trust. But it seemed he was not a man who could trust others. He gave off an obscure air of distance, like a photo just out of focus. A field of self-protectiveness separated him from the world even as he acted charmingly in it. He ate with unabashed pleasure; delighted in music, movies, and comedy; told dumb jokes; mixed it up; laughed an infectious, face-scrunching laugh. But he stayed subtly, palpably apart. He did not return the deeper, more authentic intimacy he was capable of receiving. And so he was and remains a puzzle to me—an unscratchable itch.

For decades, I assumed that my mother was the one person who was privy to those parts of my father that he kept from everyone else—the person who had as near to a full picture of the man as anyone could possess. At the time of my father's death, the following March, he and my mother had been married for twenty-eight years, a number of them tumultuous, uncertain, and nearly catastrophic. As I have written elsewhere, when I was five my father had a nervous breakdown precipitated by his long concealment of the fact that he suffered from a psychiatric symptom known as "command hallucinations." He heard voices telling him what to do. Their commands were mundane. They told him to move this glass from one side of the table to the other, to use this pen instead of that pencil. But they were voices nonetheless—prototypical signs, psychiatry insisted, of schizophrenia—and since adolescence, through high school, college, law school, marriage, and the birth of his three children, he had told no one about them, lest his life implode. When he found he could no longer carry the secret alone, he collapsed, confessed, and checked himself into the psychiatric unit of North Shore University Hospital, on Long Island. He thought he might never emerge.

Scared, confused, angry, humiliated, my mother considered leaving my father. He now seemed like a different, and more dangerous, person. Her own therapist declared, in an act of blithe malfeasance, that my father was a hopeless psychotic. In the house lived three boys under eleven who knew only that there was "something wrong with daddy's brain." On my father's first night in the hospital, he had been hysterical with dread and panic. They had to tranquilize him to sleep.

But my mother didn't leave my father. She stayed, for whatever complex of reasons, and saw him through the most fraught and vulnerable period of his life. They saw each other through. In the process they deepened a partnership that, by the time I was old enough to notice—though still ignorant of the truth of what had occurred—seemed as close, open, and inviolable as any marriage could be. They endured this and other crises. They held each other's secrets, which is a high form of intimacy. To my mother and my mother alone my father opened his heart.

Or so I imagined, with the enduring hopefulness and idealizing need of the child we all carry around in us. And so I was taken aback when, recently, my mother told me that to her, too, my father remained a mystery. She did, she presumed, know him better than most. He did show more of himself to her than he did to others, and more so as time went on. But always, right up to the end, when his heart began to fail, there was a barrier she could not breach. Always there was a sadness and sensitivity she could sense but was not allowed to see or touch. If she encroached too far into the spaces he was most intent on protecting, he warded her off, as he had warded me off, with frustration, irritation, and anger. He bared his coffee-stained teeth, widened his green eyes, and growled.

It was just shame, she said. My mother is a therapist. Like all good therapists, she has an acutely tuned radar for the traces and signals of shame. She knows how stealthily it hides, and how fiercely it defends.

He was improving, she said. He was evolving. We were sitting across from each other in my living room. Her arthritic knee, soon to be replaced, was in a brace, and her leg was propped up on the coffee table between a catalog of paintings by Helen Frankenthaler and a mess of pink plastic Barbie accessories. She could feel my father softening and opening up, she told me, loving himself more. But he needed more time. They both did.

"When you were little," my mother said, "there was so much shame in that house. Dad never stopped being ashamed of his voices. He always, always refused to talk about them. I was ashamed of his voices, too, of what people would say if they knew. Until you wrote your book I don't think I told more than one or two people. Dad was ashamed that he didn't make enough money, and so was I. I was ashamed of my panic attacks and my anxiety. I was ashamed of crap from my childhood." When my mother was ten, her own father had died, of a rheumatic heart. Like my father, he had kept his ailment a secret from his wife and family. After his death, my mother's classmates teased her for being fatherless—a bitter, formative experience for her.

"I tried to shield you boys from it, I tried to make everything seem normal. But you felt it. There were weeks when Dad barely got out of bed, he was so depressed. I'm sure you felt it. He missed a lot of work. He was barely functioning. I had to keep you quiet and out of there. 'Dad's resting.' 'Dad's trying to sleep.' But listen, kids know. Even when they don't know, they know. It's in the air. It's floating around. I did my best, but I'm sure it affected you."

She grimaced and reached for her knee. She lifted her leg and lowered it gingerly, slowly to the ground.

"How do *you* think it affected you?" she asked.

•

In 1972, a young psychologist named Ed Tronick conducted a simple experiment the results of which still resonate today. In a small, nondescript laboratory at Harvard Medical School, he gathered together seven mothers and their infant children. The oldest child was a year old, the youngest only four months old. One by one, Tronick invited each mother to sit opposite her child and just engage: play. This was Phase One of the experiment. Tronick filmed the proceedings, as he would film many iterations and replications of the experiment in years to come.

In one recording, a mother with straight brown hair and a broad smile sits across from her round-faced eleven-month-old daughter, who wears a bright red-and-white striped sweater. The mood is one of delight, affection, joy, and love. The mother coos; the baby clucks. The mother raises her eyebrows; the baby mimics her. The baby points at something in the room; the mother looks to where she has pointed. They smile and giggle and touch. The two are responsive to each other. They are *communicating*.

Then comes Phase Two. As per Tronick's instructions, the mother turns away for a moment. When she turns back, her face is an expressionless mask. She looks at her baby, but she does not interact. She does not respond. She is totally, consistently impassive—a flat, blinking face.

The baby realizes at once that something is wrong. Something has changed. She tries to reengage her mother. She smiles. She lifts an arm. She points at something in the room. "Da!" she says. She reaches out to be touched. These moves have worked before. But they don't work now. Her mother remains unreachable—there but not there. Now the baby becomes distressed. She grimaces and moans. She screeches. She puts a hand in her mouth and bites herself. When these moves fail too, when her mother will not attend even to her suffering, she gives up. She turns away, contorts her body, and cries.

All this takes less than two minutes, though it feels, watching it, much longer. Finally, in Phase Three, the mother returns. Her face becomes animated again. She reaches out to her baby. "I'm here!" she says, her voice light and sing-song. "Oh yes. Oh what a big girl!" It takes her daughter a second to accept this reunion, but she does. She relaxes and smiles, and mother and daughter are once again in sync.

This has come to be known as the Still Face study. Over the past half century, it has been conducted with mothers and older children; mothers and newborns; fathers and infants; strangers and infants; mothers and children with autism; mothers and children with Down syndrome; and even with adults facing adults, each playing one of the original roles. In every configuration, the results are the same. Connection and pleasure followed by stonewalling and agitation followed by reconnection and relief.

How should we interpret this? What should we make of this tight, poignant drama? We have to interpret it, we have no choice, since in almost all instances of the experiment the primary subject, the child, can tell you nothing about what she is thinking or feeling. She has little to no verbal language. Her mind is a mystery. She isn't passive. She acts. She exhibits agency, desire, and purpose. She *wants*. But she can't make sense of what she wants, let alone describe it to you. She is utterly vulnerable, quite literally strapped in for the experience. She can only adapt to what occurs.

When Ed Tronick talks about the Still Face study, he talks hopefully. In his experiment he sees what he calls "the power of discord." What he means by this is that perfect attunement between parent and child—unbroken, harmonious connection—is neither possible nor productive. To build a healthy mind and a resilient spirit, you need the dynamism of departure and return. Life is not all soulful communion, parents are never infallible, and systems that do not move die. What matters—what "provides the nutrients that allow our minds to grow"—is the study's third and final act: the meaning-making, reorganizing, generative leap from rupture to repair. That is where wisdom resides.

Tronick is no doubt right. When the parent returns, the child learns that distance is not necessarily abandonment. She learns that she can advocate successfully for what she needs. She can participate and endure. Still, when most people look at the experiment, this isn't at all what they see. When I look at the experiment, through the lens of my own past and pains, it is not what I see. What people see, what we see, with a squirming empathy, is an innocent child in agony. We see absence, desperation, confusion, frustration, panic, loneliness, and loss. We see cruelty and distress. We see what is arguably the signal fact of childhood: that we are created through a process of countless interactions we can scarcely understand and mostly not remember, with interlocutors who are to us as powerful, life-giving, and volatile as gods. More vividly and succinctly than any other experiment I know, the Still Face study shows how our emotional lives are forged in response to the emotional lives of our parents, and how little say we have in the matter.

When my mother asked me how the shame in my family affected me, I thought immediately of the Still Face study. I thought of it for two reasons. The first is that I have no idea how the shame affected me. I don't remember. I was only modestly sentient at the time. I have clues, feelings, mysterious hollows and unexplainable reflexes. In intimate relationships I react in ways that seem at once instinctual and implanted, natural and neurotic. Where did they come from? How could I know? Discerning how our childhoods affected us is a sideways, glancing project, riddled with guesswork. It is like the work done by quantum physicists, who only know what they are studying by the traces they leave.

The second reason I thought of the Still Face study is that one way I interpret it is as a compact display of how shame is transmitted, not like a gene but like a virus, from one generation to the next. Tronick did not set out to research shame, but shame is what his study seems to show, on both sides of the exchange—the mother's mask and the child's shrinking collapse. These two presentations, these two postures, are the faces of shame.

Or maybe it is more appropriate to say that they are the *non-faces* of shame, since shame's defining features are its furtiveness and ambiguity. Shame dreads being seen for what it is, or at all. Other emotions broadcast their essences. Joy has its smiling brightness, anger its snarling intensity, fear its protective recoiling. These are emotions any alert witness could pick out of a lineup, finger for the crime. They are outward, memorable, and bold. But shame is not so easily identified. Shame is wily and wary. It abhors detection and has devised clever methods of concealment and disguise. In this sense, shame is similar to guilt, with which it is often paired. But the differences between shame and guilt mean that their attitudes toward concealment are different. They may even be antithetical. Guilt is about the wrongness of a specific act—a harmful or unethical behavior, like theft, betrayal, disloyalty, or dishonesty. As such, it may hide itself away, but its true instinct is to be found out. A person suffering from guilt can only find relief in confession and forgiveness. He can only dilute the emotion's corrosive acidity by saying aloud the wrong he has done and seeking repair.

But for shame there is no possibility of forgiveness, and confession is anathema. Shame is about the wrongness of the self: the whole self. It is a vision of the self as corrupted, inferior, stained, worthless, deformed. A person suffering from shame knows himself to be set ignominiously apart from the mass of normal, worthwhile others. At the same time, the ashamed person is desperate to stop others from learning the truth about his ignominy. His worthlessness is a deep secret, but so is his shame about his worthlessness, for the emotion reveals the existence of the rot he believes to be at his core.

The shameful feeling points to the shameful self. And so there is nothing for the ashamed person to do, in the final analysis, but to conceal the whole contaminated system from public view, like a maximum-security prison. Concealment is shame's prototypical act. To say, "I am ashamed," wrote the psychoanalyst Otto Fenichel, is to say "I don't want to be seen." The word "shame" derives from the Indo-European *skam*, meaning "to hide." From this root also derive, the psychiatrist Donald Nathanson points out, "our words *skin*, and *hide*, the latter in both of its meanings: the hide which covers us naturally, and that within which we seek cover."

There are a number of different ways that we can hide within our own skin. Which is to say, there are a number of different ways we can throw others, and even ourselves, off the scent of our shame. One way is diversion. Just as porcupines raise and rattle their quills to protect the soft flesh beneath, people who are ashamed may lash out in anger whenever someone penetrates too far into the true territory of their pain. They may rave and rage, forcing others backward and gaining for themselves a safer, if lonely, isolation. Or, just as pufferfish cope with threat by inflating themselves to twice their normal size, a person mired in shame may inflate his own worth and self-regard, presenting himself as an exalted, incomparable figure in the world, a royal among serfs. He will transform his shame into narcissistic grandiosity, which is shame's mirror image. Both shame and narcissism take a stark, polarized view of the self. They both make what psychologists call "global attributions." It is just that shame sees the self as completely terrible and narcissism sees the self as completely wonderful. What neither do, when casting their pernicious spell, is admit any complexity.

But there is a more common way to avoid the exposure and judgment that shame fears, a way that allows for more plausible deniability, a way that keeps people close even as it holds them at a remove. This is simply to withdraw: to retreat into the dim privacy of one's own solitary mind. To be there but not there, simultaneously, and in this way to live life at a middle distance, without the great reward of full intimacy but without the desolation of full rejection.

When that mother turned back to that little girl with that face, that immovable mask, what did the face convey? What did her expression say? Her expression said: "I am not accessible to you. I will not allow you to see me. I will be here physically, but not spiritually. Not as you really need." To be clear, this isn't cruelty. When that expression arrives in the course of regular life, it is rarely spite or sadism or an act of willful, punitive retreat. It is just avoidance. It is the plain, reflexive terror of being observed when you consider the object of that observance to be repulsive—a disgrace. And no one observes more openly and acutely than a child.

And what does the child see? What does the child feel in response? What do you feel when the lines of connection between you and someone you love and cherish, someone of great importance to you, are severed, and severed unilaterally, without warning or explanation? What do you feel when you are ghosted? When you are given the silent treatment? What would you feel if you returned home one evening to find half the furniture missing, the pictures gone, dark rectangles on the walls, not even a note on the mantel? Would you feel shocked? Confused? Disoriented? Agitated? Angry? Would you call and text the person to reestablish contact, desperate at the very least for some recognition that you are here, you are still here, and that you matter, you still matter? And what if that didn't work? Would you begin to wonder if you yourself are the problem? Would you begin to suspect that you yourself are to blame for this calamity? After all, why would someone remove her love from you unless you were unlovable? Why would someone distance herself from you unless there was something in you, some defect or inadequacy, that was intolerable? If you were worthy of connection, you would have it.

And if you got to this point, wouldn't you suffer what the psychiatrist Helen Block Lewis has called an "implosion" of the self? Wouldn't you, as the little girl did when she could not reach her mother, at last turn away from the world, fold in on yourself, and hide your face, afraid to look at the accusing absence before you and afraid to have your worthless, defective self revealed?

"Oh my God," said the biblical scribe Ezra, "I am ashamed, and blush to lift up my face to thee, my God."

•

An early memory: I am seven or eight years old. My father and I are at the stationery store in the nearby strip mall, buying gum or crayons or stickers. We have just gone grocery shopping. We have paid and I am dragging my feet before we leave, thumbing through the Spider-Man comics on the thin, wobbling wire rack. As I spin the rack around I notice a boy, only slightly older than I am, at the register. He is buying a candy bar. That is, he is trying to buy a candy bar. He has brought a little plastic bag with coins in it, and he has emptied the coins onto the counter. The clerk, an old man with a bulbous pocked nose, counts the coins, slides each from one side of the counter to the other. He shakes his head. Not enough. The boy is twenty cents short. A line has formed behind the boy. Impatient grown-ups with their pens and greeting cards. Now, in view of these staring others, the boy must gather the coins from the counter and place them back in his plastic bag. This is not an easy task. The coins are hard to lift from the smooth countertop. He levers them up with his grubby fingernail and they clatter back down. I watch him. He knows full well that he is being watched. His face is like a McIntosh apple, mottled with shades of red. When he has finally managed to get all of the coins in the filmy plastic, he rushes to the door, his shoulders slumped, his eyes on the linoleum floor. The door dings its jaunty welcome as he leaves.

Now, all at once, I am ashamed. I am ashamed for the boy, vicariously ashamed. It feels like the shame is mine, that it is owned by me. His shame is now my shame, in my own body and mind. My face is aglow. I don't want to look at anyone, and certainly not at their eyes. What do I want? I want to get home as soon as possible, hurry to my room, and get under the covers. I want to cry, but out of sight.

A confusion, a kind of psychic haze, overtakes me. I have forgotten what I am meant to do, or what I want to do. The comics no longer hold my interest. They are frivolous, or simply absent. My father is outside in the breezeway. I can remedy this situation, I realize: the boy's and my own. All I need to do is to ask my father for twenty cents, find the boy, and hand it to him. I resolve to do this, but I find that I can't. The act, however charitable, seems terrible and extreme. My father will detect my oversensitivity. He will see and judge my susceptibility to the emotions of others. Already I have a reputation in my family. I am the crybaby. The tattletale. The wuss.

My father asks me what's bothering me. I start to tell him—I can see the boy now at the end of the breezeway, getting on his bike—but the words won't form. They won't cohere. So I say that nothing is wrong. Nothing. I'm fine. Can we go home now? And the blood rises to my face again, to my ears and my neck. For I know that I have missed an opportunity to do good. I have proven myself a coward, without speech and without action. Full of nothing but useless, pitiable, pointless emotion.

•

> While we have no idea consciously of the hidden purposes and impulses of another person, unconsciously we may react to them as sensitively as a seismograph to a faint subterranean vibration.
>
> —THEODOR REIK, *Listening with the Third Ear*

There are many ways to cause a person shame. There are many ways to make a person feel that there is something wrong with him, something that it would be best to hide. You can berate him in public, place him before a crowd and pronounce his misdeeds, as the Puritans did when they punished a sinner in the public square. You can strip him naked, exposing his genitals, his flab, his skinniness, his physical vulnerabilities. You can violate him. Cause a trauma. Beat him. Mock him. Degrade him. You can learn his secrets, the things he wants no one else to know—his infidelities, his inactions, his errors, his missteps—and broadcast them. Tell his peers. His colleagues. His lovers. His friends. The world. In what way does he feel defective? In what way does he feel inadequate and apart? Focus on these. Underscore them. Shaming someone is easy, if that is what you want to do.

But this is not the kind of shaming that interests me. I am not interested in purposeful shaming. I am not interested in the parent who wields shame like a pointed pistol to keep an unwitting child in line. I am interested in the atmospherics of shame. I am interested in how shame exists as a mood, as a kind of weather. I am interested in how shame rises from one person and falls like mist onto someone else, inadvertently, quietly. I am interested in how one person's shame becomes another's, and another's, and another's. I am interested in the *epidemiology* of shame.

In one sense it is misleading to focus on the communicability of shame. *All* emotions are communicable. Spreading from person to person is one of the basic things that emotions do, negative and positive alike. Thinkers have taken note of "emotional contagion," as psychologists now call the phenomenon, since at least Aristotle, who included it in his accounts of how theater and political speech affect audiences. Adam Smith argued that the tendency to imitate the emotional expressions of others was practically a reflex in people, in particular those of "delicate fibres and a weak constitution of body." In the late nineteenth century, the French sociologist Gustave Le Bon wrote, "Ideas, sentiments, emotions, and beliefs possess . . . a contagious power as intense as that of microbes." Emotions spread through crowds, he observed, as rapidly and thoughtlessly as a "panic that has seized on a few sheep will soon extend to the whole flock." What the specific emotion is hardly matters. What matters is what the psychologist Silvan Tomkins has called the "principle of contagion": "the fear-arousing potential of fear, the anger-arousing potential of anger, the excitement of excitement, the joyousness of joy, the distressing quality of distress."

Emotional contagion, then, is mundane. We are social, mimicking creatures. We aspire, out of some immemorial gene-preserving impulse, to conform (which is not nearly so dirty or ignoble a word as we are told). We need to be thought well of, to be retained in good standing in the community. We do this without knowing it. We match our expressions and movements, our postures and intonations, with those of our interlocutors as automatically as an octopus matches the color and texture of a stone on the ocean floor. And we have the capacity, thank goodness, to empathize with others. We have acquired the talent to feel our way into others' experiences—to tune our nervous systems into the unique frequency of whomever we desire with any fervency to understand. Hallelujah.

And yet it is hard to shake the impression that there is something singular about the contagiousness of shame. Shame seems to transmit in a way that is different from other emotions: more destabilizing, more immediate, more total. One encounters this point again and again in the literature on shame, especially the clinical literature. All the relevant manuals urge the conscientious therapist to take careful heed. When we are confronted with the typical signs and cues of shame—the fitful silence, the barely restrained turbulence, the groundward glance, the abrupt, conspicuous reddening—we are particularly likely to adopt the emotion as our own, to take it on and shoulder its weight. Or: We are particularly unlikely to be able to resist taking it on and shouldering its weight. It happens in a flash. Shame begets shame with an unmediated and plague-like virulence.

Why is this? What could account for shame being more catching than other emotions? One plausible answer is that shame is less specific than other emotions. It has fewer identifying marks that allow the prospective infectee to look it over and say: "No, this isn't mine. Sorry. This is yours." Emotions have targets. An emotion is always about something. I feel annoyed that my teenage daughter left a plate of food to rot in her room. I feel sad that my friend has been diagnosed with cancer. I feel scared that this plane will catch fire and tumble into the ocean. You may very well contract these feelings from me. My annoyance, sadness, and fear may, if they are intense or prolonged, or if I am particularly animated about them, atomize into the space between us and find their subtle way into your interior. But it is more probable that you will sympathize and remain aloof. You are able to remain aloof. After all, it was not your daughter who broke the house rules. It is not your friend with the tumor in his gut. You are perfectly comfortable with flying. Your individuality, your sense of distinctiveness, is the stick with which you can bat the feeling away.

But shame is not so easily differentiated or disclaimed. Shame may have a trigger—a secret revealed, a fault exposed—but its objects are diffuse and general. What is shame about? It is about belonging, security, connection, the need for love. What are shame's targets? They are failure, separateness, unsuitability, lostness. Strike these targets and they will always reverberate. You cannot help but sense the movement. These hungers are your hungers, too. These aches find ready analogues in your own experiences. Shame is a skeleton key. Who has not felt inferior, incompetent, lost, or separate? Where is the vaccination against *that*? How could you possibly inoculate yourself?

If you take this answer and flip it around, you find another answer, which is that shame extends its reach down, far down, into our most vulnerable and embryonic selves. I mean embryonic literally. We start our lives wholly attached to another, sharing in kind oxygen, nutrients, antibodies, drugs, and illnesses, drawing from the blood what we require to flourish and returning in the blood what we do not. We start fused, two as one. Then we are severed—in body. But of course we remain attached. We remain for a long time in total and desperate need. In need of food. In need of fluids. In need of warmth. In need of cleaning. In need of protection. Not least: in need of recognition. In need of the affirming and steadying presence of our parents. Here, hovering heavily above us, are our creators and our models. Here are the hands cradling us and the eyes staring down. Here is how we know that we will be cared for, that we will be held, that we are safe, that we are cherished. Here is how we know, quite simply and terribly, that we *are*. How else would we know? We poor humans, with large heads and long infancies, are born abject. Our parents are the wellsprings of our identities. They are the gravity that holds us together.

Shame is what happens when that gravity disappears. It is a second severance, a sudden and annihilating sense of disunity. A falling away. This doesn't mean that it is permanent. It only means that it is expansive. It is a kind of cataclysm. A disconnection from the source, shame cannot be anything but a cataclysm.

"It is joy to be hidden," wrote D. W. Winnicott, "but disaster not to be found."

•

My great-grandmother, I recently learned, died in a mental institution, of rectal cancer. Delusional and paranoid (she was convinced she knew who killed Lindbergh's baby), she was institutionalized repeatedly over the years, all throughout my grandmother's childhood. My grandmother never spoke about this. My grandmother's father was a traveling salesman, and often absent. Later my grandmother married a man who bore scar tissue in his heart, and held it a secret.

My grandmother was agoraphobic. She was afraid of crossing the street. She told no one this until she was in her seventies. She held it a secret, something to be endured alone.

My grandmother mocked my mother for liking sports and wanting to play ball in the street. "What's wrong with you?" she asked. "You should be wearing a skirt, and crinoline. You act like a boy!" My mother's father died when she was ten. Later she married a man who heard voices, and held it a secret.

My father's father heard voices as well. He held it a secret.

My father's mother suffered from agoraphobia and depression, though she never spoke of it or sought treatment. Her own father had abandoned the family when she was a child. After her husband, my grandfather, died, she wailed, "He promised not to leave me! He promised not to die first! He left me all alone!" She continued wailing this until her own death. She died only months after my father. She had not known that he was gravely ill, because he did not tell her. He kept it a secret, something to be endured alone.

•

After the age of twenty-five, a character in Julian Barnes's novel *England, England* believes, you are no longer allowed to blame your parents for your problems. This is generally true. But you are allowed, and at times perhaps obligated, to trace the lineage of problems within your family. You are allowed, and would be well advised, to bring your curiosity to bear on the patterns of behaviors, difficulties, and pathologies, secrets and predicaments, that give form and structure to what might otherwise seem, falsely, to be a life of struggle and confusion all your own.

My mother, who is now dogmatically opposed to secrets of any kind—she has become a late-in-life apostle of openness, like a child of alcoholics who bans all booze from the home—begins each course of treatment with a new client by drawing up what is known as a "genogram." A genogram is a sort of family tree of pathology. It is a chart that allows the therapist and her client to lift themselves above the client's complaints, as if in a hot-air balloon, so that they can see the contours of the territory of which the client is only a small and relatively new part. Using a complex of designated markings—lines, squiggles, squares, slashes, arrows, shadings, denoting everything from physical abuse to bankruptcy, sibling estrangement to suicide—the drawer of the genogram maps the client's deep psychological history, revealing to her, often with a shock, that she is the product of an idiosyncratic system that has been functioning, or malfunctioning, for generations.

Does this help? Not necessarily. It only provides context. Even if a disorder is inherited, its treatment is individual. And the information gained is anyway too blunt to offer much in the way of guidance or insight. To know that secrecy and shame run in your family does not give you an understanding of why they run. To see the problems transmit, parent to child, parent to child, does not give you an understanding of the mechanisms of transmission, the particular forces that, in living room and bedroom, kitchen and nursery, backyard and backseat, have imbued you with what you now realize are, for whatever it's worth, the torments of your ancestors. For that you need emotion, memory, and narrative. You need the finer grain.

"How did our shame affect you?" my mother wanted to know. I have my guesses, my suspicions. The bafflingly persistent homesickness and terror of abandonment. The grandiosity and perfectionism that quickly toggle to self-loathing and despair. The inability to be contentedly alone. The voice that perches like a parrot in my brain and squawks, "Failure. Failure. Failure." But these are my problems now. They are under my supervision and care. The more salient mystery lies at the site of exchange: the synapse where the poison slipped unwittingly through a matrix of good intentions.

When my father returned from the hospital, chastened and abashed, the law firm where he worked would not take him back. He had been truant and unproductive even before he went away.

At loose ends, he eventually accepted a job at a personal-injury firm whose ubiquitous advertisements, on TV and billboards, were cheesy, tasteless, and, on Long Island, a communal joke. It may have been during that period that I began to think of my father as a failure, and to be ashamed to be the kind of son who could think such a loathsome, ungrateful thing. It may have been during that period that I resolved to avoid his fate. (Even to write this down, a quarter century after his death, makes my throat feel thick and constrained, my mouth dry.) My mother confesses that she too felt ashamed—that she understood the firm to be "for losers"—and that she believes my father did as well. But it was all unspoken. At home he watched TV and movies, cooked dinner, tucked us in. My father, my brothers, and I developed a common language cobbled together from song lyrics, movie quotes, and comedy routines. We eschewed sincerity. We policed each other for moments of sensitivity, and when we spotted them we pounced. We were without mercy.

Oh but the love! The atmosphere of affection! I never doubted it for a moment, even as I detected less wholesome currents in the air. My father never spoke about work, except to say that he did not like what he did, and that if he had felt free to do what he wished he would have been a writer. He never talked about money. He rarely talked about his past. He in fact rarely talked about himself or his views on the world at all. My brothers remember his rages, the speed with which they would come on, and the color and cast of his face. My mother remembers her caution around him—her fear, in those tenuous early days, of setting him off or disturbing his hard-won, newly medicated calm. He refused to see a therapist, though he took his medication dutifully, then and for the rest of his life. He wanted to, or thought he had to, go it alone. And so, for the most part, he did.

I read the journal articles. I read the books of psychoanalytic theory and clinical practice. I consult the venerable experts.

I read: "The absence of an idealizable parent during crucial times in development is part of what leads to shame sensitivity."

I read: "Shame follows in the wake of the child's frustrated yearning for connection."

I read: "If the child is in a shame-filled environment, he will empathically feel shame."

I read: "To feel shame . . . we do not need the presence of an actual shamer or even a viewing audience; we need only these internalized figures that have become part of who we are."

And I read, further, about the treatment of shame, which is precisely the paradox you will have expected, for what else is there? "The therapist's task is to remove the masks of deception and expose shame, to speak of it directly and respectfully, and then to try to find ways to lift its burden through genuine self-acceptance."

"In attempting to lessen shame, we must risk self-exposure."

•

My father did not just refuse to see a therapist. In a way, he refused to seek connection at all. If he had truly intimate friends, I don't know of them. There was camaraderie, and laughter, and shared meals, wine bottles and bungalows and beach houses. He and my uncle seemed to enjoy each other's company. He had friends; he did. I don't know one person who disliked him, sweet and clever as he was. But did he ever disclose himself? Did he ever unfurl himself? Did he ever look for real solace, which is, as I have come to understand it, a starkness, a bold and fearful nakedness? Did he ever seek that exacting prize?

There was one incident, one story that my mother tells in weighty, regretful tones. Clearly, understandably, it is one of her worst memories. But when I imagine it now, I see a wild and reckless courage. I see a radical act for which I have, the more I think of it, enormous respect. I see a stripping down, like Lear on the heath.

It happened just before my father entered the hospital. He and my mother were driving home from I don't know where, down the quiet side road leading to our house. The pressure mounting inside him must have been tremendous. All those years of secrecy. All that fear. Three children. Work. Money. Mortgage. The months of anxiety and depression. The voices.

My mother was behind the wheel. My father started to cry, then to sob. They were only a block from home when he told her to stop the car. He pleaded with her to pull over. Shouted. She pulled to the curb and he tumbled from the car. Howling in the gutter. Wailing while my mother, aghast, pleaded with him to get back into the car. To let her take him home, behind closed doors. The neighbors. Sweetheart, the neighbors! Let me take you home.

It was the next day that my father confessed his voices, called the hospital, and arranged for his intake.

Now, tell me: Why would he do this? Why would he leave the car just yards from his own home? Why would he scream his pain in public, on that silent suburban street at night? *Yards* from home. This was a man, mind you, who abhorred exposure. This was a man mired in shame, which is to say in silence and exile. For years he had hidden. For years he had kept his secret from his family. This gentle, sane, jovial man in the two-story house in the middle of the cul-de-sac. And now he tells the world? Now he rends his garments in the public square?

My mother says it was a panic attack. The confinement of the car. An involuntary, adrenal flight into the open air, like that of an animal in a corner. Maybe. Probably I should defer both to her superior clinical experience and to her superior knowledge of my father's character and habits. And yet here my humility balks. I picture my father on the speckled asphalt over which my bicycle tires would later spin a hundred thousand times—the trim green grass, the crimson fireplug, the gaping storm drain—and what *I* see is a great, foolish, admirable gambit for freedom. I see my poor, dear, frightened father making a brave, blind vault toward the razored lip of his own jailhouse walls. I see an announcement: I am done. I am tired of the dark. I see the shattering of an extended silence . . .

And then a retreat. A permanent retrenchment. But okay. All right. (It's all right, Dad.) A life is what it is, and shame is an inheritance not so easily shed. I too feel the cascade of the past emptying into me, the murky pull of concealment. I feel the shame of you all, and let me tell you: It is not shameful. It is just where we start.

chapter six

ENVY

In late 2022, Emily and I bought a house in what the real estate agents call, after the prevailing architectural style, Victorian Brooklyn. For the previous five years we had lived in a squat, narrow, rented house three miles to the north. We liked it there. The house had its problems. When it rained hard, water flowed down the back steps into the kitchen. We were frequently invaded by ants and, sometimes, mice. There were no closets, not one, and the "backyard" was a desolate expanse of cracked concrete and ineradicable weeds. Still, the rent was reasonable, the location desirable, and the landlord responsive and fair. We were relatively content with the place, and we might have stayed much longer had we not literally screwed ourselves out of it. By 2021, we had a teenager and two children under the age of three, and each day the house felt less like a home and more like a crowded, noisy Salvation Army outlet.

The house we found was much larger and much nicer than any other we considered, and much larger and nicer than anything either of us had experienced in our adult lives. It was a three-story Victorian with a driveway, a finished basement, and a wraparound porch. It had a dining room with a stained-glass window. Four-and-a-half bathrooms. A room for the younger kids to share. Home offices. It had closets. It was glorious. It was quiet. It was perfect.

It was also, this being New York in the twenty-first century, expensive to the point of obscenity. There was no house on the market, from dump to palace, that wasn't obscenely expensive. Here was the snag. To the marriage I had brought, financially speaking, only liabilities and a hazy, unmet potential. Emily, who is as frugal as a pioneer and as industrious as a honeybee, had spent years saving for just this moment. Since her early twenties she had survived on little more than kale, cottage cheese, and chewing gum, working late into many nights to supplement her income as an editor with writing assignments. Through sheer will and diligence, she had accumulated and gestated an impressive nest egg. But it wasn't enough. We still fell hundreds of thousands of dollars short of what we needed. So we decided, after much discussion and debate, to accept the help of Emily's parents. The deal was this: They would take a forty percent stake in the house, with no strings attached and no expectations of repayment in their lifetimes. This was not a loan but an advance on Emily's inheritance. Any profits from this investment were ultimately to be divided equally among their three daughters.

This simple, wise, benevolent arrangement elicited a number of strong emotions in us, foremost among them gratitude and wonder. But it elicited more complicated emotions, too, especially in Emily. A surge of shame overtook her, a sense that in accepting her parents' largesse she was doing something fundamentally, even morally, wrong. For twenty-five years Emily had lived according to an ethos of thrift, self-reliance, and charity. She worked hard, she lived modestly, and each year she gave to charity, as her parents had instilled in her, "until it hurt." Now, suddenly, she was a taker, a passive receiver of funds she did not earn and, by her lights, did not deserve. A dedicated progressive, she felt discomfited by the very notion of deservingness. It was pure, idiot luck that she had parents who were able to help us financially. Her understanding of this fact was central to her identity. It was a cherished principle, and once the wire transfer had been initiated and the contracts signed she was haunted by the thought that she had betrayed it, and all for the sake of that vulgar modern confection, the "dream house."

She was also haunted by the thought that she was acting unfairly toward her sisters, neither of whom had received the same offer. Accepting her parents' money was, Emily worried, dangerously inequitable. It threatened to dysregulate a family system diligently predicated on balance: no one daughter loved more or less than another; no one daughter treated better or worse than another; no one ranked; no one favored. Never mind that Emily's sisters were among the loudest voices urging her to for godsakes take the deal. We *want* you to do this, they said. We want you to have this house. But there seemed no amount of blessings they could give that would ease Emily's conscience. She did not want to be, in any way, preferred.

And there was a third thing, too—a set of feelings and behaviors that emerged immediately after we moved and soon hardened, as it were, into a complex. This complex was most apparent when we had people come to visit, or when we even talked about having people come to visit. Emily, normally the most eager and gracious of hosts, would become fretful and reticent. On the one hand, she wanted to share our home with our friends, to welcome them, cook for them, throw parties, have houseguests. To open the doors wide. On the other hand, she dreaded each visit like a dental exam. It was bad enough, in the age of Zillow, that anyone with a phone could look up how much we had paid for the house. But for people to see it with their own eyes? To witness the ostentatiousness of the thing? The bay windows! The hardwood floors! The strangely tuneful "smart" appliances! It was almost too much for her to bear. Our friends are not wealthy people. They are cartoonists, novelists, critics, literary journalists, academics, teachers. What would they say? What would they *think*? Would their opinion of us change? Would they feel alienated or diminished or uncomfortable? Would they judge us—rightfully, righteously—for our bourgeois acquisitiveness?

The worst part was that we would never know. Any negative evaluation would take place either in their own heads or out of earshot, on the ride home. In front of us they would say the polite, supportive things. And so Emily, to quell her anxieties, was forced to employ a strategy of preemptive self-criticism. In essence, she would nervously blurt out everything she feared our guests might be thinking about the house, and about us in it. She would confess not only to the excessiveness of the purchase but to her embarrassment at the excessiveness of the purchase. She would lay bare her discomfort, wincing through the obligatory tours, undercutting every expression of admiration with her own expression of ambivalence. She would point out that the roof often leaks! That the backyard was filled with strange bits of metal and broken glass! That the floors are still often very dirty! All of it true, none of it enough. While I, further deepening the comic recursiveness, would make clear that we were all fully and fondly aware of Emily's painful self-awareness. We were all in on the joke.

Not in enough for Emily, though. There was still the matter of the money itself—the cold, clear facts—and Emily could not fully breathe, it seemed, until she had diminished our potential complicity by spelling out the exact terms of her parents' involvement in the purchase. The figure itself was crucial and emanated a certain magic. Forty percent. Her parents, and not we, owned forty percent of everything our friends saw—from the roof, say, to the third floor, plus the main bedroom and en suite bathroom. *Forty percent.* They needed to know this! I came to think of it as a kind of emotional arithmetic. As awkward as Emily felt, she could feel two-fifths less awkward if she could articulate the details of our ownership stake. It was as if she were asking people to discount their judgment of us by the appropriate amount. It was as if she were asking them to conduct all necessary calculations before they formulated their opinions.

Or let me put it another way: It was as if she were saying to our friends, "See? Do you understand? We aren't as bad as I imagine you imagine us to be. We are, still, the same. Or, at the very least, we know exactly how bad we are."

•

In 1967, after more than two decades of fieldwork, the Berkeley anthropologist George Foster published a book called *Tzintzuntzan*, about a village of peasants in the Mexican state of Michoacán. Centuries earlier, Tzintzuntzan—"the place of the hummingbirds"—had been the capital of the Tarascan Empire, and a great and vibrant city. By the time Foster first visited, just after World War II, it was a poor, insular community of around two thousand people who lived, as he put it, "a biblical style of life." Pottery-making and farming were the main occupations. Some people fished. Few earned enough to live on.

Tzintzuntzan has many of the features typical of ethnography: the dutiful charts and maps, the arid facts and figures. But what makes the book unusual, and strikingly original, is that it uses all of its information to explore a single emotion in the lives of its subjects: envy, the feeling of "resentful longing," as one eloquent definition has it, for the advantage of another.

Foster was a social anthropologist, which means that he was primarily interested in teasing out the hidden viewpoints and accepted, unquestioned beliefs that lead people to behave as they do. In Tzintzuntzan in particular, he came to believe that much of the way the villagers acted toward each other—the ways they courted, worshipped, quarreled, grieved, and raised families—could be explained only by way of a shared worldview about the meaning and distribution of the "good things in life." Tzintzuntzeños believed that everything worth having, from wealth and health to virtue and virility, from love and friendship to power and honor, existed in "limited and unexpandable quantities." Life, as they saw it, was a win-or-lose game. The pot of desirable stuff was both lamentably small and permanently fixed. No one could do a thing to increase it, and no one ever would be able to. Foster called this vision of how the world worked the "Image of Limited Good."

The Image of Limited Good was a mostly subconscious assumption. It was a "cognitive orientation" that structured the villagers' daily lives, and it helped Foster to make sense of some classic and peculiar Tzintzuntzeño behavior. From the very start of his fieldwork, he had been struck by the villagers' tendencies toward reticence and stinginess. No one seemed to praise anyone else. No one gave compliments. No one seemed able to *take* a compliment. If you told someone that the meal they prepared for you was delicious, they would tell you all the ways in which it was inadequate. If you praised their home, they would point out the flaws. For some years, Foster chalked up these behaviors to selfishness and bad manners—mere peasant idiosyncrasies. In time, however, he came to understand them as parts of a larger, coherent pattern. Tzintzuntzeños weren't just withholding and self-effacing; they were averse, almost allergic, to any suggestion of difference in their ranks. They went to extraordinary lengths to downplay and conceal even the hint of an advantage. Expectant women hid their growing bellies under heavy cloaks and referred to pregnancy as an "illness." Mothers kept their children dirty and clothed them in rags. Those wealthy enough to have homes with glass windows kept the shutters closed all day. Even the children ate in silence, so as not to exhibit undue pleasure. The entire town was devoted to maintaining a sense of equality among its members.

When Foster looked at these behaviors through the lens of the Image of Limited Good, they took on an unassailable logic. *The good things in life come in finite amounts. The universe is zero-sum.* If Tzintzuntzeños believed these statements to be true, it followed that no one in the village could improve his position without reducing the position of someone else. No one could enrich himself without impoverishing his neighbor. No one could gain in social standing without diminishing the social standing of another. The Image of Limited Good required the villagers to uphold a delicate, eternal balance, or else.

Or else what? Here was where envy entered the equation. Central to Foster's insight was the recognition that Tzintzuntzan's equilibrium, such as it was, was held in check not by mutual compassion or egalitarian fervor or Christian charity. What held Tzintzuntzan's equilibrium in check was fear. All that denying and apologizing, all that secrecy and silence, all that dodging and covering and hiding—it was all there for a single purpose: to prevent the poison of envy from creeping in and corrupting the system. Envy was the ever-present threat that loomed over Tzintzuntzan. Envy, with its seething indignation and quiet malice, envy which is the "rottenness of the bones" (Proverbs 14:30), envy which "breeds unkind division" leading to "ruin" and "confusion" (*Henry VI*, 4.1)—envy which, above all, carries with it the threat of sanction, punishment, and violence—had to be suppressed at all costs. The stability of the village and the safety of its residents depended on it. In a Limited Good society like Tzintzuntzan's, Foster wrote in a later essay, any improvement, real or perceived, conjures the specter of envy. Anyone who advances beyond the average "knows that his neighbors may convert their envy into direct or indirect aggression, because they see his success as being at their expense." At the same time, this specter of aggression drives a desperate desire for an advantage. "The ideal Tzintzuntzeño," Foster writes, "spends his life walking a psychological tightrope, on which a single misstep, to right or left, will spell disaster."

With these ideas Foster could finally understand why, whenever he asked a question related to status or difference, he received the same response, the same canned, anxious, conversation-stopping insistence: "Here we are all equal!"

·

In the previous two chapters, we examined negative emotions from two crucial vantage points. What we feel and how we understand and express what we feel—the whole complex weave of our emotional lives—exist on the one hand at the level of temperament and personal impulses, and on the other at the level of family experience, parental influence, and our early emotional educations. We are faced with our emotional nature and what to do about it, and we are faced with how we were nurtured and what to do about that. Foster's work now presents us with a third realm we will have to explore if we are to fully understand our negative emotions and learn to live wisely and well with them. That is the level of culture, or how the spaces and societies we live within codify, communicate, and police our emotional norms.

This is the most difficult level to talk about, since it has the greatest number of variables and moving parts. Even in a society as relatively self-contained and uniform as Tzintzuntzan's, people are of course different from one another. They have different personalities, different upbringings, different experiences, hopes, desires, needs. Moreover they, like everyone else, feel and act differently in the different domains of their lives. Sibling relationships, friendships, the marketplace, the church, the schoolyard, the field, the pottery studio, the bedroom: With each shift in setting the emotional picture shifts as well, however subtly. Everywhere people adjust depending on where they are and whom they are with.

The medieval historian Barbara Rosenwein has written persuasively about what she calls "emotional communities" within a given culture. She defines these as groups of people who "adhere to the same valuations of emotions and how they should be expressed." Emotional communities are like social communities, and often map on to them more or less directly. To use a personal example, my group of college friends tends to value irony, irreverence, and a kind of loving rejection of intellectual airs. We give each other license to act goofy, to tease each other without censure or (usually) complaint. In effect, we acknowledge that we knew each other when we were young clueless idiots, and within the group we have permission to return to the emotional expressions that we associate with that time. By contrast, with my friends from the worlds of publishing and journalism, this would never fly. There is a greater expectation of intellectual and moral seriousness, an understanding that although there is great envy in our world (who's up? who's down? whose book sold well? whose book won an award?) and fear in the work that we do, it would be déclassé to express those emotions. "Don't let 'em see you sweat" is more the emotional ethic in this group. And when, in my early forties, I entered graduate school to become a therapist, I claimed citizenship in another distinct emotional community. In this group the most valued emotions are empathy and compassion, but with an allowance for particular forms of professional grousing: about clients who repeatedly cancel at the last minute; about the money-grubbing byzantine ways of health insurance companies; about rival therapeutic approaches. These are only three of the emotional communities of which I am a member. There are many more, and in each of them I am expected to adhere to different emotional rules—rules that dictate not only what I can say without censure or exclusion, but, in a more subtle, stealthy way, what I actually *do* feel. In each of my emotional communities I am, in ways I typically don't even notice, a different emotional creature.

Sometimes the codes governing different communities clash with one another, causing strain. When I was in college, I was for a time a member of a comedy improvisation troupe. This community, which was filled with skilled performers, valued courage, spontaneity, flamboyance, speed of reaction, and emotional volubility. My closest friend in the troupe possessed all of these attributes at levels that were at times almost too much to bear. He was, I think, something of a comedic genius, and one weekend I brought him home to meet my family. I did not anticipate how uncomfortable I would feel, how caught in the middle between two emotional modes—one in which high expressiveness was held up as a virtue and one in which there existed expressive boundaries that were real but invisible, and that you knew you had crossed only when you caught a skeptical, appraising glance from one of your brothers that seemed to say: "Tone it down, Dan. You're embarrassing yourself."

Rosenwein's concept of emotional communities helps us to see the sheer variety of emotional contexts in which each of us live, and between which we shuttle not only in a lifetime but often in a single day. Home, work, school, church, gym, bar, family gathering, community meeting, self-help group: Each sphere is its own emotional universe, with its own unspoken protocols. But there is a related concept that takes a much wider view of the situation, one that emphasizes not difference but commonality: The "emotional regime," as the anthropologist and historian William Reddy has called it, governs what it is "normal" and "abnormal" to feel and express for an entire society at any one point in time. An emotional regime is a bit like the old notion of national character—the fatalism of the Russians, the stiff upper lip of the English—except that it focuses more on the power behind the existing rules. Every culture develops rituals, rites, and social practices, political and economic systems, that structure emotional possibilities and convey emotional expectations for everyone who lives within that culture. It is like a regime because we feel we have to live by it, even if we don't necessarily notice that it is there.

We tend to think of our emotions as private, intimate things, and so we have accustomed ourselves to a more personal apportioning of blame. For example, when a client comes into my office struggling with feelings of anger toward her children, that anger will almost invariably come hitched to a belief in the inappropriateness and shamefulness of that anger. There is the anger, which is primary, and there is the belief "I shouldn't be feeling this," which is secondary. Our work together can then move along three different tracks. We can address the anger itself: what it feels like, when it occurs, what behaviors it gives rise to, and what methods might reduce it. We can address the origins of the anger: the way she was raised by her parents, the expectations placed on her and the expectations she has for her children. But we can also address, indeed we must address, the client's belief that it is improper or contemptible to feel anger toward your children. Where did this belief come from? The client didn't invent it whole cloth. And even if she absorbed it from her upbringing, from her own mother's aversion to feeling anger toward *her* children, this doesn't explain what caused her mother to take on the belief. It doesn't address the cultural roots of the belief that a mother is supposed to feel a certain way toward her children, that the ideal of motherhood is benevolence, nurturance, kindliness, harmoniousness. It doesn't address the association of anger with masculinity, or the disproportional allowance made for men's negative emotions over women's, or the innumerable representations of angry women as undesirable, shrewish, emasculating, and repressive. In short, we cannot fully understand the client's experience of anger without taking into account how the culture at large views anger.

Another way of saying this is that every emotion has a biography. Every emotion occurs within a specific time and place. We are continuously receiving and responding to cultural messages about what emotions are appropriate and inappropriate to feel, as well as when, where, and how it is appropriate to feel them, and we have no choice but to look carefully at these cultural messages. If we don't, we risk omitting a major part of our emotional lives. We also risk putting too much blame for our negative emotions on ourselves and our intimates.

Which returns us to envy. Every culture on earth seems to have some concept that relates to our notion of envy. It is an emotional state that is present in every era and every society. Envy is, I think, our most social emotion, since it is almost literally about appearance and exposure. The word itself derives from the Latin word *invidia*, meaning "to look upon." The person who envies not only looks but looks covetously, with malice.

As the scholar Tiffany Watt Smith has observed, envy is also one of the very few emotions explicitly concerned with notions of fairness and justice. Anytime we gaze upon what others have, or are gazed upon by others, we are in the potential presence of envy. And in America, in the twenty-first century, gazing is a national pastime. Our entire market economy runs on it. Tzintzuntzeños closed their windows to avoid being seen. We spend hours each day, eyes on our phones, peering into the lives of our friends, our colleagues, actors, musicians, moguls, models, politicians, chefs, influencers, countless strangers.

How do *we* view envy?

•

Once upon a time, there lived two brothers. Cain, the older brother, was a farmer, and he was very unlucky. He worked tirelessly, but he couldn't seem to get ahead. His crops often failed. He was honest but shy. He didn't have any friends. Abel, the younger brother, was a cheerful, talkative, wealthy shepherd. He played the flute and had loads of friends. Everyone loved the guy. One day, the two brothers were walking in the fields. Abel (who truth be told was a bit of a jerk) was droning on about how great his life was. Cain grew more and more frustrated. A voice in his head told him to cool it, but eventually he couldn't take it anymore, and he punched Abel square in the face. He felt better until he realized that his brother was on the ground dead. Then he was horrified.

He hadn't meant to kill Abel! He just wanted to give vent to his emotions! After that, his life was pretty much ruined.

This is a condensed version of the foundational biblical story as told by the educator and activist Felix Adler, founder of the Society for Ethical Culture, in his 1892 book *The Moral Instruction of Children*. The original is of course a lot different; it involves animal sacrifice and direct communication with God, and there isn't any flute. Adler thought it important, however, to retrofit the story to suit the sensibilities of nineteenth-century American children. He encouraged parents to tell it in this way, and to be sure to follow up by underlining the story's moral, which, he wrote, was this: "Do not harbor evil thoughts in the mind.... Cain's sin consisted in not crushing the feeling of envy in the beginning; in comparing his own lot with that of his more favored brother and dwelling on this comparison, until, in a fit of insane passion, he was led on to the unspeakable crime which, indeed, he had never contemplated." Envy, Adler needed his audience to understand, was a sin defined by measuring your worth against another's. It was dangerous. It had to be controlled and contained. If it wasn't, morally abhorrent things would happen.

Adler's approach to moral instruction was characteristic of its time and place. In the late nineteenth century, moralists of all kinds—teachers, clergymen, civic leaders, journalists, essayists—portrayed envy as a perilous vice and a social scourge. In writing geared not only toward parents but toward children, businessmen, farmers, and middle-class women, they extolled the idea of the Great Chain of Being. Social and economic hierarchies were natural and right, part of God's design. The only proper response to your divinely ordained place in the universe was to make peace with it. These moralists cited the tenth commandment: "Thou shalt not covet . . . anything that is thy neighbor's." They cited Saint Paul's injunction that, whatever condition you find yourself in, "therewith to be content." In every way possible, they upheld the traditional understanding of envy as a rebellion against moral law and the cause of unhappiness, strife, and fruitless dissatisfaction.

Then, fairly suddenly, all that changed. Somewhere between the death of Queen Victoria and the stock market crash of 1929, the cultural meaning of envy in America did a complete one-eighty. One moment everyone was preaching the gospel of restraint, thrift, stability, and contentment. The next moment everyone was preaching the gospel of aspiration, material desire, emulation, and discontent. A new "emotional regime" governing envy arose, one that would have been all but unthinkable just years before. In his novel *Billy Budd*, written in the 1880s, Herman Melville observed that envy was "universally felt to be more shameful than even felonious crime." (In his book, envy *causes* a felonious crime.) The new regime waved away this familiar stigma. It touted envy as something instinctive, vital, and useful, a spur to personal advancement and an engine of national growth. In short: a virtue. In a 1921 textbook on economics, Ray Osgood Hughes worried that Americans had become too complacent and too static. To progress in life, they needed to feel envy.

> Let these same ignorant people once... become acquainted with the pleasures and luxuries that some folks have in abundance. Immediately discontent sets in, and a striving for higher and better things may follow. And then gradually from this, a new contentment comes.... This higher kind comes from realizing what one ought to have and knowing that one is actually making progress toward gratifying those needs. In many cases, then, a certain discontent is almost desirable.

This was a textbook for high school kids. After 1920, they would be inundated with such messages.

How did this happen? How did envy transform from a sin to be extinguished into a quality to be encouraged in schoolchildren? The historian Susan Matt answers this question in her book *Keeping Up with the Joneses* (2003). She gives a number of answers, including urbanization, the devastation of World War I, the decline of religious belief, and the increasing influence of Darwinian thought. But her main answer is, not to put too fine a point on it: money. In the early years of the twentieth century, there occurred a radical transformation in the American economy—an explosion in wealth, technology, communication, and manufacturing capacity. This was the era that saw the rise of the radio, the automobile, the movies, the mass-circulation magazine, the department store, and the mail-order catalog. Nineteenth-century America still adhered closely to Foster's Image of the Limited Good. There wasn't enough to go around. Now, everywhere you looked, you saw abundance. Goods that were once available exclusively to the rich were now available—in mass-produced facsimiles, but available nonetheless—to just about everyone. In the city, you could admire them in the windows of department stores that filled entire city blocks. In the country, you could admire them in the pages of the Sears, Roebuck & Co. catalog. You were enticed by elegant advertisements on billboards, in magazines, and during radio programs. You were enticed to want, you were enticed to emulate, and you were enticed to buy. America turned, in those decades, into the consumer economy that we still are today.

The story of the relationship between consumerism and envy has a number of parts. As Foster has shown with the Tzintzuntzeños, the first way people seek to tamp down envy is through concealment. If you hide what you have, others won't envy you; if you can't see what others have, you won't envy them. Envy is spurred by sight. It was almost inevitable, then, that as American culture became more visual, envy itself would increase. More images mean more desire. Envy is also spurred by an awareness of inequality and difference—an awareness driven home by all those images of beautiful people wearing beautiful things, having wonderful times. The consumer economy, Matt argues, delivered a kind of double blow to the prevailing emotional regime. On the one hand, it increased the occasions for envy. On the other hand, it offered a ready solution to the feeling of envy: Buy stuff. Get what you want. By buying lots of stuff, or the right kind of stuff, you may not gain status in any literal sense; that hat, that dress, that face cream won't make you rich or gain you entry into high society. But you will *feel* as if you have gained in status. You will *feel* less deprived and less shut out. Your envy, that nagging sense of inferiority you carry around with you like a rash, will be assuaged.

But only temporarily. That's the catch. The phrase "keeping up with the Joneses" entered into common circulation in the 1920s. At the time, it carried no negative connotations. "Devoid of any moral overtones," Matt writes, "it portrayed envy and emulation as innocuous, ordinary, and expected social instincts." But envy is not innocuous. Envy is an agitation that increases in the pursuit to relieve it. It tends toward insatiability.

In *The Theory of the Leisure Class* (1899), perhaps the most influential book ever written on the psychology of consumption, Thorstein Veblen described the cycle of discontent into which "invidious comparisons" lead a person.

> So long as the comparison is distinctly unfavorable to himself, the normal, average individual will live in chronic dissatisfaction with his present lot; and when he has reached what may be called the normal pecuniary standard of the community, or of his class in the community, this chronic dissatisfaction will give place to a restless straining to place a wider and ever-widening pecuniary interval between himself and this average standard. The invidious comparison can never become so favorable to the individual making it that he would not gladly rate himself still higher relatively to his competitors in the struggle for pecuniary reputability.

The agitation has no cure. Hunger, once satisfied, does not inspire more hunger. But envy isn't like hunger. It is more like alcoholism. It is a chronic condition. It can't be destroyed. It can only be held in abeyance.

In early twentieth-century America, the wealthiest and most powerful members of society were coming to recognize that the very features of envy that had given earlier leaders pause—its fractiousness, its insidiousness, its restlessness—were precisely what the new economic conditions required. People have always desired. People have always compared. People have always envied. But now the nation, in its striving for greater power, influence, riches, and growth, needed those traits unleashed. Envy came to be thoroughly redefined in this era not just because there was more stuff to buy, and more ways to see and buy that stuff. Envy came to be thoroughly redefined because very powerful people—corporate leaders, politicians, economists, and bankers—*wanted* it redefined, and relentlessly sought to reeducate the public in what one corporate adviser of the time called "the new economic gospel of consumption."

It is striking just how explicit this project was. In 1929, Herbert Hoover's Committee on Recent Economic Changes (convened not long before the stock market crashed) surveyed the American economy and beheld a nationwide demonstration that human wants "are almost insatiable; that one want satisfied makes way for another." The committee saw "a boundless field before us . . . new wants which will make way endlessly for newer wants, as fast as they are satisfied." That same year, Charles Kettering, an executive at General Motors, published an article claiming that in the new economy "there is no place anyone can sit and rest. . . . It is a question of change, change, change, all the time—and it is always going to be that way . . . for the world only goes along one road, the road to progress." The title of his article was "Keep the Consumer Dissatisfied."

And how were consumers to be kept dissatisfied? The answer was straightforward: by manipulating their emotions. The leaders of the age recognized that envy—always latent, always just barely subcutaneous—could be teased to the surface to increase sales and profits. "Teased" is perhaps too passive a word, because in many cases their methods couldn't have been more direct. Advertisements made open use of envy as a sales tactic. They targeted customers by stoking their fears of inferiority and their desire for superior status. "Every Woman's Wish—Clothes that other women will envy," read a 1924 ad for Butterick dress patterns. The makers of Pompeian face cream urged potential customers, "Don't Envy a Good Complexion—Use Pompeian and have one." They went on to ask, "Why cast envious eyes at another when all you need to do to have an equally enviable complexion is to use Pompeian MASSAGE cream yourself?"

The Royal Tailors, in *The Saturday Evening Post*, published an illustration of a dapper man on a streetcar, openly admired by the shabbily dressed men who gaze at him. "All Eyes Envy the Tailor-Dressed Man," the ad read. Elsewhere, the company proclaimed that "envy of the man with a good tailor lies inrooted in the soul of every untailored clothes wearer. That envy need no longer remain ungratified in *you*." That envy lurks in the soul of man is an idea with which no medieval theologian could disagree. This was the very problem of envy, after all: its spiritual inrootedness. The suggestion that the solution to envy was to buy a custom-made suit was an entirely new innovation.

But that was what the bottom line required. Two new professional fields, advertising and public relations, emerged to serve that goal. Before 1900 or so, most ads were dry, text-heavy displays, dedicated to the simple delivery of information. By the 1920s, they had become carefully designed tools of mass influence intended to cause emotional discomfort in the reader. In *Propaganda* (1928), Edward Bernays, the so-called "father of public relations," declared this work to be essential to the national interest.

The conscious and intelligent manipulation of the organized habits and opinions of the masses is an important element in democratic society. Those who manipulate this unseen mechanism of society constitute an invisible government which is the true ruling power of our country.... It is they who pull the wires which control the public mind, who harness old social forces and contrive new ways to bind and guide the world.

Bernays was well placed to lead the new movement in public relations. His uncle was Sigmund Freud (in 1920, he facilitated the American publication of *Introductory Lectures on Psychoanalysis*), and Bernays was shrewd in applying Freudian insights to commercial ends. He grasped that a superfluous consumer good, a luxury item, derived its power not from what it was but from what it represented. A person will often desire an item, he wrote, "not for its intrinsic worth or usefulness, but because he has unconsciously come to see in it a symbol of something else, the desire for which he is ashamed to admit to himself," because "it is a symbol of social position, an evidence of his success." The psychology of consumption is basically a retailer's version of Freud's concept of displacement.

Other advertisers and publicists took note of the work of Freud's dissident follower Alfred Adler, who in 1907 began to outline the dynamics of the "inferiority complex." Matt quotes an advertiser of the time as stating that we all "suffer from an eating sense of our unimportance, insignificance, inadequacy, whether we know it or not. And, whether we know it or not, a large part of our energies are directed to making ourselves feel important, significant, equal to anything."

The operative word, as ever, was *feel*. The consumer wouldn't, of course, actually become a movie star or socialite by purchasing the right hair cream or soap flakes or brand of cigarette. But by tying a product to a prominent figure, and then getting the consumer to purchase that product, an advertiser could produce in the consumer that "grand and glorious feeling"—namely, that our supposed betters "have 'nothing on us.'" Fortunes could be made by targeting people's emotional vulnerabilities.

•

Toward the end of his nearly century-long life, Charlie Munger, Warren Buffett's partner at Berkshire Hathaway and one of the most successful businessmen ever to live, noted a glaring contradiction in American society. Since the end of the Great Depression, Munger observed, living standards in the industrialized West had grown to a level unprecedented in five thousand years of recorded history. By 2022 Americans were healthier, wealthier, safer, and more comfortable than they had ever been before. At the same time, they seemed to be much less happy than ever before. A pall of dissatisfaction—of anxiety, depression, and pessimism—had settled over the nation.

Munger offered a "simple explanation" for the incongruity. "The world is not driven by greed," he said, "it's driven by envy." And envy is triumphant in twenty-first-century America. All anyone thinks about today "is somebody else having more now and it's not fair that he should have it and they don't." He denounced the sophisticated political and commercial networks designed "to pour gasoline on the flames of envy," as well as the lemming-like willingness of consumers to be engulfed by the emotion. "Who in the hell needs a Rolex watch so you can get mugged for it?" he asked. "Yet everybody wants to have a pretentious expenditure. That helps drive demand in our modern capitalist society. My advice to young people is: Don't go there."

It was a cheeky thing for a billionaire to say. Berkshire Hathaway owns Borsheims Fine Jewelry, Helzberg Diamonds, and Ben Bridge Jeweler, as well as sizable stakes in Amazon, Apple, and American Express. Munger devoted most of his arch-capitalist life to stoking demand, in many cases literally for Rolexes. Still, his assertion about the ascendancy of envy in American life deserves consideration. So, too, does his assertion that envy is the preeminent emotion in human life in general.

Munger was born on January 1, 1924. A week earlier, in southern France, another man was born who would make Munger's latter claim the centerpiece of a grand, vastly influential theory of human experience. René Girard, a literary scholar and philosopher who ended his long career at Stanford in 1995, was the architect of what is known as Mimetic Theory. It is an idea with many byways, reaching into numerous disciplines including anthropology, mythology, history, theology, and economics. But the heart of the theory has to do with the nature of desire. We tend to believe, Girard observed, that our desires are our own, formed by our unique personalities, histories, and needs. Our particular desires—for this mate, for that lifestyle, for that experience—mark us as individuals. But no. In this, Girard argued, we are completely deluded. "Individualism is a formidable lie." We don't develop our own desires; we copy what others desire. It is congenital, and usually unconscious. When it comes to what we want in life we are clueless, and we "turn to others in order to make up [our] mind."

Girard outlined two ways in which this process takes place. In the first, we adopt the desires of some "external mediator," someone outside of our immediate social circle who can serve as an ideal—a model for how to be. In literature, the classic example is Don Quixote, a lowly Spanish nobleman, formerly known as Alonso Quijano, who dreams himself into the role of a gallant knight-errant. Quixote reads so many overwrought chivalric romances that he adopts the character and purposes of a chivalric hero. But we don't need to turn to literature to understand external mediation. It is what drives all celebrity-based advertising. When you see Beyoncé in a L'Oréal commercial, or LeBron James in an ad for Nike, or Timothée Chalamet on a billboard holding a bottle of Chanel cologne, you are seeing an appeal to external mediation. You are seeing an attempt to get consumers to adopt the alleged desires of these accomplished, famous, beautiful people.

Over the past century, this kind of effort has metastasized, exacerbated by television, celebrity culture, targeted marketing, the commercialization of public spaces, and the internet. External mediation is the old faithful of modern advertising. It works, and it may be what Munger had in mind when he fretted about the supremacy of envy in American culture. There is an economic logic at work here, too. Once people have secured for themselves the basic necessities of life—food, water, shelter, safety—they turn to the acquisition of what economists call "positional goods." These are goods that people desire because they place the owner at a high status relative to others. Gucci handbags, Cristal champagne, Air Jordans, infinity pools . . . the wealthier a society grows, the greater the importance of positional goods.

None of this is new. But our own era has seen another, distinctly powerful innovation, one that has vastly increased the opportunities for envy: social media.

According to Girard, there's not just external mediation but something he called "internal mediation." The difference is in proximity. If Taylor Swift is an external mediator, an internal mediator is your friend, your neighbor, your colleague, your cousin, your high school English teacher, your college roommate, your boss. An internal mediator is someone with whom you interact, with whom you share a social environment. This both deepens and complicates the process of mimetic desire in that it introduces legitimate competition into the mix. It is a kind of love triangle (Girard used the phrase "triangulated desire"), but one in which the desired object becomes less important than the rivalry itself. You see what your peers have and you feel almost metaphysically diminished. This other person seems to possess a "fullness of being" that you lack. They seem to be living better than you are. They know the score. They are winning. That this is almost always false doesn't make it any more tolerable. The difference eats at you. You feel compelled to respond—to prove that you are on par, even superior. It is an existential dogfight with no natural resolution.

If this sounds like a description of how Facebook and Instagram work, that is because Girard anticipated these developments. He saw that the distance between people was collapsing. The world was getting smaller. Mass media, economic globalization, and the digital revolution were making everyone feel like peers—which is to say, in his worldview, like rivals. People to envy. Girard, who has been called both the "prophet of envy" and the "godfather of the like button," explicitly defined modernity as "the universalization of internal mediation." Ours is an age in which "one doesn't have areas of life that would keep people apart from each other." We see everything, and it rankles.

And there is another, more practical reason that Girard's ideas are so well-suited to the social media age: In an indirect but very real way, he helped to create it. One of Girard's most enthusiastic acolytes was the future venture capitalist and technologist Peter Thiel, who attended Stanford as an undergraduate in the late 1980s. Thiel has said that Girard's work transformed him. The concept of mimetic desire influenced how he ran his companies, how he chose his investments, how he managed his employees, and even how he conducted his personal life. The clearest example of this is also the most famous. In 2004, Thiel invested $500,000 with Mark Zuckerberg, a Harvard dropout who had developed a website that was becoming popular on college campuses across the country. This was no arbitrary or idle bet. Thiel saw perfectly the market potential of a website in which people are exposed to practically endless numbers of internal mediators—billions of people brought into rivalrous daily contact with one another, cycles upon cycles of comparison, agitation, envy, and one-upmanship. Here, in Facebook, was the ideal Girardian machine—a "worldwide theater of imitative desire," as the scholar Robert Pogue Harrison has called it. Eight years later, Thiel cashed out most of his shares in Facebook and took home a profit of more than a billion dollars. "I bet on mimesis," he has said.

Thiel remains a committed admirer of Girard, who died in 2015. In 2008, Thiel founded a nonprofit called Imitatio, which funds efforts "to press forward the consequences of René Girard's remarkable insights into human behavior and culture." But Thiel's is a ruthless, cynical kind of admiration. Girard saw mimetic desire everywhere, but he wasn't in favor of the phenomenon. On the contrary, he wrote again and again about how it leads humanity into cycles of frustration, anger, hatred, conflict, and ultimately violence. The more people are encouraged to want the same things, the more they become like fractious siblings. They become simultaneously beholden to others for a sense of identity and belonging and desperate to distinguish themselves. Their fixations grow. Their compassion shrinks. They bicker and fight. They recruit others to their sides. They look for scapegoats to relieve the pressure built up in the system. Societies that slip into this cycle enter into what Girard called a "mimetic crisis." This never ends well. A civil war is a mimetic crisis: "brother against brother" until the body count becomes unbearable or the fever breaks.

A major feature of a mimetic crisis is cluelessness. People are driven without quite knowing why. Girard wondered whether his own work had found success because "mimetic crisis" serves as a handily oblique way to talk about envy. People don't like to talk about envy, Girard observed. As emotions go, it is an embarrassment: an admission of weakness. Even as we feel envy, we hide from it. Even as the culture thrusts envy upon us, even as it makes envy an engine of immense and concentrated profit, we avoid naming it. The idea that our desires are being manipulated at all is so distasteful that we pretend that it is not happening. We are willfully oblivious about our suffering.

And suffer we do. Over the past decade, more and more research has been looking into the relationship between social media and depression, and the role that envy plays in this relationship. A 2015 study in the journal *Computers in Human Behavior* asked, "Is Facebook depressing?" The answer was yes. "We found that the more people use Facebook, the more likely they would develop envy," one of the authors explained, "and then that envy, over time and more Facebook usage, can lead to depression." A 2018 article in *Frontiers in Psychology* confirmed that the more people are exposed on social media to the impeccably curated lives of their peers, the more envious—and sadder—they become. A 2020 article in *Current Opinion in Psychology* laid out the Girardian mimetic spinout in all its self-perpetuating misery. People use social media, compare themselves to others, and feel bad. These bad feelings then "ironically cause people to engage in further damaging social comparisons, creating a vicious downward cycle." To deal with their feelings of inferiority and envy, people pump themselves up. They post photos of their smiling kids, their beach vacation, their gourmet meal. This makes other users feel bad in return, and the "envy cycles" spread across the network.

•

Mark Zuckerberg, then, is a jerk. The people who run Snapchat and Pinterest and TikTok are jerks. People who make vivid commercials that stoke our envy so we will buy useless stuff are jerks. The celebrities who sell their images for the purpose of aspirational consumerism are jerks. Psychologists who use their expertise to help corporations better manipulate the minds of their customers are jerks. Peter Thiel is an enormous jerk. They are all opportunists, confidence men plucking the taut strings of human frailty to the tune of unspeakable profits.

But so what? That's just City Hall, which every fool knows you can't beat. That's the great tide of History, Technology, Mass Media, and Economics—elements of such breadth and motive force that to outline their pernicious effects on mere individuals is about as helpful as pointing to a barrage of missiles falling from the sky and saying, "Those are bad." Thanks a million. We know it. Even as we open our social media apps and re-up our Amazon Prime memberships, we know it. Even as we hold congressional hearings, publish white papers, produce documentaries, and warn our kids, we know it, and live as our great-grandparents did and our great-grandchildren will, which is to say vulnerably. The human propensity for envy is the same as it always has been, and each year the profit-makers devise new ways to harness it. That is the world as it is.

So what do we do? After all of this history and theory, all of this business about mimetic crises, the malignant innovations of consumer capitalism, and the voraciousness and tenacity of Silicon Valley—after all this thorough, dispiriting, and not necessarily surprising diagnosis of our emotional precarity in an exploitative world—what do we do that might still guide and keep us? What are we left with?

We are left—alas, alack—with the verities. We are left with the old sturdy truths about how to live well among distraction and disorder, those fortune-cookie clichés about gratitude, contentment, and the dogged, indefinite cultivation of the peaceful self that, for all their fusty, dust-caked familiarity, are in the end the only slogans we can trust.

•

I have been reconsidering my description of Emily's attitude toward our house and how our friends view us in light of it. Emily read a draft of this chapter, and she had questions. She had notes. I have been giving her notes serious thought.

In a 1972 essay, "The Anatomy of Envy," George Foster outlines the four major ways that people who fear the envy of others act to protect themselves and minimize their exposure to harmful consequences. There are two extreme ways and two moderate ways. The extreme ways are to conceal or to share fully: Don't let anyone see what you have and they lack, or divvy the envied thing up equally so there is no longer anything to envy. The moderate, and more common, ways are to deny that anyone has any reason to envy you, or to offer what Foster calls a "sop"—a "symbolic sharing of good fortune" in the form of a gift of some sort, a token to acknowledge your advantage and, in a sense, to apologize for it. When you deny, you claim that what you have is really not so great after all, and certainly not superior. *Sure, I got this big award, but everyone knows awards are arbitrary. It's nice, but I don't fool myself that I actually deserve it.* To offer a sop is to carve off a small piece from what you have, something that carries the spirit of the thing, and hand it over as compensation. When the bride tosses her bouquet to the unmarried women at her wedding, or when the traveler returns from his vacation with a bag of gifts to distribute to friends and family—macarons from Paris for you, a ceramic dish from Athens for you—they are offering sops.

When Emily enumerated our house's hidden flaws, those leaky ceilings and uninsulated walls, and revealed the particulars of how we paid for the house, I saw acts of denial. When she invited people in and cooked them elaborate meals, soaked beans, rehydrated mushrooms, baked fresh breads and cakes, then sent them home with three or four pounds of leftovers and even, sometimes, our own potted plants, I saw sops. Influenced by my reading, I saw rituals of self-defense—anxious, unconscious efforts to ward off what one philosopher of envy calls "the malignant gaze, the evil eye that . . . [is] a blight of relations," and that humankind has feared, across cultures, for five thousand years.

Maybe, Emily says. She's willing to entertain the suggestion, and she won't deny her occasional uneasiness and her urge to relieve it somehow, or her discomfort now at my exposing her and us to wider scrutiny, to many more appraising eyes. There are truths here, she admits.

Still, she asks, could I take off my pith helmet for just a moment, please? Could I lay down my clipboard and make room for other, less anthropological interpretations? Is it worth considering the possibility, for example, that my analysis skews too far in the direction of the negative, of threat, vulnerability, danger, and fear? Could it perhaps be that my relentless focus on the psychology and economics of envy is maybe just a little bit . . . cynical?

What about thankfulness, she asks? What about self-awareness? What about her commitment not to fool herself that any of the privileges we have, any of the comforts we enjoy or nice things we own, have come to us through any channel other than blind, dumb, stumbling luck? What about the discipline of holding this truth, and it is a truth, consistently in mind, so that one's humility doesn't crumble and give way, as it so easily can, to indolence, entitlement, and selfishness?

And what, she asks, about the *joy* of giving? What about the plain delight she feels when she feeds people and sends them off with more food? Defensiveness? Sops? Please. It's a pleasure! It is a pleasure and a privilege to give. It always has been, no matter where she has lived. There is a sense of wholeness and belonging that grows the more generously we act. And there is a pleasure in being among people who know you for who you are, for your chatty self-consciousness and reflexive apologizing, your beautiful and personal neuroses, and who love you still, or even more for it. See it as the mechanics of envy if you want. See it as self-preservation. That's your prerogative. Just don't pretend those are the only ways to see it.

I am grateful, she says. I am grateful for—amazed, disbelieving, and yes, a little embarrassed, a little scandalized by—our good fortune. And I refuse to forget it. I don't forget it even when there is no one here. I don't forget it when I'm alone! I don't want to forget it. Who would I be if I forgot it? Not me.

And anyway, she continues, after all this talk about desire and the invidious look, status and possessions, wealth and measurement, where are you in this chapter? Daniel, where are *your* envies? You write about my alleged involvement in the workings of envy, but you don't for a moment fess up about your own active and vocal envy of others. Where are all the restless, paralyzing comparisons you make between your own labored literary work and the fluent, prolific, celebrated work of your peers? Where is the sense of inferiority you feel at not having published enough books? Where is the envy you feel of people who have more bylines than you, more renown, more respect, a house outside the city, a nicer car, fewer responsibilities, who send their kids to private school, who have nannies and maids, who have better bodies and more discipline, who went to better colleges . . .

You talk about denial. You talk about concealment. But you have concealed everything. You have run away and hidden yourself behind me. What is that about? What are you protecting *yourself* from?

And she is right. Of course she is right. Where am I?

Oh, it is a gift, a great and terrifying gift, to be seen.

PART THREE

chapter seven

BOREDOM

By the time I met Emily, in 2015, I had decided not to have more children. I had a seven-year-old daughter with my first wife, and one of the lessons I had learned in raising her was that, on the whole, I wasn't built for fatherhood. Most people who knew me disagreed. They saw that I was caring, devoted, and compassionate, and they took these qualities to mean that I was a "good dad." In this sense, they weren't wrong. When my daughter was born, the cord wrapped around her neck, I discovered, as many do, that my love for her was more profound than I could have anticipated. I had friends and relatives whom I loved deeply enough that to save any one of their lives I would have given my own. So visceral was my love for my daughter, so instantaneous and complete, that to save her life, I felt, I was prepared to do the far worse thing and take someone else's. To protect others, I was ready to die. To protect my newborn child, I was ready to kill.

Ready to kill, but not necessarily happy to be living. I know few people for whom becoming a parent isn't a jarring experience. No amount of forethought will prepare you for the enormity of the responsibility or for how that responsibility alters your values and perception of the world. Compared with the toothless, incontinent, half-blind child in your arms, all else becomes at once featherweight and foreboding, wispy and fanged, and you and your child blink your way together into a precarious new existence.

But this wasn't my problem. My problem was less grand and more upsetting: I didn't like being a father. I didn't find it enjoyable. This was a shock. I was sure that a baby would be the wellspring of new delights. Instead my life seemed to have been abruptly drained of delight, and a painful irony phased into view. What had motivated me to want a child in the first place? A sense of potential and exuberance. I had taken such pleasure in my days and felt such gratitude for this one single existence—for the thrills of art, literature, food, and sex, for the vibrancies of friendship, conversation, and thought—that I felt driven to expand the scope of existence itself. Experience was too wonderful to hoard and too interesting to restrict. I wanted it all. Why should life not contain everything? So I had a child ... and in doing so I distanced myself from the very pleasures I wanted to expand and share. Overnight, the activities that most enlivened and sustained me— reading, watching movies, seeing friends, making love, sitting quietly by myself—were placed at a terrible remove. From the wide vital world I entered a small dark room containing a stack of parenting manuals, a white noise machine, and a red-faced, hysterical child, helpless as a guppy and destructive as a warhead. From a life of freedom and agency I entered a life of constriction and tension, and what I asked myself in those early days, repeatedly, was, "What have I done?"

Those same people who assured me of my virtue assured me that I was being ridiculous. My situation was hard, no question about it. Our daughter was colicky. Tough luck. Still, what I felt was common enough, the result of a nearly universal stage of sleeplessness and strain. Soon it would pass and I would adjust. Soon ("Just you wait and see!") I would be reunited with my former enjoyments. I would regain my sense of pleasure and possibility.

I didn't buy it. I was old enough to know when I was being sold a line, when some indoctrination was being attempted. What these people were trying to indoctrinate me into, I sensed, were their own desperate rationalizations: their compromises, their half-furtive, guilt-laden unhappiness. Many of these people, I couldn't help but notice, had stains on their sweaters and new lines in their faces. They had become a little heavier, a little paler, a little less sharp. The artists among them were giving up their studios and getting regular jobs. The hallways outside their apartments were cluttered with jogging strollers, puffy coats, colorful lunch boxes, umbrellas made to look like ladybugs. Their smiles were suspicious, grim, and forced.

Around this time, I spent several days with an older writer, one of my idols, and I shared my distress with her. She waved it off. Raising a child to maturity, she said, was "just a blip on the spectrogram" of life. But this woman had let me read her journals, and I happened to know the immense cost she herself had paid for being a parent: the years of worry and fear, the burdens of time, focus, energy, and money. *So much money!* Also, I could do the math. Eighteen years isn't a blip. Eighteen years is almost a quarter of the lifespan of the average American male. It was more than a third of the lifespan of a specific American male, my father, whose death at fifty-two was never far from my mind.

I could concede the point that I shouldn't generalize completely from the first, acute phase of parenthood—that it was a crisis to be endured as one endures a hurricane or earthquake. Indeed, the months passed and something like a new, post-crisis equilibrium emerged. Our daughter's nervous system began to gel. The shrieking settled. We clicked off the noise machine, yanked open the blinds, and stepped outside. A novel pleasure, call it parental pride, made its appearance. How lovely our child was! When she giggled, her throat pulsed in and out like a bullfrog's. She had round cheeks, blue eyes, and fine blonde hair, like a Renoir. On the street strangers beamed at her, and at me, happily implicated in her freshness. What a doting father! Look at him carrying his baby to the park, to the greenmarket, to the playground, tying a bonnet to her head, slathering her plump pink arms with organic sunblock. I could feel the vigilant, protective forces radiant and alive inside me. I cherished this feeling. This feeling was half, or more, the point. This feeling was my reward.

But at the same time, shadowing this love, a darker feeling was gaining force, threading its opportunistic way into the fabric of my experience. This other feeling had found its toehold in those chaotic early months, when my wife and I inflated a large black exercise ball and tried to bounce our daughter to sleep, trading off shifts like factory workers. My mind slackened by fatigue, battered by the baby's cries, I could do nothing to get through those episodes but count. *One, two, three, four, five, six* . . . all the way to a hundred. Then again, silently counting. *One, two, three, four, five, six, seven, eight, nine, ten, eleven, twelve* . . . Over and over again, over and over, one to a hundred, one to a hundred, bounce, bounce, bounce, bounce, bounce, until relieved of my post.

The repetition and tedium, the muscle-slackening, assembly-line monotony: Now *this* aspect of parenting I hadn't anticipated. No one had warned me! Or had they? One day at 4 a.m., between shifts, a line from an essay by the writer Nora Johnson suddenly returned to me. In the essay, Johnson describes the job of raising a child with an arresting disdain for sentimentality. Being a parent, she insists, isn't about nobility or beauty. It isn't about pride or pleasure. Rather, it is "the simple, nerve-wracking, mindless, battering-ram process of trying to teach a savage to use a fork." I remembered this line now the way Julius Caesar, his blood pooling on the senatorial marble, remembered the line, "Beware the ides of March."

Like my love, this feeling had staying power. Long after I had deflated the exercise ball and stowed it high on a closet shelf, I was struck by the insidious way this mind-numbing sensation entered my days. The rapturous baby-gazing, the blissful passages spent mooning at this miraculous chip of sentience in butterfly pajamas, made up a small fraction of the experience of being a parent. Much of the rest consisted of nothing more than blunt, basic, run-of-the-mill boredom. Boredom, front to back, back to front. The boredom of diapers. The boredom of breakfasts. The boredom of naptimes. The boredom of play dates. The boredom of playgrounds. The boredom of picture books. The boredom of blocks. The boredom of snacks. The boredom of birthday parties. The boredom of Cheerios, pasta, peanut butter, and Goldfish. The boredom of milk. The boredom of sippy cups. The boredom of dishes. The boredom of whining. The boredom of tantrums. The boredom of daycare drop-offs. The boredom of daycare pick-ups. The boredom, distilled and perfect, of the demand, *Again! Do it again, daddy! Say it again! Sing it again! Read it again! Play it again! Build it again!*

Again again again again again again.

Love and boredom. Boredom and love. This, I found, was the essence of my education as a father. These were the immutable poles of parenting, though one was discussed more openly than the other. About boredom there seemed to be a conspiracy of silence, as if acknowledging the emotion without a wink or a footnote of self-accusation would cause it to break free and metastasize. With certain intimates I could confess just how monotonous I found parenting to be. With the rest, in Brooklyn in the second decade of the twenty-first century, it would have been like confessing to drowning kittens or robbing liquor stores. Children, that great adventure, boring? The care and feeding of a human soul, tedious? Maybe the parents of the previous generation felt entitled to these judgments. But we knew the harm they could do. We, children of the '70s and '80s, knew who got hurt when parents placed too high a premium on their own pleasure. And we must not repeat the mistake. We must prize our children's needs high above our own. We must strike a parental stance of commitment and wonder. A thousand books, articles, and blogs broadcast this dictate.

In this way I came to see my parental disposition as at best anachronistic and at worst terminally deficient. That my marriage to my daughter's mother ended in divorce, and that our divorce, while managed with comparative civility, caused our daughter abiding pain, hardened my resolve to cap my output at one. From that point forward, my sexual goals (beyond the pursuit of pleasure) were to avoid fertilization and venereal disease, in that order. My parental goals were to be a good, loyal father until the time of my daughter's legal and financial emancipation. After that, freedom. Freedom and the clear, clean, brisk atmosphere of benign self-interest.

Then I met Emily, and love, never tax-free, scrambled my understanding of self-interest. On our fifth date, walking hand in hand down Flatbush Avenue to her apartment, Emily stopped abruptly and announced that she wanted children, she was sure of it, and if I wasn't willing to at least entertain the prospect then the only gentlemanly thing to do would be to save her, a healthy and attractive thirty-eight-year-old woman, the time and trouble and scram. "Listen," she said, "I'm not saying I want children with *you*. I'm saying don't think you'd be doing me any favors by sticking around." With that, having said her piece—and having doubled my admiration for her—she again took my hand.

The details of what followed hardly matter. The tortured perseveration, the tumultuous breakup and joyful reunion, are themselves, in this context, fairly boring. What matters in this context are the two children, a boy and a girl, who resulted—two children in relation to whom I feel the same militant love and persistent, depleting, frustrating, resentful boredom I felt the first time around. What matters is what to do with this feeling of boredom: how to understand it, what is the right relationship to it, and how to endure it. What matters, as with all emotions, positive and negative, is what the emotion is trying to say, and whether, and how much, to listen to it.

•

When I look closely at my reluctance even to admit to my boredom, I see the effects of an emotional upbringing that held boredom in almost unique contempt. It is startling to realize this after all these years.

Like, I suspect, many Americans of my generation and economic class, I was raised to approach my emotions unskeptically. With my brothers and at school with my friends, the atmosphere was one of emotional surveillance: Express a vulnerability, one sensed, and someone would target and exploit it. But my parents, and especially my mother, offered a blanket acceptance of the emotions. The sentimental law of our household was "validate." Behaviors, including acts of speech, could be proper or improper, praiseworthy or offensive. Thoughts, too, could be dubious and maladaptive. But emotions were inarguable. My mother would no sooner criticize someone's emotions than she would someone's height or skin color. Emotions had a bedrock legitimacy. You may not like this or that emotion, you may not want it or be proud of it, but it's yours, it's okay, and no soul on earth has the right to tell you otherwise. To this day, I rarely see my mother angrier than when she sets her jaw and says, in the middle of an argument, "Don't you tell me how to *feel.*"

This happens to be a strange position, historically speaking. As we saw earlier, the idea that emotions are neither correct nor incorrect, but just are, like clouds or sea currents, cuts against just about every major Western philosophical and religious tradition from the past 2,400 years. Most Greek authorities held that we are eminently responsible for what we feel. For the Stoics, to submit to emotions such as envy, pride, and anger was to live wastefully, out of rhythm with the workings of the universe. (Are you still moping because your wife died? Dummy, everyone dies. Get on with it.) The traditional Christian view of emotions is even sterner. For the Christian, to submit to such feelings is to cut yourself off from God's grace. It is to live in deadly sin—"deadly" because it may result in the death of your eternal soul.

I can't speak for other people's childhoods, but during mine, in the middle-to-upper-middle-class New York suburbs from the Carter through the first Clinton administration, almost none of this remained. All emotions were granted the luxury of licentious, prepardoned expression, as if our house itself was a psychotherapeutic office or the set of *Mister Rogers' Neighborhood*. When my parents were at their most self-possessed and least distracted, you felt that you could confess to any painful emotion whatsoever and you would be met with empathy, curiosity, and concern, as well as guidance as to how to see your way through and out of that emotion. You could tell them anything at all.

Anything, that is, but that you were bored. Boredom alone inspired little to no parental sympathy, and was the cause of almost uniform censure and dismissal. Of all the human emotions, only boredom retained some of that ancient moral stigma—a blot of weakness, if not of sin. Recently, I overheard a woman tell her son on the playground: "Don't say, 'I'm bored.' Boredom is a bad word." It was in this spirit that boredom was rejected in my home. Not rooted out, not sermonized against, but simply and firmly rejected, as one rejects a logical fallacy: What you believe cannot be the case. Why? Because reality is abundant. It will deny you nothing, if only you approach it with curiosity. What interests you, child? *Something* must interest you. Your interest is a hard little lever. Poke it into reality, apply pressure, and hold your breath. Watch the dam break.

The message this response delivered was not only that boredom was verboten but that it was the opposite—the shadow side—of engagement. To be bored was to suffer from a self-imposed blindness to just how rich in wonders the world actually was. Boredom was a delusive emotion, and for my own good it needed to be dispelled. In conveying this to me, my parents had plenty of help. Nearly every children's book in our house trumpeted the same message. As a parent myself, I can better see how children's literature is a kind of anti-boredom propaganda. From Eric Carle to E. B. White to Margaret Wise Brown, the express purpose of children's literature is to exemplify and nurture in children the ability to find and take an absorbed interest in the world. Behold, these books proclaim, the wonderful beauty and oddity of the world, of the stars and moon and animals and plants. Behold the strange and passionate lives being lived just beyond your ken. Within that mote of dust thrives a community in mortal danger. In that humble New England barn, an epic drama unfolds. See all that a little boy like you can create *ex nihilo*, with only a purple crayon. When boredom does occur in children's books, it is only as a fleeting negative state. It is there expressly to be overcome. Boredom, in children's literature, is nothing more than the precondition of imagination—the stillness before the Big Bang.

> Alice was beginning to get very tired of sitting by her sister on the bank, and of having nothing to do.

> *I sat there with Sally.*
> *We sat there, we two.*
> *And I said, "How I wish*
> *We had something to do!"*

> There was once a boy named Milo who didn't know what to do with himself—not just sometimes, but always . . . "there's nothing for me to do, nowhere I'd care to go, and hardly anything worth seeing."

Bang! The white rabbit dives down the hole. Bang! The manic

cat bursts through the door. Bang! A package arrives containing a tollbooth and a map of "the Lands Beyond."

Boredom's purpose is to spawn its antitheses—ingenuity, pleasure, wonder—and then die. This is the traditional narrative arc, and it is occasionally made explicit. In *The Phantom Tollbooth*, Milo begins in the Doldrums and eventually makes his way to the Kingdom of Wisdom. When he at last returns to his own room and life, his vision has shifted irrevocably and for the better: "Outside the window, there was so much to see, and hear, and touch—walks to take, hills to climb, caterpillars to watch as they strolled through the garden. There were voices to hear and conversations to listen to in wonder, and the special smell of each day."

One of the things these books convey so beautifully is the great luxury of time that children, especially young children, possess. The stories customarily start with idleness. At a child's feet lies an expanse of time she doesn't know how to fill. There is just too much of it, and not enough direction or structure. A child's complaint of boredom is usually a whine that there is nothing to do: "I'm *booooored*." This helps to explain why parents tend to have little patience for these complaints. They know that what awaits the child is a different kind of boredom: the obligated, dull boredom of adulthood—of parenthood. Most parents, after all, are choked to the gills with things to do, many of those things uninteresting and wearying, and for the benefit of their idle, whining children, who should know better. Bored? When you are on hold with the insurance company, when you are rinsing vegetables to roast for dinner, and emptying the dishwasher, and wiping down the counter, and fielding emails and texts from colleagues, clients, your boss, your ex, your mother, the nursing home, the school, the collection agency—when you are straining simultaneously to address and bear up under the weight of numerous, ever-proliferating pressures, then a confession of boredom from anyone, but especially from the primary beneficiary of your efforts, can only strike you as an insult.

Bored? You're bored? Are you putting me on? I'd *kill* to be that kind of bored. You want something to do? Fine. Go clean your room. Take out the garbage. Dust the sconces. Go count fucking squirrels for all I care. Dinner's in twenty minutes.

•

In 1960, the Italian author Alberto Moravia published a novel titled *La Noia*, or *Boredom*. The novel is narrated by a thirty-five-year-old failed painter, Dino, who suffers from what he defines as "the lack of a relationship with external things." All his life Dino has felt a pained, restless detachment from the world. And all his life he has struggled to understand this feeling. As a schoolboy, Dino writes, distressed and embarrassed by his disinterest with his lessons, he conceived of an ambitious "universal history" according to which all events since the beginning of time were motivated not by biology, economics, or the desire for progress, but by simple, humble boredom.

> In the beginning was boredom, commonly called chaos. God, bored with boredom, created the earth, the sky, the waters, the animals, the plants, Adam and Eve; and the latter, bored in their turn in paradise, ate the forbidden fruit. God became bored with them and drove them out of Eden; Cain, bored with Abel, killed him; Noah, bored to tears, invented wine; God, once again bored with mankind, destroyed the world by means of the Flood; but this in turn bored Him to such an extent that He brought back fine weather again. And so on. The great empires—Egyptian, Babylonian, Persian, Greek and Roman—rose out of boredom and fell again in boredom; the boredom of paganism gave rise to Christianity; that of Catholicism, to Protestantism; the boredom of Europe caused the discovery of America; the boredom of

feudalism kindled the French Revolution; and that of capitalism, the revolution in Russia. All these fine discoveries were noted down by me in a kind of summary, then I began with great enthusiasm to write the true and proper history. . . . Then I grew bored with the whole project and abandoned it.

It's a pretty good gag, if not a new one. Friedrich Nietzsche said something similar in *The Antichrist*, sixty-five years earlier. (Not surprisingly, the Catholic Church banned the work of both authors.) But even as a joke, or half-joke, the idea underscores just how accustomed we are to thinking of boredom as something repellent from which we want to escape. In Dino's grand history, boredom isn't merely an unpleasant emotion. It is an intolerably unpleasant emotion. It is so unpleasant that even an omnipotent deity can't take it. ("Against boredom," Nietzsche writes, "even gods struggle in vain.") To shake off boredom, in Dino's telling, people will do just about anything. They will create and they will destroy, they will drink and murder, they will build and revolt. Whatever it takes, so long as the feeling goes away.

That boredom feels bad no one would dispute. When we are bored for any length of time, we may feel confused, jittery, hemmed in, detached, hazy, despondent, unmoored, overwhelmed, or some combination of these. There is an important difference, however, between feeling bad and feeling desperate to stop feeling bad. Sometimes we positively want our negative emotions. We encourage and cling to them for what they give us: the punishment we believe we deserve, the sense of superiority or refinement we believe we require, the vigor that so often accompanies agitation. We hold on to guilt to atone for our wrongdoings. We hold on to disappointment to shield us from more disappointment. We hold on to anger to maintain our energy and focus. A friend of mine told me she stoked her own anger when she was going through a divorce in order to fight more effectively with her ex-husband and his lawyer.

Boredom isn't like this. We always yearn for our boredom to end. We always want to slip out from under its shadow. Boredom is almost purely aversive, a "bestial and indefinable affliction," as Dostoevsky put it. By nature or training, boredom is a problem we urgently need to solve.

Any emotion that we flee from becomes a motive force. Any emotion we can't abide turns into action. Fear turns, in a twinkling, into literal flight, or, if flight is impossible, into aggression. But fear is the most deeply physiological of our emotions. Fear is a warning signal that our physical safety is at risk. Boredom, more expansive, less directive, is also a warning signal—but what is the warning? What is the problem in need of a solution? When we run from boredom, what are we running from?

Over the past twenty years, an intellectual cottage industry has developed around this question—an entire sub-discipline called Boredom Studies. Plodding through the endeavor's dense, varied, and occasionally tedious output, which includes papers with titles such as "More Bored Today Than Yesterday? National Trends in Adolescent Boredom From 2008 to 2017" and "Boredom, Time, and Modernity: An Example from Aboriginal Australia," two dominant answers emerge. One is that boredom represents a breakdown in our ability to pay attention to what we are doing. According to this explanation, boredom occurs when there is a mismatch between person and task. Either the thing we are meant to do is too difficult ("Read and summarize this dissertation on minimum entropy deconvolution") or it is too simple ("Peel these apples"). In both instances, mind and action can't connect. The gears won't catch, and we feel the gnashing and grinding. We feel it, we blame the action, and we are bored. The opposite of this conception of boredom would be the almost mystical bliss of a flow state, in which consciousness and action merge into one, our perception narrows to a clear fine beam, and our awareness of time drops from our shoulders.

It's an appealing and intuitive theory, and no doubt relevant in a lot of cases. But it is complicated by the fact that sometimes there is an obvious gulf between what we are capable of doing and what we are doing—and boredom never comes. An English factory worker in 1941 might feel totally content working a double shift stamping out rivets on an assembly line if those rivets are going to make tanks with which to fight Nazis. A father may cheerfully shovel the snow from the front steps knowing he is aiding his child's walk to the bus stop. What bridges the gulf between ability and action in these examples is a sense of meaning. We believe that what we are doing serves a valuable function, so we aren't bothered by it; or we believe that what we are doing does not serve a valuable function, is mere tedium or repetition, and we are bored. Boredom, as one paper puts it, is "a barometer of meaning." It is an emotional instrument, an existential Geiger counter wildly pinging whenever we enter the territory of the pale, the senseless, and the empty.

This is the second answer, and it has on its side centuries of evidence chronicling the insane lengths humans will go to in order to imbue their ordinary lives with "purpose": sieges, crusades, cults, wild and doomed voyages across the oceans and to the poles. One of the best contemporary writers on boredom, the philosopher Andreas Elpidorou, emphasizes exactly this motivational aspect of the emotion. Boredom, Elpidorou argues, is a state that seeks its own extinction. When we feel bored, "we're moved to think of alternative situations and goals, ones that are more interesting and meaningful to us than our current ones." Boredom propels us away from itself. It wants to thrust us into the arms of some other, less boring activity.

This makes boredom a potentially dangerous emotion, since it is resolutely agnostic about its alternatives. "Boredom is the root of all evil," claims Kierkegaard's character A, in *Either/Or*. In fact, numerous studies suggest, people who are prone to boredom are more likely to gamble, abuse drugs and alcohol, and drive recklessly. One report on the causes of violent extremism, produced by the United States Agency for International Development, concludes that "it is difficult to over-estimate the extent to which boredom significantly enhances youth vulnerability to extremist ideas and activities." In one well-known study, published in the journal *Science* in 2014, a number of subjects grew so bored with their own quiet thinking that they willingly gave themselves electric shocks—just to feel something.

But boredom doesn't need to be destructive. Treated with care and consideration, it can be just the prod we need to identify our strengths and our most ardent, unique desires. The discomfort of boredom, even the anguish of boredom, can spur us into flights of imagination, resourcefulness, and invention. That is why so many today lament the ubiquity of the iPhone: It destroys a mental state of incalculable value. Some studies correlate boredom with curiosity and a propensity to daydream. When we are bored, we are more likely to seek out more absorbing and congenial circumstances than the ones we are in: a career better aligned with our interests, a partner better aligned with our personality, a livelier town, more enriching hobbies, new forms of beauty and inspiration. In Elpidorou's optimistic account, this is the redemptive power of boredom, as well as its paradox. In alerting us that we are on the wrong track, boredom can guide us to the good life. Through pain, it puts us right. Boredom, Elpidorou writes, "can set us free."

•

I'd like to think so. If I believed this, maybe my experience of boredom would change, and I would be happier. As it stands, my experience bears little resemblance to this account. I can't remember many times in which my boredom led to feelings of openness, engagement, gratification, or a more capacious and vibrant creativity. What I can remember, what is the upsettingly regular occurrence, is my boredom leading to feelings of resentment, frustration, guilt, shame, and bouts of self-contemptuous distraction: long nutritionless spells goggling slack-jawed at celebrity news on my phone while the living and professedly tedious world throbs around me. What I personally know of boredom is not, as Elpidorou has it, that it is "a beneficial regulatory psychological state" that aids in "the construction of a meaningful life." What I know of boredom is something like the reverse: that it is a destabilizing psychological state that infects even, or especially, those experiences that constitute for me the very essence of a meaningful life. It is hard to understand how I can praise boredom for reorienting me when its targets are exactly those things to which I want to be better oriented.

This book itself is a case in point. This book that is so important to me and to which I have devoted countless hours of my life. Years, in fact. Each day I sit here in a quiet room, walled in by stacks of books and papers, my dog-eared, over-highlighted notes that I've read a thousand times—and I plead with it all to interest me. I beg it to draw me in and give value to my day. Sometimes it does. There are times when I feel enraptured by discovery, when I feel amazed at my good fortune to be this very person doing this very work, reading, studying, learning, playing with words, and I leave my desk trembling with caffeine and insight. But these moments are relatively rare. Many of my working days, in fact the majority, are as flat and uninspiring as a parking lot. Many days I have to all but lash myself to my chair, or force myself through that turgid, thirty-page journal article ("Temporal discrimination and the indifference interval: Implications for a model of the 'internal clock' ") that may, if I am lucky, contain a wisp of information that advances my understanding of my subject. Many days I sit soaked to the bone with boredom, dreaming of Netflix. Should I heed this feeling? Should I allow it to push me into new circumstances?

"The life of the creative man," Saul Steinberg said, correctly, "is led, directed, and controlled by boredom." "It should surprise no one," writes Annie Dillard, "that the life of the writer—such as it is—is colorless to the point of sensory deprivation."

Or, leaving off myself, take the case of prayer. Over the centuries, boredom has shown up in many different forms, among them *acedia*, a "foule sinne," according to Chaucer's Parson, "a ful greet enemy to the lyflode of the body" that "maketh [man] hevy, thoghtful, and wrawe." In his treatise *The Eight Evil Thoughts*, the fourth-century ascetic Evagrius Ponticus gives a comprehensive account of *acedia*. This "most oppressive of all demons," Evagrius writes, causes the hermit to leap out of his seat and look outside, imploring time to pass more quickly.

> And it forces him to look around, here and there, to see whether any of his brethren are near. In addition the demon makes him dislike his place, his life itself, and the work of his hands. It makes him think that he has lost the affection of his brethren and that there is no one to comfort him. If, during these days, anybody annoyed the hermit, the demon would cause this to increase his hatred. It stirs the hermit also to yearn for different places in which he can easily find what is necessary for his life and carry on a much less difficult and more profitable profession. . . . The demon employs all his wiles to cause the hermit to leave his cell and to flee from the racecourse of his vocation.

Some did flee, of course. In holy callings, there is always attrition. But thousands stayed and kept to their devotions. Despite the monotony, desolation, tedium, restlessness, doubt, anxiety, despair, and anger, they stayed in their dreary cells in the Egyptian desert, drinking dirty water and praying among the snakes and scorpions, fleas in their beards. They weren't prisoners. They could have left at any time and gone back to whatever city, town, or village they came from. But they stayed on. They kept at their hard task.

Why? Why did they stay? Because they loved God and feared Hell? No doubt that was part of it, but I refuse to believe that it was all, or even primary. The principal reason they stayed, I think, is that for all the awful power of the demon of *acedia*, it was not then and is not now absolute. No state of mind is absolute. No emotion is a fixed point. As persistent and painful as their boredom was, it must have been endurable so long as it was punctuated, now and then, by feelings of deep, sustaining connection: love, joy, communion, comprehension, peace. A feeling that one has temporarily plugged into the central line of existence and experienced the wash of true meaning.

The boredom was the labor, in other words. It was the price exacted for the reward, if you could pay it. What the demon said was, "Flee! This is not your path." What the demon *meant*, however, was that you were on exactly the right track, which is to say the track of full, fierce commitment. The trick is in telling the difference.

•

The finest document on boredom that I know of is a speech that the poet Joseph Brodsky gave in praise of it at Dartmouth College's commencement ceremonies in 1989.

Brodsky's must be one of the strangest graduation addresses ever delivered. It is definitely one of the most Russian. He offered no false comforts, flatteries, or easily digestible pablum. Instead, he told the 1,100 assembled graduates that as soon as they left campus a large proportion of their lives would be claimed by the "incurable malaise" of boredom. If they thought they already knew this malaise, they were wrong. "The worst monotonous drone coming from a lectern or the eye-splitting textbook in turgid English is nothing in comparison to the psychological Sahara that starts right in your bedroom and spurns the horizon." What they were to discover out there, among their lovers, spouses, children, and work, was that "life's main medium is precisely repetition," and repetition is "boredom's mother." They might escape this fate for a while. They might try hard to escape it, changing jobs, houses, countries, and careers; embracing hobbies, travel, promiscuity, or psychoanalysis. Eventually, though, boredom would get them. It would crawl under their skin, for each and every one of them.

A troubling valedictory, but an honest and grown-up one. And not inevitably bleak. The heart of Brodsky's speech is his desire that his "young and newfangled" listeners eventually give up trying to evade boredom and start respecting it for what it is, which is a "window on time." Brodsky understands boredom as the voice with which time speaks to us, the messenger that whispers in our ear, "You are finite . . . and whatever you do is, from my point of view, futile." Not futile, full stop; futile from the perspective of infinity. Futile in the widest—the ultimate—frame. Boredom exists, Brodsky says, "to teach you the most valuable lesson in your life . . . the lesson of your utter insignificance." It isn't a pleasant message, but it beats self-deception. It beats the frantic delusion of "specialness." This is why Brodsky praises boredom, because it tells the truth. It puts us in our tiny, fragile, temporary place. And thank goodness it does, for the infinite of which boredom is an emissary is not a terribly warm or fertile place. Only the finite is "charged with life," with love, pain, excitement, and fear. When boredom reminds you of your insignificance, glory in the knowledge, for "passion is the privilege of the insignificant."

This is the point, if there is one. Boredom is the distress that includes its own remedy. It is the wound that saves. If you try to distract yourself from boredom, if you run from it, all is lost. Brodsky quotes an imperishable line from Robert Frost's poem "A Servant to Servants": "The best way out is always through."

A note that the novelist David Foster Wallace wrote not long before he killed himself makes a similar point:

> Bliss—a second-by-second joy and gratitude at the gift of being alive, conscious—lies on the other side of crushing, crushing boredom. Pay close attention to the most tedious thing you can

find (Tax Returns, Televised Golf) and, in waves, a boredom like you've never known will wash over you and just about kill you. Ride these out, and it's like stepping from black and white into color. Like water after days in the desert. Instant bliss in every atom.

But I don't think we need the promise of mystical joy to endure and learn from boredom. Enlightenment is welcome should it want to come, but awareness, mere awareness, a calm and loving truce with pedestrian reality, is the more democratic and realistic goal.

"Everything that displays a pattern is pregnant with boredom," Brodsky told those flabbergasted undergrads. Of course, much of what displays a pattern—lifelong friendships, enduring marriages, serious scholarship, the making of art, prayer—is also pregnant with meaning.

Meaning and boredom. Boredom and meaning. Hand in hand like twins.

•

Sunday morning. Winter. I work for a couple of hours at my desk in a prefabricated toolshed in the backyard. My desk faces a wall. To my right, above stacks of boxes, camping gear, old gym equipment, bags of hand-me-down clothes, broken appliances, tools, paint cans, and an unused stroller, a pair of windows provides a view of a cinderblock wall. Behind and above me, a trio of narrow windows lets in little light. It is dim and cold. I have toe warmers, the kind you use while skiing, in my boots, and I'm wearing a down jacket.

The work is going slowly, as usual. This morning, for the umpteenth time, I am going over my notes, hoping to find something for my brain to latch on to, some idea or quotation or scrap of narrative that will tell me what, if anything, I have to say. What, besides the coffee, will wake my interest this morning? What will turn the engine over? Anything? Anybody? You, Kierkegaard? You, Nietzsche? Nothing? Nothing at *all*? The corners of the notes are curled with use. I have been staring at them for years now, hauling them from place to place. I have carried them to the beach and to the mountains, to Oregon, North Carolina, Maryland, Mexico, Florida, and Arizona. I hate them. I would burn them, but my book is two years late and I need the money. What strange choices I have made. What strange, stupid choices. On the first page of the notes I have jotted down something from Spinoza. "An emotion is only bad and hurtful, insofar as it hinders the mind from being able to think." Beneath this, for some long-forgotten reason, I have written: "DIVORCE."

My ex-wife is now married to a lovely, practical man who cooks often and knows how to use computers. When she and I were first dating, in our early twenties, we toured the Pacific Northwest and stopped to visit an older writer I had met at an artists' colony. This writer served us dinner and drinks, and introduced us to his daughter. Then he questioned me. Did I really want to write books? Was it really necessary? Think carefully. To be a writer, he said, "is like having a term paper due—for the rest of your life." I smiled. Ha. Ha ha ha ha. Twelve years later, one of the reasons my wife cited for wanting to split up was that she could no longer tolerate living with a writer. All that agitation. All that solitude. I was indignant. How dare she? But I came to understand. Of course. Of course.

At noon, it is time to go in and watch the kids. My wife is a writer, too, with her own deadlines. I enter the kitchen wearing what she calls my "haunted" look.

"Not a great morning?"

I shrug. I am practicing being stoical.

The floor is littered with markers, crayons, and sheets of paper. The children are . . . what are the children? Ceaseless. The children are ceaseless. They need witnessing. They are desperate to be seen.

"Look, daddy! Look, daddy! Daddy, look!" How nice. What a nice sticker. Well done, sweetheart. "Look, daddy! Daddy! Daddy, look!" Yes I saw. Very nice. "Look, daddy!"

The four-year-old is in a questioning phase. Question after question after question. Are penguins cold? Are lions scary? What does "exhausted" mean? Is tea hot? What is air? It is like having termites colonize your brain. It is impossible to think even a single independent thought. I refill sippy cups. I police conflicts based on inanities. I toast toast. I am living the life of the mind. Have I ever been so bored? In the study of boredom in which people self-administered electric shocks, they reached that point in only fifteen minutes.

"Daddy has to poop," I lie. On the closed toilet I stare at my phone. I read half a paragraph of a *Times* article about Taiwan and play most of a word game I no longer enjoy. How constipated can I pretend to be? At what point will a four-year-old become suspicious, or worried? When I leave I flush the toilet and run the faucet, for verisimilitude.

Finally it is time for the little one to take her nap. I read her a book about ducks and another book about ducks. The boy seems to have continued speaking the whole time I was gone, and falls immediately back into questioning. "Daddy, is it true that"—sorry, no time, kid. We've got errands to run. It takes him a full seven minutes to put on his Velcro sneakers, and another two to zip up his jacket, which he insists he must do by himself. ("Are zippers for closing things?") I lift and twist him into his car seat, and in doing so bonk his head on the roof of the car. Miraculously, he doesn't cry.

We need carrots, broccoli, bread, milk, cheese, tampons. The day, and my mind, start to loosen. The thin light of some minor pleasure starts to glow. Is it nostalgia? The memory of shopping with my own father? That I am now engaged in a (heaven help me) "goal-directed" activity? No matter. Let it in, I tell myself. Why hold tight? The boy loves it here. The colors. The smells. The possibilities. His hair juts topsy-turvy from under his wool hat. I have shopped for groceries a million times, at a million stores. His hand is so warm. He is so young and so warm.

In one day, Emily is turning forty-six, and I still need a card. I know of a gift shop around the corner. I happen to know this neighborhood well. I lived here for five years. These were the years after the divorce, confused, bleak, dispassionate years during which I hardly published a word and wasn't sure I wanted to. The gift shop is crowded. The boy brims with excitement. He is eager to display what he knows: that this is Santa, that we celebrate Hannukah and not Christmas, that these are pine cones and these little pictures with strings are decorations you hang on a tree. I choose a card with a picture of a seed-covered bagel and the words "You Are My Everything," and an ornament for my ex-wife and her husband, and I let the boy hand both to the clerk.

The sun is already going down and the temperature dropping. I notice the boy shiver and ask him if he would like some hot chocolate. I may as well have asked him if he wants a pony. He all but drags me by my arm to the deli, and hops up and down as I order. An obese woman in a motorized chair sits by the window. I am running out of money. Soon my oldest will graduate from high school and I have little savings. I need to work harder. I need to break the logjam and find some purchase in the material, some plan or order in the mass. But where? After all this blank time, where?

In front of a bar, near the park, we find a small table and sit across from each other, my son and I. The hot chocolate is too hot to drink, but he wants to hold it anyway. He wants to see the steam rise, and to tell me that steam is different from smoke, that one is wet and one dry, and to show me that he can read the letters on the paper cup, and that in front of the drugstore he sees a mechanical dragon and remembers trying one and being scared by how it moved and played strange, tinny music. He tests the hot chocolate, recoils, blows on it, tries again, recoils again. This heat is a trial and the cold is now his ally. The tip of his nose and the tips of his fingers are red. He points out a pigeon, an airplane, a motorcycle, a parked school bus, a plain garbage can. Then he is silent. He blows steadily into the cup. When at last he drinks, the hot chocolate streams down his chin and coats his upper lip. Later I will take him to get a haircut, and afterward he will climb down from the chair and smile up at me, his face covered in fine brown hair, bearded like a grown man.

chapter eight

REGRET

The vanishing volatile froth of the present which any shadow will alter, any thought blow away, any event annihilate, is every moment converted into the Adamantine Record of the past.

—EMERSON

No one confines his unhappiness to the present.

—SENECA

Here is an image I have never been able to shake. Once it entered my mind, fifteen or so years ago, it stuck there like a burr.

The image occurs at the start of Henry David Thoreau's *Walden*. Thoreau has read, he writes, of Hindu mystics who engage in the most astonishing acts of religious devotion. To purify themselves and do penance to their gods, these men hang by their ankles over open flames, roasting like shawarma. They inch on their bellies across the span of continents. They sit at the center of four blazing fires and stare at the sun, bleaching their retinas. They live out their strange, strenuous, restricted lives shackled to the trunks of trees.

And then there is this. Some of these men, Thoreau reports, some of these ash-covered yogis, spend years on end looking over their own shoulders, so that in time (here Thoreau quotes his source directly) "it becomes impossible for them to resume their natural position." Their necks become so contorted and cramped that eventually "nothing but liquids can pass into the stomach."

These men waste away. They reduce to nothing, twisted around themselves like ivy. They spend so much time looking backward that they are never again able to look forward.

Now here is a story. This story has been told countless times, in countless variations, for almost as long as there has been writing. It is the story of Orpheus and Eurydice.

On the day of Orpheus and Eurydice's wedding, one version of the story goes, a jealous, drunken satyr pursues the bride with the aim of raping her. Eurydice flees into the tall grass, and a snake strikes her ankle. She dies of its venom. Naturally, Orpheus is bereft.

Unnaturally, he refuses to accept that Eurydice is gone. He is so intent on the impossibility of her death that he will not even attend her funeral. Apollo, Orpheus's father, implores him to accept the fact of Eurydice's absence. She is dead. That is reality. Orpheus disagrees. He believes he can change reality.

Orpheus descends to the underworld and asks Hades and Persephone, king and queen of the dead, to resurrect Eurydice. His case is weak: There is no precedent for such a thing. Even his presence in the underworld is a violation. But Orpheus is a great musician, and he sings a beautiful, plangent song that makes even the Furies weep. The gods relent. Fine, they say. Go ahead. Take Eurydice. But there is a rule. The rule is: *Don't look back.* Lead Eurydice home and don't turn around until you have reached the surface.

Orpheus very nearly succeeds. He travels for hundreds of leagues. Marathons upon marathons in the gloom and dark. Then, just before he makes it out, he loses his faith, or his nerve. He looks over his shoulder. Eurydice fades back permanently into death.

Now Orpheus is again bereft. But this time his pain is worse, since he himself is the cause of it. There is no panting satyr to loathe. There is no startled serpent. The blame, every last drop of it, lies at his sandaled feet.

This knowledge undoes Orpheus. He cannot forgive himself. He cannot move on. Having once looked back in error, Orpheus never stops looking back—*at that error*. In one telling, Orpheus builds a second tomb for Eurydice on which he engraves the words: "Killed by her husband at the gates of Hell." In another, he retreats to the wilderness, where, among the rocks and trees, he sings an endless sad song about what could have been but, for his one mistake, wasn't. Never will be.

Stupid me, he sings. *Stupid, stupid me.*

•

With the exception of anxiety, about which I have written elsewhere, regret has preoccupied me longer than any other emotion. It has dogged me since adolescence, latching on to experiences as small as a disagreement with friends and as large as the loss of my virginity, my choice of career, my choices of intellectual and journalistic subjects, and even, or especially, my children. Regret has played the role in my life of an emotional parasite, siphoning off faith, fortitude, commitment, and poise, and secreting in their place doubt, confusion, vacillation, and fear. That I have often regretted my decision to write this book, that I have wondered whether it was a terrible mistake, is one indication of the emotion's particular force in my life.

I hate regret. This alone distinguishes it from other negative emotions I feel. Other negative emotions I dislike and resent. Other emotions are unpleasant. They disorient me. They cause disorder and conflict. But for all other negative emotions I nevertheless feel a respect, even an affection. I take it as a matter of principle that it is always better to love than to hate an emotion. To hate an emotion is to wish it dead. It is to exert a belief that the emotion is too foul to to merit a place within the self. This is both unwise and dangerous. It is unwise because our emotions, each and every one of them, are articulate emissaries from our inner lives. They have vital information to impart—information we can't get elsewhere—about our vulnerabilities, furtive desires, hidden assumptions, and half-remembered experiences. If we silence them, we silence a part of ourselves, and thus stunt self-knowledge. It is dangerous because there is no healthy way to kill an emotion. There is no way at all. One of the enduring insights of psychoanalysis is that, like energy, emotions don't die; they only change form. And they tend to change frightfully. Try to exile an emotion, Freud observed, and it is likely to emerge down the line as a symptom. It will go underground. It will transmogrify. It will burble and sour and find its expression. To vilify or reject an emotion, then, is not just futile, it is masochistic—a kind of psychological self-abuse.

Yet I hate regret, and I do reject it. I do wish it dead. I consider regret to be a uniquely stupid and harmful emotion. I struggle to find in it a single redeeming quality, a single constructive or enriching purpose. Of all the human emotions, regret alone, with its brooding, neurotic, self-consuming fixation on what came before, seems to me valueless and barren, a purely execrable outlier.

I think none of these things about regret's closest cousins, guilt and remorse. These emotions share regret's primary characteristics: looking backward and blaming the self. Yet at their centers they are patently moral. They want us to improve ourselves. We have hurt someone, broken some rule, gotten something we don't deserve, and guilt, the nag, won't let us forget it.

Guilt sits by our bed at night rapping its knuckles against the headboard. *Hey. You. Schmuck. Remember? Remember that thing you did? Make it right.*

Remorse delivers a similar message but in a wilder tone. If guilt knocks, remorse drags you out of bed and cuffs your ears. *Oh, no. No rest for you, monster. You don't deserve to sleep.* (Remorse, from the

Latin *remordere*: to torment.) Remorse hauls the criminal to the station house, the perpetrator to the victim's doorstep, the sinner to the confessional. Remorse, pitiless, insistent, delivers the hard wisdom of permanence. That terrible thing you did can never be undone. Even forgiveness, should you be lucky enough to get it, won't repair the damage you caused. You will carry this weight with you forever and it will serve as a reminder: *Do better. Be better.*

Emily Dickinson wrote of remorse that it is a disease "Not even God — can heal — / For 'tis His institution — and / The Complement of Hell." Regret, too, is a hellish emotion. Like guilt and remorse, it weaponizes memory. It localizes and klieg-lights the painfully concluded event. But it doesn't do these things in order to repair, rehabilitate, or enlighten. Regret's core appears to be not a moral but an aversive impulse—a plain, petulant dissatisfaction with the way things are. A compulsive and punishing distaste for the facts on the ground.

The facts, the blunt facts, say, "This is how it is. This is reality. Now let's deal with it." Regret says: "The facts are a bummer. This is how it might have been."

Regret says: "Your life would have been better if only you had . . ."

Regret says: "Follow me. Spend some time wallowing in the muck of your grievously lost opportunities."

What I would like to know is, where is the wisdom in this? What is the use? I mean the *possible* wisdom and the *possible* use. Even our most exalted emotions have the capacity to be dumb and destructive. Love, directed at the wrong object, can be ruinous. Reverence for a corrupt ideal will almost certainly corrupt. At the same time, even our most reviled emotions can serve us well. Anger may pervert the soul, leading to meanness and violence. But anger is also, as Audre Lorde has said, "loaded with information and energy." Anger alerts you to the moral disfigurements and fixed, customary cruelties of the world. It tells you who is your enemy and who your ally. And it rouses the will, without which change of any sort is impossible. The dark side of anger is that it over-narrows your focus. The bright side of anger is that it makes things happen. It drives you onward, spine steeled.

What is regret's bright side? What is regret's "adaptive function"—that kernel of every emotion that explains its original self-protecting or self-flourishing purpose? These questions are of enormous importance to me. I feel that a lot rides on whether they have answers or not. For I am lousy with regrets, and I don't know what to do about them. When I feel joy in my new career as a psychotherapist and I say to my wife, "If only I had done this twenty years ago, I would have been so much happier!"—what am I to make of that statement? When, lying sleepless in bed, I writhe on some pointed memory—getting a little too drunk on my wedding night; quitting that prestigious job on a whim; yelling in my daughter's face when she was seven and out of control—is there information to be gleaned from the experience? When I need quiet to write and my son, my big-hearted, dimpled, guileless son, is wailing over some domestic injustice, and I think, "I should never have had him; children are ruinous"—should I give that thought any credence at all? Should I attend to it? Should I *love* it? Or should I cut it dead as a monstrous blasphemy?

What is regret's bright side? The question is eminently practical. For if regret has a bright side, then it has a meaning; and if it has a meaning, then it has value; and if it has value, then it deserves respect; and if it deserves respect, then it can be tamed. To understand what good an emotion is trying, however wrongly or perversely, to do for you—what frantic hurt it is ventriloquizing, what raw vulnerability it is guarding—is to begin to rein in its power. There is no better way to reduce the force of a negative emotion than to thank it sincerely for its (often misguided) service. Conversely, there is no better way to increase the force of a negative emotion than to treat it like a cancer or a sin.

Pain, writes the classical scholar Margaret Graver, "even the crudest physical pain, is a kind of awareness."

•

A woman in her mid-thirties, an engineer, walks into my office for help with symptoms of mild depression. Her problems began six years earlier, when she moved from Seattle to Manhattan for what she considered to be her dream job. She wasn't wrong. In New York, she found herself doing work that was more engaging and substantive, and significantly more remunerative, than any she had done before. But there was a hitch. Within days of her arrival, she became racked with anxiety, homesickness, fear, and dread. She wept uncontrollably and without warning, she panicked in the grocery aisles and at the gym, she spent full weekends cloistered in her studio apartment, barely getting out of bed. Slowly, and seemingly on its own, her condition improved. Her career flourished. She met a man, fell in love, and was engaged to be married. She became an avid runner. Yet her former state of contentment never quite returned. Things got better but not completely, not as they had been. This fact gnaws at her. She believes that by moving to New York she made an egregious error for which she continues to pay, and likely always will. Week after week, month after month, she comes back to this one tenacious thought. It has gotten so that I can almost see it coming. Her back stiffens. Her eyes seem to unfocus. She fiddles with her necklace.

"As soon as I started to feel bad I should have gone back to Seattle," she says. "Right back. I should've packed my bags and turned around again. I really don't know why I didn't. I thought about it. My friends were there. My brother. My mom. I was *happier*. I could've just turned back."

One afternoon I ask her: Why do you think you return so often to this regret? What do you believe it does for you?

She looks at me as if she can't fathom my ignorance.

"It protects me! That's what regret is, isn't it? It stops me from screwing up again. It reminds me to listen, to really listen, to what I need."

The clinical and academic literature on regret is curiously meager. Psychoanalysis and psychiatry are mostly silent on the subject, and psychology tends to approach it from an experimental perspective that is thin in real-life examples. Yet from the substantive work that does exist, I immediately recognized my patient's answer as the most common current explanation for why we feel regret. This explanation maintains that regret exists so that we can avoid repeating our mistakes. Regret, in this view, is one of the human mind's behavioral safeguards—a kind of stopgap measure. We possess weak memories, or weak wills, and we are prone to what Freud called a "repetition compulsion." Like Charlie Brown presented once again with Lucy's football, we have a difficult time learning from our experiences. Hope springs idiotic. Regret is there to keep us alert and rational. It does this in the most effective way possible: with pain. Regret presses its bony finger into the tender old scar. It dials up the biting memory and thrusts it into consciousness, center stage. As the Dutch psychologist Marcel Zeelenberg puts it in a 2016 lecture, regret "elicits reparative behavior." It is there "to help us make better decisions. . . . It is there to increase our wisdom."

This explanation of regret is close, if a great deal less morally concerned, to the one I offered for guilt and remorse. It stakes out a strictly functional position. The explanation allows that regret, like all emotions, can malfunction and over-assert itself, but it focuses on what regret, when working correctly, intends to do for us in practical terms. Regret acts as a warning signal, a flashing red light. It is the "fool me twice, shame on me" of emotions.

Is this the meaning of regret? Is this its face: a stern but beneficent mentor smiting us for our own good? I don't want to dismiss the possibility. The explanation undoubtedly applies to many situations in which regret arises. When I remember with regret some of my behavior in my first marriage—my iron rigidity about my work, my anxious, passive-aggressive avoidances, my jealousy of past lovers—I feel compelled to behave with greater openness, flexibility, and humanity in my second. More mundanely, when I gorge myself on pizza, have trouble sleeping, and feel regret at my gluttony, I become less likely to indulge like that in the future, or at least in the near future. My regret, as Zeelenberg says, "leads to behavioral change." The analysis fits.

What gives me pause is that it doesn't seem to fit all that broadly. What we might call the self-corrective theory of regret does not feel capacious enough to account for the full, complex, lived experience of the emotion as I know it, and as I see it in others—that is, not just regret's consequences for behavior but its wolfish persistence, its abscess-like throb, its tendency to metastasize beyond its original causes, and its self-distorting, self-abusive, self-confounding qualities. When I look at the kinds of situations to which the theory seems most neatly to apply, and what those situations have in common, I become skeptical that it can offer anything like the best or final word on the subject.

Two examples can serve as cases in point. In his lecture on regret, Zeelenberg tells a story about what happened when he moved to a new city and needed a haircut. A colleague directed him to a salon downtown, where he was assigned to a hairdresser whom he calls Maryann. Maryann gave Zeelenberg a decent haircut, but at the end she accidentally snipped his right ear with her shears. Bleeding down his neck, Zeelenberg understandably felt disappointed and irritated. A few weeks later, he decided he needed another haircut, and he returned to the salon. Reluctantly, not wanting to make a fuss or embarrass Maryann, he agreed to be served by her again. At the end of this haircut, Maryann accidentally sliced open his left ear with her electric clippers. Bleeding a second time, Zeelenberg now felt regret. He shouldn't have been so passive or polite! He should have made his desires known! Bolstered by this feeling, Zeelenberg resolved never again to return to that salon.

The second example appears in *Regret: The Persistence of the Possible* (1993), by the psychologist Janet Landman. Some years earlier, Landman writes, she decided to shop for a used car. She was meticulous and methodical in her search. She combed through the relevant statistics in *Consumer Reports*, she decided on the make and model that best suited her needs and that she could afford, and she insisted on a test drive. But she made a crucial mistake: She didn't have a mechanic inspect the car before she bought it. It was the weekend, her own mechanic was not available, and she felt pressured by the seller. She wanted to complete the sale. As it turned out, the car's transmission was shot and she was out six hundred dollars. Landman writes that she felt "a good strong pang of regret" over this error. She also writes that she feels grateful for this pang. Through the sting of regret, she was able "to clarify exactly where I had gone wrong." She would be able to "avoid making the same mistake in the future."

Zeelenberg and Landman are both apologists for regret. They lament regret's at once neglected and poor reputation and, each in their own way, offer revisionist accounts of the emotion. Their stories are intended as object lessons in those accounts, and it is worth noticing just what they share. Most obviously, they are both stories that center on economic interactions: money freely offered in return for a good or service. More specifically, they are stories about *unsuccessful* economic interactions—unsuccessful, that is, from the point of view of the buyer. Both Zeelenberg and Landman got bad value for their money. Something went awry in the exchange. The hairdresser wasn't careful enough. The car was a lemon. The outlay ended up exceeding the anticipated return. In both cases, too, the buyer traces the problem back to his or her own error in judgment. Zeelenberg should have spoken up. Landman should have resisted the seller's pressure and had the car thoroughly inspected before finalizing the purchase. They each believe that, had they acted otherwise than they did, it would have led to a happier result for them.

At first blush, the main problem with using stories such as these to exemplify a theory about a human emotion is that they are just too simple to do the job. We can accept that Zeelenberg's and Landman's distress will return to them, a phantom pain, whenever they are in situations similar to those that created the emotion. They will feel the former bite, the lashes that their past selves inflicted as punishment, and they will remember: "Tread carefully now. Act differently. Don't repeat your error." The difficulty is, the circumstances that cause regret are rarely so clear, our mistakes rarely definitive. Life is not a hair salon or a used-car lot. Our deepest, most resonant regrets seldom emanate from purely economic exchanges. *If a hairdresser almost chops off your ear, find a new hairdresser. Before you buy a car, look under the hood.* These are lessons to which the word "wisdom" applies only superficially, if at all. It is relatively easy to claim a positive meaning for regret when the stakes are not only low but narrow—uncomplicated by competing, mercurial needs and unclouded by sentiment, desire, fear, obligation, ambivalence, and run-of-the-mill, universal human ignorance. To prove that regret aids us in our growth and development as human beings, we would need to look at cases that are more complex and then see how the theory holds.

Upon closer inspection, however, the problem becomes not that these cases are too simple but that they possess a complexity that they fail to admit or explore. There is a sleight of hand, an unrealistic stripping down, operating in these stories, whereby events and conclusions that are in fact fraught with ambiguity are made to seem as if they aren't.

Take the fundamental assertion that Zeelenberg and Landman made errors in judgment—that they acted in imprudent, incorrect ways. By what measure are we able to say that this is true? One answer, the one implicit in the stories, is that the regret itself serves as evidence of an error. The emotion is the instrument that spotlights the mistake; that is after all its job. We of course have to take Zeelenberg and Landman at their words that in the wake of these incidents they felt regret; they experienced distress coupled with self-blame. Their subjective emotional states are by definition theirs, and only theirs, to report. The question is: Does the existence of regret prove that a past action was regrettable? Some of the time it does, but there is not a direct correspondence between the two. Emotions provide us with information about the world and our own experiences, but they don't always perform that job accurately. Our emotions lead us astray all the time. We fall in love with people who reveal themselves to be unworthy of our love. We hate people not because they are hateful but because they pose a challenge to our self-image or safety, or because they remind us in some inchoate or superficial way of someone who previously caused us harm. Our emotions are not objective facts, they are responses to which we have to respond in turn, determining not only what we are feeling and why, but whether we *want* to feel that way. Indeed, a good working definition of insanity would be the reflexive acceptance of every emotion that comes along. Conversely, a good working definition of maturity would be the ability to deem our emotions valid and valuable but always provisional.

Were Zeelenberg's and Landman's actions mistakes by virtue of their unhappy results? Certainly neither person got what they bargained for. Zeelenberg wanted a haircut that wouldn't make him bleed. Landman wanted a working car. Neither achieved these aims. Still, in order to label the results unhappy we would have to compare them to some alternative, supposedly happier results. We would need to know for certain that things would have gone better if they had acted differently. *And this is something that we can't do.* Neither they nor we can claim with any confidence or honesty to know the results of their contrary actions. It is at least possible that Zeelenberg would have had a worse experience in some other hairdresser's chair: a nick to the jugular, a verbal or physical altercation, inadvertently shaved eyebrows. If Landman had passed up the opportunity to buy that car, perhaps she would have had to wait months for another opportunity to arise, during which time her current car might have died, or been stolen, or stalled on the freeway, all at greater financial cost to her. Maybe she would have been forced to walk to work, and crossing at the light a cement truck, barreling down the road, the driver distracted . . . The point is not that these other results are likely. The point is that these stories have illustrative utility only in strictly binary terms: injured ear vs. intact ear, out six hundred bucks in the moment vs. not out six hundred bucks in the moment. It is only by cleaving off all other variables that we can label these events as not simply regret-causing but, as their authors profess them to be, regrettable.

We can in fact go further and say that, even if we accept that the results of Zeelenberg's and Landman's actions were unhappy, it by no means follows that the actions themselves were worthy of correction. The express purpose of these stories is to show how regret can educate and reform us for the better. Presumably, regret alerts Zeelenberg that he should be more assertive in the future, and Landman that she should be more cautious and patient. But suppose events had played out in more gratifying, pleasing ways. Then a completely different, and equally or more valuable, pair of lessons might have been learned. A spiffy, injury-free haircut from Maryann might have taught Zeelenberg that he was right to give her a second chance. It is morally important, after all, not to judge people hastily. It is important to be generous, charitable, and forgiving. A fully operating car might have taught Landman that she was correct to grab the bull by the horns. Her diligence and her instincts served her well. She had been self-sufficient, shrewd, and profitably bold. In other words, if the purpose of regret is to "repair" our behavior, then we have to be certain that our behavior is worth repairing. Otherwise the signal that regret offers is arbitrary—a matter of what just happened to take place rather than of how we "should," in any meaningful sense, be.

All this leaves out, meanwhile, what might be the most basic limitation of these stories, which is that they draw conclusions about regret's meaning and purpose based only on a particular, circumscribed form of regret. The cases Zeelenberg and Landman outline are real and relatable enough. We can easily transpose them to events in our own lives. But these events would only be ones in which we are compelled to make a decision in the short term. They would be events in which we have to act more or less immediately. Do this or that? Accept or decline? Buy or pass? They would entail regrets produced in the tumult and force of the moment, like Orpheus's lamented turning. In short, they would be about actions taken. But this is not the only type of regret. It may not even be the most consequential type.

•

Probably the most famous literary statement on regret appears in Soren Kierkegaard's *Either/Or*, under the heading "An Ecstatic Lecture."

> If you marry, you will regret it; if you do not marry, you will also regret it; if you marry or if you do not marry, you will regret both. Laugh at the world's follies, you will regret it; weep over them, you will also regret it; if you laugh at the world's follies or if you weep over them, you will regret both; whether you laugh at the world's follies or you weep over them, you will regret both. Believe a girl, you will regret it; if you do not believe her, you will

also regret it; if you believe a girl or you do not believe her, you will regret both; whether you believe a girl or you do not believe her, you will regret both. If you hang yourself, you will regret it; if you do not hang yourself, you will regret it; if you hang yourself or you do not hang yourself, you will regret both; whether you hang yourself or you do not hang yourself, you will regret both. This, gentlemen, is the sum of all practical wisdom.

Kierkegaard is joking—sort of. At the very least, he is being self-consciously perverse. (You can't regret anything after you've hanged yourself.) He is also articulating a point of view that is not necessarily his own. The presumptive writer of this passage is a fictional character named A, an incorrigibly ironic, melancholy, too-clever-by-half "aestheticist" who lives always on the knife's edge of paradox: neither this thing nor the other thing, both this and that, at once fluid and frozen and so . . . what, exactly? Anything at all? As A's more sober correspondent, B, observes later in the book, A is "a strange being"—protean, restless, and slippery. Yet even if A is only being half-serious, reveling in his talent for contradiction, his meditation recognizes and conveys two features of regret that are fundamental to the emotion, and that are critical to understanding its meaning and effects.

The first of these features is so broad as to be existential. It is that the general conditions of human life are always and forever suffused with the conditions for regret. Regret is not just one emotion among many; it is what you might call one of the inevitable emotions. It is inevitable because we live, each and every one of us, in the flow of inexorable, forward-moving time. Nothing stops, ever. Nothing pauses. You can't hop off the bus and still make the journey. Indeed, like it or not, you are the bus driver. And it's a lifetime position. No coffee hour, no vacation, no breaks. No *brakes*, even. You can decide not to steer, but that still qualifies as making a decision. You can decide to turn left, but you will then have to live with the knowledge that you are simultaneously deciding not to turn right, or to continue straight ahead, or to ram headlong into the median strip. Every choice you make is haunted by all of the choices you are at the same time and as a direct result not making. Every move negates other, alternative moves. This is the crux of the "practical wisdom" that A extols, however cartoonishly: Regret is the price of the ticket for existence. Face it or not, it's always there.

It is possible, and should be acknowledged, that this position is too extreme. It is possible that it does not, in fact, apply to everyone. There are those among us, after all, who appear to slip the noose of regret through sheer force of temperament. I know a few. It isn't that these lucky elite are unaware that the choices they make cancel out alternative choices. They know, they just seem unbothered by the knowledge. They have imbibed the rules and somehow it has not given them heartburn. They marry and cheerfully leave behind all consideration of what not marrying, or marrying someone else, might have meant for them. They embark on a career and do not brood on all the alternative careers they might have had. They oversleep, fail a test, say the wrong thing, miss their flight, make their kid cry . . . and they carry on. *Je ne regrette rien.*

The question that sometimes preoccupies me is: Are these people for real? Is it actually possible to live without regret? Can one really go through life with blinders on, eyes forever forward? If so, what consequences might this have for self-awareness? Is the statement "I regret nothing" aspirational, the equivalent of the frightened child who faces down a bully and says, "I'm not scared of you!"—in short, a useful lie? Or maybe these contented people have simply not yet received the jarring blow—the rupture, the loss, the leveling humiliation—that will snap regret squarely into the center of their awareness? Maybe they are living in bad faith, unconsciously dodging a full reckoning with reality. Whatever the answer, it does not seem to me to undermine the essence of A's statement. To live is to be forced to choose, to choose is to be forced to reject. Life is finite. Each decision contains the seed of regret.

The second feature of regret that Kierkegaard captures is the emotion's dual nature. We feel two basic types of regret: that which comes from having done something we wish we had not done, and that which comes from having not done something we wish we had done. There are regrets of action ("If you marry...") and there are regrets of inaction ("If you do not marry..."). The two kinds of regret have a lot in common. Both are counterfactual experiences. That is, both look to the past, imagine it otherwise, and extrapolate from there. Both are charged with self-reproach, that characteristically regretful phrase "If only I..." Both are consequences of the inevitability of choices, the inevitabilities of life. But regrets of action and regrets of inaction are hardly equal.

Regrets of action may be anywhere from moderate to catastrophic, but they always have the virtue of being clear. A regret of action has a discrete focus. Something objectively happened in the world. You behaved in a way that now strikes you as incorrect or detrimental, maybe even tragic. You slept with the wrong person. You totaled the car. You trusted the wrong barber. You re-killed your wife at the cusp of Hell. The distress you feel in the immediate aftermath of your behavior is likely to be acute, like a broken bone or a stab wound. You will look back and kick yourself purple. As the psychologists Daniel Kahneman and Amos Tversky have shown, people seem to know intuitively not only that regrets of action hurt sharply, but that they hurt more sharply than regrets of inaction, and are especially to be avoided. In the early 1980s, Kahneman and Tversky devised the following scenario:

> Mr. Paul owns shares in company A. During the past year he considered switching to stock in company B, but he decided against it. He now finds out that he would have been better off by

$1,200 if he had switched to the stock of company B. Mr. George owned shares in company B. During the past year he switched to stock in company A. He now finds that he would have been better off by $1,200 if he had kept his stock in company B. Who feels greater regret?

When this scenario was later presented to respondents, the results weren't even close. A full ninety-two percent of the respondents believed that Mr. George, who took an affirmative step resulting in a financial loss (or in a missed opportunity for financial gain), would feel more regret than the simply passive Mr. Paul. Which makes good sense. As Kahneman and Tversky put it, there is a difference in the "imaginability" of the two situations. "It is often easier to mentally delete an event from a chain of occurrences than it is to imagine the insertion of an event into the chain," they write. In other words, in the stories we tell ourselves about what might have been, a regret of action involves a relatively simple narrative maneuver: a clean edit.

The research that Kahneman and Tversky conducted on regret helped to inform what ultimately became their Prospect Theory, an influential approach to understanding how people make choices when there is risk involved. It is a psychological theory, but it is a psychological theory grounded in the concerns, methods, and language of economics. That is, the problems the theory dissects and interrogates are, as in Zeelenberg's and Landman's stories, immediate problems: vivid snapshots, life lived under pressure. In fact, work of this sort tends to view human emotion itself as something that happens under pressure. Emotions are "triggered by changes," Kahneman has said, and are most powerful and consequential in the moment. "The long term is not where life is lived."

Kahneman is right, up to a point. But what happens after that point? With regret, what happens after that first explosion of distress, that initial mania of self-laceration? What happens *long* after? As the psychologists Thomas Gilovich and Victoria Medvec have observed, the results of the Mr. Paul and Mr. George survey are "intuitively appealing," but they cut uncomfortably against the grain of a well-known feature of regret: that when we stop and look back on our lives, it is not what we did but what we failed to do that tends to trouble us most. Our *shouldn't haves* recede and our *should haves* step forward. *I should have left my marriage when I was young. I should have pursued my love for music. I should have told my father I loved him before he died.* In the short term, we may feel the jarring blow of our actions, but in the long term we feel the deep ache of our passivity. If Orpheus is the incarnation of regrets of action, the incarnation of regrets of inaction is the unhappy old man at the center of Samuel Beckett's masterful one-act play *Krapp's Last Tape*, the lonely, constipated writer brooding over the old memory of a lover whom he did not pursue: "Be again, be again. (*Pause.*) All that old misery. (*Pause.*) Once wasn't enough for you. (*Pause.*) Lie down across her."

Gilovich and Medvec have described how and why this should happen—how and why Orpheus should give way to Krapp. "What is it about the way people think about their choices and their lives," they ask, "that diminishes regrets of action but strengthens dismay over regrettable failures to act?" Among their answers is that, because regrets of action sting so sharply in the moment, we notice them more, and therefore are more likely to reverse course in an attempt to regain our equanimity. We are more likely to take "compensatory steps" to feel better. We hurt someone we care about; we make amends. We take a job we hate; we quit and find another. We have an affair; we end it. Quite aside from the fact that regrets of inaction are not always clear in the moment, it is more difficult to compensate for them, because opportunities forgone are often opportunities lost. If you don't take off work to sit at the bedside of your dying friend, you will never get the chance to do so again. You will have missed the train.

Another answer they give is that people do more "psychological work" to reduce the pain of regrettable actions. The most common and generic form of this work is to look for the "silver lining." *Yes, I drove halfway across the country for a man who turned out to be a sociopath. But at least he didn't take* all *my money! And I love Wyoming!* Or: *Okay, fine, I got wasted at my sister's wedding and urinated in the swimming pool. But without that experience I would never have gotten sober.* This kind of mental response doesn't usually pertain to regrets of inaction, which are often the consequence of simple inertia. You did not act when you wish you had because you adhered to the status quo, which retains its insidious appeal. Where is the opportunity to say, "I learned so much"? You learned from what—not doing anything? Perhaps, but you will have been unusual to have realized it.

Then there are the processes that cause our regrets of inaction to metastasize and swell. Here time itself is the culprit. As Gilovich and Medvec write, many of our regrets of inaction "arise from an inability to conquer our fears or overcome our doubts when the 'moment of truth' is at hand." Uncertainty immobilizes us. We will be rejected, humiliated, exposed, thrust into intolerable anxiety and confusion. So we remain on the bench. We don't dial the phone, chase the opportunity, express the intimate feeling. But uncertainty has a way of lessening with the years. We live on (if we are lucky) and accumulate wisdom and understanding. Now the fears that once oppressed us seem frivolous. Now we are someone new, someone different, and we look back on our past self—that frozen, frightened, rationalizing youth—with amazement, or with contempt. How absurd, how wasteful, it was to be afraid. Indeed, time doubly conspires against us, for as we get older we have a harder time recalling our former reasoning. Kurt Lewin, a pioneering psychologist of the twentieth century, observed that the forces that compel us to act loom larger in our minds than the forces that restrain us from acting. In the short term, when a regret is fresh, the gap between the two is relatively negligible. But it widens. It widens progressively. From the distance of decades the question "Why didn't I at least try?" may become not just haunting but literally unanswerable, our youthful reasoning lost.

Time may also conspire with our imagination to torture us for our former passivity. Because our regrets of action are sharply defined, we can sharply define their consequences. We acted stupidly. As a result this particular bad thing, or set of bad things, happened. They *actually* happened. We lived the consequences. A regrettable inaction, by contrast, reverberates into a void that we fill as we wish. We failed to act. What good things might have happened had we overcome our fear and inertia? What benefits, joys, and enrichments might have accrued to us if we had only taken that step? The answers have no limit. None at all. We can spool out as many possibilities as our imagination allows. Wealth, contentment, ease, great accomplishments, great respect, great love, adventure, fame. Beautiful dreams. Pure beautiful dreams that must live alongside complex, adulterated actuality.

Gilovich and Medvec give one last, eminently disquieting answer to the question of why our regrets of inaction tend to grow over time. This is that they "often belong as much to the present as they do to the past." The case of a regrettable inaction is rarely really closed. Our failures to act persist as living, aching possibilities. We can still redeem ourselves. *We can still act.* The particular object may be forever gone—the lover married, the parent dead, the neglected child grown—but the general object survives. To love better. To learn bravely. To apply ourselves to matters of abiding value. To dive headlong into meaning. To grow. To act. To overcome. To live.

To live! The injunction never ends, and every time we remember what we did not do we are reminded, with a fresh and mocking challenge, what we still can. Then we are faced with a choice. We can change our lives, with courage and anxiety, or we can slip further into the terrible familiarity of regret.

•

In 2015, the Bank Street Arts Centre, in Sheffield, England, mounted an exhibition called The National Facility for the Regulation of Regret, or the NFRR. Conceived and designed by Rachel Genn, a neuroscientist turned artist and novelist, the NFRR was a fictional institution, founded and run by a fictional psychiatrist, that catered to patients suffering from "regret-related disturbances." These patients included Lassie, a middle-aged woman who repeatedly modifies her body with injections and plastic surgery; Johnny, a soap-opera actor infatuated with a more famous soap-opera actor; and Karl, a gambler and neat freak who is "crippled by superstition." Each patient received their own room, furnished to reflect their particular difficulties, as well as their own tailored course of treatment.

Genn has said that her intention in this installation was to explore "the nature and function of regret," but the most interesting and illuminating thing about the project is how obliquely she went about accomplishing this goal, and what her approach tells us about the emotion. The two most common elements in all definitions of regret are looking back and self-blame, yet none of Genn's characters seem to look back, and none seem to blame themselves. What these people have in common isn't a fixation on some lamentable past event or botched opportunity. What they have in common is a fixation on a fantasy of transcendence—a compulsion toward modes of thought and action that serve as replacements for, or escape hatches from, their own limited, disappointing realities. All of Genn's inpatients are unsatisfied with their lives. They aren't pretty enough, or celebrated enough, or rich enough, or safe enough. They are not where they want to be. So they go elsewhere. They flee their discontent. They bend themselves into more desirable shapes.

Genn is here explicitly linking the concepts of regret and compulsion—and more explicitly, as she has said, regret and addiction. It's a shrewd and revealing association. There *is* something overpowering, something seductive and drug-like, about regret. Also something habit-forming. The addictive element in regret is the devilish possibility that it dangles before your eyes: the possibility of an alternative. Time, again, precludes do-overs. All sales are final. But as 130 years of psychoanalysis have shown us, the human mind is endlessly inventive in its efforts to evade distress. It will devise all sorts of mechanisms to reduce dissonance and provide relief.

What regret gives you is the distress and the relief in one place. The emotion constitutes a dialectic of suffering, though it never advances. Any torturer will tell you this is the most horrifying method. Pain, then comfort, then pain again, then a craving for that same withdrawn comfort. Heroin, if it could speak, would advocate the same approach. Dependence requires a feedback loop, an oscillation from pole to pole that generates its own energy and its own logic.

The pain of regret is the bitter knowledge that a choice you made was permanent and (you judge) wrong. You embraced a career that hasn't really panned out. You don't have the talent you thought you did, or the passion. You certainly don't have the success. You are stuck, unadvanced, underappreciated, underpaid, worn down. Face it, you chose poorly. The antidote to this stinging conclusion is as soothing as it is simple: Imagine otherwise. Rerun the tape. What if you had decided to, say, go to medical school, as you had considered all those years ago, as your parents had wanted you to? What would have happened? It's your fantasy. It's your private solace. Go crazy. Let's say, then, that today you would be swimming in self-esteem, your practice booming, your coffers stuffed, your summer house sun-drenched (a handsome skiff bobbing off your private dock), your kids happier, better educated, better adjusted. Just imagine it. Why not? It's a victimless exercise. Perfectly sane. After all, things could very well have gone that way. It's not *so* crazy to think so. It's not crazy at all. So play it out.

Only now you are in trouble, for you have misused your imagination. We tend to praise imagination in our children indiscriminately, as if invention of any kind is a gift. But there is a difference between imagination as a creative force and imagination as a compensating force. The former grapples with reality by means of adding to it, however floridly or strangely. The latter is a flight from reality. The imagination at work in regret is a compensating imagination, and it creates nothing but a further demand for itself. It has nothing to do with actual change—with an honest accounting of one's needs, circumstances, strengths, opportunities, responsibilities, and weaknesses—and everything to do with escapism. It is far easier to dream a pretty dream of self-revision than it is actually to revise, with all the limitations and strictures that suggests.

But of course the dream always ends. The present always reasserts its primacy, and now seems even dingier and harsher than before. You fled into your bright counterfactual illusion. You awake from your dream in the same bed, in the same situation, at the tip of the same familiar narrative. Who wouldn't feel the pull to go back to sleep? Who wouldn't want again to ease their own distress?

•

And so I am right, perhaps, to find regret uniquely pernicious and dark. I am right to consider it without practical value for the self. I am right, even, to hate it as I hate no other emotion.

Yet where has my hatred gotten me? What benefit has it brought me? My regrets continue undeterred and undiminished. They are so persistent and fecund that they routinely contradict themselves. On Monday, I regret that I did not pursue a doctorate. On Tuesday, I regret that I did not become a neurologist. On Wednesday, I regret that I did not begin to write fiction in my twenties. On Thursday, I regret that I did not pursue a career as a performer. On Friday, I regret that I did not become an editor. On Saturday, I regret (briefly) that I did not dedicate my life to making money. On Sunday, I regret the waste of my regretting. The regrets proliferate, clash, pile up, clamor, and overlap. My hatred means no more to them than would my love. They are deaf to my assessments.

In this, too, I think I see a similarity to addiction. It is useless to hate one's addiction, just as it is useless to hate the things to which one is addicted. The vodka can't hear you; neither can your thirst. Your thirst is barely more than a reflex. It is a response to your discomfort with reality as it stands. It is not a thing; it is a movement. It is a fleeing-from. That is why so many addicts find sobriety only in the act of submission. The key to the struggle against addiction is often, paradoxically, the abandonment of the struggle against addiction, and the strenuous acceptance of . . . everything: all that was, all that wasn't, all that still is, all that never will be, all that always will be. The full embrace of reality is the bulwark against relapse.

But the analogy only carries so far. Regret is more than an escape hatch. It is what you risk, always, when you look back on your life. It is the hazard posed by self-examination, and therefore a possible side effect of an invaluable cure.

"Life must be understood backward," Kierkegaard wrote, but "it must be lived forward." We turn as we advance. We can do no other. Did Orpheus lose his faith or was he hungry to know? Did he forget his desire for Eurydice or did he choose his desire for knowledge? Who could blame him for wanting to see for himself? Isn't it a virtue, a human virtue, to want to understand what lies at our backs?

No, where Orpheus went wrong was not in his turning to look behind him. Where Orpheus went wrong, I think now, was in the attitude with which he turned forward again—that is, with loathing and horror. Where he went wrong was in allowing his vision of the past to infiltrate and corrupt his experience of the present. It is reasonable enough to turn around. The past pulls at us like a planet. But can you leave the past where you found it? Can you come home again?

By way of an answer I offer another parable, about another son of a deity who would travel to the underworld in breach of the long-standing laws. This is a parable about Jesus, from Nikos Kazantzakis's 1955 novel, *The Last Temptation*.

Toward the end of the novel, Jesus, at the peak of his agony on the cross at Golgotha, blinks and suddenly finds himself in a field in the full bloom of spring. An angel appears: "Don't be disturbed, beloved," the angel says. "No, you weren't crucified." It was all a dream. The sacrifice, the humiliation, the betrayal, the torture: all dreams. Now Jesus is free, by the grace of God, to live his life again. He relives it as an ordinary man, with ordinary pleasures: sex, children, satisfying labor, the ease of time flowing forward into senescence.

It is only in the final pages of the novel, when Jesus is old and visited by his enraged former disciples, that he recognizes his terrible mistake. The angel was Satan, exploiting Jesus's pain and terror, his urgent bleeding desire to be anywhere-but-here. In his desperation on the cross, Jesus had allowed himself to be duped. It took only a split second, and it was ruinous. He "lost courage and fled."

When *The Last Temptation* was published, members of the Greek Orthodox Church tried to have Kazantzakis excommunicated. The Vatican placed the novel on its list of forbidden books. American evangelicals denounced it from the pulpit. It isn't hard to understand their anger. Any theology that insists on the pure divinity of Jesus will balk at the suggestion that he was susceptible to satanic wiles, and the novel includes a sex scene between Jesus and Mary Magdalene. But as a representation of human emotional impulse—of the common desire to flee from painful actuality—the novel takes nothing whatsoever from Jesus. For he doesn't stay in his soothing counterfactual. He returns, willfully, triumphantly, to the present tense. Jesus had blinked himself into fantasy. Now he blinks himself back to reality, to the cross. And what he feels is joy.

chapter nine

DESPAIR

... to be restored, our sickness must grow worse.

—T. S. ELIOT

The closest I ever came to wanting to die was in a parked car in late December of 2015. I was thirty-eight years old, and for a year and a half, ever since my wife and I had formally separated, I had been living in a near-constant state of nausea, confusion, and a muffled, dreamlike terror. This was a state of mind I had never experienced before and for which I found myself totally unprepared, to the extent that one can prepare for a calamity and its consequences. That marriages have a tendency to end prematurely I knew to be a verifiable truth. That my own marriage might end prematurely I took to be an impossibility, a result rendered absurd on the one hand by the devotion my wife and I shared, through all hardships, to the sanctity and permanence of our public commitment to each other, and, on the other hand, by the fact that I didn't want it to happen. Some psychological defect or moral rigidity prevented me from even imagining it happening. When, despite my wishes, it did happen, I was in for a second shock, for I discovered that somewhere along the way I had developed a wildly incorrect understanding of what divorce felt like.

For reasons having to do with a lifetime's consumption of popular movies, I imagined it would feel like leaving home—which is to say, unsettling but thrilling, jittery with opportunity, the excitement of the newly paroled. There would be a short, agonizing period of grief and anger. Then: resurrection. Renewal. In time, new love found at (why not?) some cinematic locale: a train platform, a garden party, the poetry aisle of a used bookshop, Rome.

As it turned out, this was not what divorce felt like. What divorce felt like was an act of sudden and catastrophic violence. A building collapse. A collision on the freeway. In short: a trauma. In the aftermath of a trauma, the destruction and your experience of the destruction blend together. You stagger, you reel, your senses simultaneously hazy and heightened. An acute disorientation reigns. What just happened, and why? Are you only lightly wounded or have you been disemboweled? You enter what feels like a cocoon of bewilderment, so that the pain, needs, and even kindnesses of others register only as shadows on the wall of your own personal, private ordeal, and this isolation worsens the ordeal.

The bewilderment of divorce is, I think, the bewilderment of an identity lost. It is the bewilderment of a precious self-understanding exploded by events. One moment you are party to something sacramental; the next moment you are not. A dense web of connections and meanings falls under agitating scrutiny. What now is your relationship to Uncle Jerry? Is he now just . . . Jerry? Can you still go to Mets games together? What do you do with the anniversary card claiming undying love, the one with the pandas sharing a bamboo stalk à la *Lady and the Tramp*? It's just a juicer, sure, let's not be melodramatic—but it's a juicer that *entered your life on your wedding day*. It's a wedding juicer! How can you in good conscience push more raw beet through the thing? There ought to be a ceremony. You should strap the juicer to a virgin and heave them both into a volcano. Anything else would be profane.

When I was at the height of my distress over my divorce, a friend told me that it can take ten years or more to adjust to the new reality. At the time I thought this was a shocking thing to say to someone in pain. Today I can attest to the statement's accuracy. Divorce is a complex, creeping process, pocked with hazards and reversals. I had a hard time of it. Still, looking back I am convinced that I would have traversed the territory more quickly and with fewer concussions had I not made, right as my marriage was ending, a decision that even in the happiest of times I might have found taxing to the point of masochism. This was the decision to write a novel. Worse: It was the decision to write a novel on the subject of despair.

It seemed like a reasonable enough move at the time. I had always wanted to try my hand at a novel. My wife, who had a firmer grasp of the fact that money is needed to purchase goods and services, hated the idea. Now her opinion didn't matter. Moreover, I was fixated on a topic that as I saw it could be fully developed only in the mode and with the techniques of fiction. As a journalist, I had already begun to explore the psychological costs of climate change, atmospheric pollution, habitat destruction, and other ecological catastrophes. I visited a farming community in eastern Australia devastated by open-pit coal mining; a therapist in Oregon treating patients for "eco-anxiety" and "eco-despair"; and, later, a festival in southern England run by an anarchic environmental group trying to reckon with their hopelessness about the state of the world. None of these projects satisfied me.

To convey the knotted and profound emotional ramifications of our age of ecocide, reporting alone wouldn't do. What was needed was unrestricted access to a single dynamic, highly articulate, deeply conflicted mind—a real wordy mess of a bastard. So I invented one. The protagonist I imagined was a twenty-nine-year-old graduate student who, two weeks before he is to marry his college girlfriend, loses his faith in the morality and value of all he has been trained to pursue. He has been radicalized, in his plentiful spare time, by his obsessive reading of climate change reports. Rather than channeling his radicalization outward, into action, however, he channels it inward, ruminating neurotically on the problem's consequences for him personally. This drives him to despair. To the dismay of his fiancée and others, it also drives him to a barren, chipmunk-infested cabin in the New Hampshire woods. There our hero remains throughout the span of the novel, paralyzed but for the compulsion to explain his paralysis. All the prizes he once fervently desired—scholarly achievement, the recognition of his peers, a home, property, children—now seem to him either hollow or sinister: corrosive agents in the inexorable degradation of the planet. His own eating, crapping, resource-devouring existence now seems like a travesty and a scandal. The poor guy is stuck. Knowing what he knows, he can't return to his past, blithe self. Neither can he move forward, since the logical endpoint of his worldview is suicide. The challenge of the novel would be to get him unstuck, but in a way that allowed him to stay true to his principles and to the terrible facts. To put this another way: The point of the novel was to solve the hero's despair.

The astute reader will notice a few hiccups in this literary scheme. The first is that the book has no detectable plot. Nothing happens. In physical terms, nobody does anything. Ishmael went out to sea. Emma Bovary slept around and (spoiler alert) chugged arsenic. Even moony Clarissa Dalloway did a little shopping and hosted a party. My guy sits in a cabin in the forest, surrounded by rodents, feeling bad about the apocalypse. He does this for, say, three hundred pages. Then he feels a little better . . . maybe. It is possible that there exists an audience for such a book, but I'm hard-pressed to say where. Maybe in France.

The second hiccup has to do with the book's ending. It is fine to declare an intention to solve someone's despair, but actually accomplishing the goal is a herculean lift, in life or on the page. In his *Ethics*, Spinoza defines despair as "pain arising from the idea of something past or future, from which all cause of doubt has been removed." There exist other, more nuanced definitions, but for our cabin-bound sad sack this one serves pretty well. No sane, undeluded person could dispute the reality at issue: There are too many humans burning too much fossil fuel into an atmosphere that can't handle it and that is reacting in ways leading to the immiseration and/or death of millions of living beings. Them's the facts, and they are doubtless. Now what? How do you help someone to hold this knowledge in his head—the knowledge of the fallenness of the world and his own, inevitable participation in that fallenness—while also allowing him to feel a sense of meaning, purpose, gratitude, and even joy? I had no idea. Most psychiatrists and philosophers don't have much of an idea. Despair is a paradox, and I had no clue how to resolve it without having my hero become either a religious nut, a psychopath, or a drunk. I had only the problem.

But let's say I was able to work my way through these problems. Let's say I was somehow able to manage, through style, wit, and ingenuity, to make a static book lively and a despairing man undespairing. That would still leave the matter of the writing itself. It takes a lot to write a book—any book. It means years of spending every day with the subjects and themes of your choosing, alone at your desk, straining to assemble something cohesive and resonant from the corned beef hash of your intentions. If your book is about frozen yogurt or golden retrievers, you will still have to contend with ample frustration and self-doubt, and an unremitting sequence of obstacles. If your book is about despair and ecological destruction, you had damn well be as sturdy as an Olympian.

I was not as sturdy as an Olympian. I was as tremulous as an abandoned kitten in the rain, with worms. The wise move, I see clearly now, would have been to do nothing at all. There are times in our life that scream for inaction. Pause the show! Put everything on ice! As I once heard a Zen teacher implore her students: "Don't just do something, sit there." But what could be harder, even in a serene time, than to do nothing at all? What could be more maddening, when you are frothing mad, than to lie in repose?

I wrote in place, spinning and desperate, like a truck in mud, getting nowhere. Every day I sat in front of the page and every day I rose hours later slick with self-contempt. No project had ever been closer to my heart or more in tune with my ambitions. And no project had ever resisted my ministrations with such mulish tenacity. It felt at times as though the book, in its reluctance to be written, was almost begging me *not* to write it, as though its concern for me was greater than my concern for myself. *Don't do it, pal. There's trouble ahead.* Like many people in pain, I took this as an insult—a challenge to my talent and courage. I resorted to the whip hand. I told myself, repeatedly, that if I did not finish and publish the book it would mean that I was nothing but a run-of-the-mill failure—yet another in a pathetic, centuries-long procession of self-deluded would-be novelists. A joke. A living obscenity. That I intended these curses to have a salutary effect on me will serve as a good barometer of my mental health at the time.

You can bully some sentences into existence, but you can't bully an entire book. After several appalling months, the thing sputtered and stalled. I tidied up the forty-odd pages I had managed to write (it was like maneuvering a corpse into a suit), tucked them away in a folder on my laptop labeled "DESPAIR_DRAFT," and sat back to consider the totality of my position. I found it to be void. To be bereft of the roles of husband and *paterfamilias* was one thing. To be bereft of the role of writer, which both predated and, to my mind, superseded the others, was a cataclysm too far. Twice a week I taught writing and literature at a small college north of the city. But what was I to do with the rest of my days? (And why did each day seem to contain hundreds of hours?) What was I to do with my ambitions?

I tried writing other things, but I was working by dead light—like making love by rote. Any hope of renewal, any expectation that the well would fill again, withdrew, and I came to dread and loathe even the sight of the pen-filled mug at the corner of my desk. When I walked past bookstores I hurried my pace, as if I were a grieving parent passing a nursery school. The despair I had proved unable to harness into prose found its living, proper home.

Then, as if on cue, a billionaire offered me a job. The billionaire's father had died, and he wanted me to research and write his biography. I could think of nothing I wanted to do less. I would have rather worked on an oil rig or field-tested industrial solvents. But teaching was neither engaging nor particularly lucrative, divorce is expensive, and billionaires pay well for vanity projects about their parents. In this way I found myself driving around New York City and its suburbs interviewing old people about a dead man in whose life, though it was an admirable and interesting one, I had exactly no native interest.

I tried to think of the job as a make-work operation, like a WPA project. It helped to pay my bills, and it got me out of bed. I tried to think of it as a stopgap. But a stopgap on the way to what? In the past when I had taken temporary jobs for money, I had not doubted that they were temporary, and subordinate to my real work. Now there was no real work to speak of, nor hope of any. The notion of "temporary" had lost its meaning. Time, the future, had flatlined.

In psychiatry, the term "suicidal ideation" has a range of connotations. It may mean that someone is making active plans to kill himself, stockpiling medication or buying a gun, or envisioning how he would do it if he did: where he would be, what he would write in a note, what he would leave to whom. Or it could mean something vague and diffuse: an openness to death. A curiosity about oblivion. What a relief it would be, not to be. Without the hope of some positive comfort, what recourse but the blunt negation of pain?

I sat in a dozen fussy living rooms, eating sugar cookies off chipped china, asking questions and feigning interest in the answers. I filed expense reports with one or another of the billionaire's overqualified assistants. I thought of cars jumping the curb and crushing me on the sidewalk. Cancer eating my liver. An aneurysm bursting as I slept. Heart disease. ALS. An electrical fire. Leukemia. Blood poisoning. A robbery gone bad. These thoughts brought relief for a moment. Then I returned to excruciating reality and found that I needed the thoughts all the more. The experience was circular, the fantasies self-reinforcing. By the winter of 2015 it was a miracle I was ambulatory. In a sense, I wasn't. I moved by habit and requirement, but remained static in my mind.

Nowhere but here. Nowhere but now. The eternal, awful present.

•

In thinking about our emotions, the temptation is always strong to explain each within the context of its opposite. Emotions are wily, slippery things. They flitter, shape-shift, blend together, swell, and disappear. They can be spectral in their elusiveness. It makes sense, then, that we would seize on some other position by which to orient ourselves, like a sailor using dead reckoning. What is hate? It is the opposite of love. What is boredom? It is the opposite of engagement. Nowhere is this temptation stronger than with the emotion we call despair. Here the polarity is built into the emotion's name. The word despair derives from the Latin *spes*, meaning hope, and the prefix *de*, meaning without. What is despair? It is the absence, the opposite, of hope.

There is a truth to this way of thinking about despair, but it is a thin truth. It is thin because it forces us to consider despair exclusively in terms of what it takes away. It focuses our attention on those expectations and ideals that despair, rightly or wrongly, negates. Throughout a period of terrible marital conflict, a man retains the belief that his union with his wife can still survive. He "has" hope. Then something happens. Something changes in him. A betrayal comes to light. She speaks her true, passionless feelings. His hope drains away. Now he despairs for his marriage; it can't be redeemed. The man sets out to write a novel. He believes, he knows, it can be done, even if he has to contend regularly with serious, paralyzing doubts. But he makes so little headway, and feels so little confidence in the meager results, that his passion and purpose abandon him. The novel will not and cannot be written. He despairs.

Despair of this kind is real. In fact, it is common. A person might experience it many times a day, sometimes with such small effect that it registers only as a kind of emotional charley horse, a spasm that soon resolves, with relief, back into hopefulness. My own days are often busy with the weather of despair. As I write, for example, it is dusk on a Sunday, and if I choose I can describe my waking hours in terms of all the hopes I have had and then lost: that I would wake feeling rested and calm; that my two young children would remain quiet long enough for me to finish a single cup of coffee in bed; that the anxiety I have felt over a disagreement with a friend would abate; that I would feel confident in my grasp of this subject; that I would trust myself; that I would feel worthy of love; that I would feel whole. A constellation of despairs, some piddling, some profound. Some indistinguishable from annoyances. Some like heartaches. Some like the throb of deep injury. But all temporary. Either the dashed hope is so minor that it can be left quickly behind—"Fine. Whatever. I'll go to the children"—or else, out of self-preservation, one waves the despair away and decides to stand again on what one philosopher has called "the ground of hope." "I can't write this book. It's impossible! I just can't do it! . . . But I have to. I *want* to. The difficulty isn't total. I'll keep at it." The void opens and the void closes. One can live in this oscillating condition for years at a time.

But this is not the kind of despair I want to talk about. The despair that concerns me is not directed toward any specific hope or the disappointment of that hope. It isn't a habit, and if it passes it passes the way a trauma passes, or childhood: It leaves its mark. When I feel despair that I will ever again experience a morning of uninterrupted leisure, I can, if I stop and breathe, feel the faint but reliable warmth of hope in the distance, like the winter sun. There is a charge of possibility in my desire for something, even if I am forced to reckon with the frustration of this desire.

What I want to talk about is true despair, which is less of an emotion and more of an estrangement. It is a shift from a state of being anchored, however tenuously, to time and purpose, to a state of being adrift—abandoned by, or to, the universe. It is a state of frantic *grappling* with abandonment. When I was *in* despair, I lost even the hope of hope. A monstrous certainty rose up in me: the certainty that nothing lasts; that death obviates all action; that under the aspect of eternity none of my ambitions or desires meant anything at all. That nothing and no one would come to save me.

What makes this certainty so excruciating is that it is not a delusion. It is fact: a revelation of how things are. Despair is gimlet-eyed and ruthless. It has no illusions about the world. The past did not redeem me, the future is short and will not redeem me, and I have no choice but to live out a life of strict insignificance. These truths are almost banal. They are the truths of a teenager who has just read Camus for the first time and won't shut up about it. Sisyphus-this and Sisyphus-that. But you are no teenager. You are probably middle-aged or older. In your rearview mirror you can see the ruins, and on the horizon, the graveyard. These truths are no longer intellectual toys. They are alarm bells. They are battering rams.

At the same time, something inside you balks. This logic cannot be complete. "As despair deepens," writes the psychoanalyst Leslie Farber, "what had meaning now seems meaningless; what seemed meaningless is fraught with meaning." How could this be so? How could meaninglessness be life's meaning? What kind of truth negates itself? More viscerally, what human truth negates life, pointing you inexorably to death—to your own death?

And so you come to live, each and every sober moment, on this pinprick of consciousness, in the nutshell of a paradox. The past provides no comfort, the future no possibility. There is only the discordant, restless now. It is the demonic inverse of mindfulness. You live afraid, angry, resentful, envious, alternately desperate and slack, like a deer tied to a tree. You know only one thing, with which you are obsessed: This can't go on. Despair, true despair, is hardly an emotion at all.

•

In those days, I took a lot of walks. I walked and I brooded over my life. What it had become. I have always been a gifted brooder. Now I became a master in the pitiable art of turning oneself over in one's mind, of holding oneself up to the light in fascination and dread.

What was happening? What should I do? Where should I turn? To whom? Was I depressed? Clinically speaking, was I now a depressed person? If so, shouldn't I be hospitalized? Shouldn't I be cared for away from the pressures of the everyday? A vision materialized, soft and cool. Tulips on the windowsill. A hot meal under a beige plastic dome. Taut linen. The nurse's strong hand squeezing the bulb that tightened the cuff on my bicep.

I thought of hospitals. I thought of ashrams. I thought of monasteries on Asian mountaintops. I thought of alpine cottages. Sanatoria. No work. No obligations. Absolute silence. No duty but to be.

What was happening? I alighted on a metaphor—a cliché, really—which I expounded to my closest friends. "Something has broken inside me," I said. Some essential mechanism, some ... spiritual gyroscope has cracked. I was attracted to the finality of this metaphor, its sharp division between youthful verve and grizzled knowledge. If accepted as true, the metaphor assured me not just compassion but admiration. The wound that brings wisdom. The trauma that sets one apart. Admiration, and also absolution. I was in stasis, achieving nothing, publishing nothing. I saw no point in writing, and, at the same time, could not bear the thought of obsolescence. Loserdom. A bookless future. It was like exile, like being shut out of the party. But it wasn't my fault. I had a doctor's note. I had an alibi: "Something has broken inside me." It was straightforward, decisive, and tragic. Didn't they see this?

They did not. Not my friends, not my brothers, not my therapist. Invariably my confession was received with condescending silence and an indulgent nod, kindly but noncommittal—the kind you offer to a perfectly healthy hypochondriac who insists he has a mortal disease. No matter how I tried, I could not get them to accept the reality of what I sincerely if self-servingly felt. No one would validate the existence of a permanent rupture in my life.

I remember being hurt and confused by this refusal. What does anyone want of their private agonies but that they be recognized? This is the emotional contract we forge with our intimates, is it not? I tell you I feel shitty. You say you get it. I feel better for having been witnessed. For having been *believed*. A tidy call and response. This is the arrangement, and for all my other negative feelings—anger at my ex-wife, fear of financial ruin, worry for my daughter, frustration with my work, grief, anxiety, shame—the arrangement held. Only in this instance was it abrogated. Only my feeling of fundamental despair fell outside the bounds of the statute.

Today, at a remove of years, I think I have a better understanding of this refusal. I have theories. One centers on charity. Simple affection. How could I ever have expected anyone who cared about me to assent to a notion as unsparing and entire as brokenness? How could I have been so selfish as to ask for it? What is a friend, faced with such a claim, supposed to do? She could deny it outright: "Don't say that. You're not broken." But this would be a direct shooting down of another's urgent reality, and a kind of violence. The most loving move, and probably the most honest one, is a plain, neutral silence: solidarity without agreement. Don't refute the belief, but don't collude with it either. Simply be present, and in your presence exhibit a tender consistency that can perhaps be used as a beacon in the dark.

Then again—theory number two—maybe they didn't know what on earth I was talking about. Maybe the feeling of a clear yet indefinable discontinuity was obscure to them—too far from their own experiences to be recognizable. To credit another person's state of mind, after all, you have to have some idea of what it feels like. And despair is a pretty exclusive condition. It is an unimaginable feeling. You can't extrapolate it from sadness, frustration, or grief. You have to encounter it in the wild. You have to see it with your own eyes. Otherwise it can sound silly and melodramatic. *I have been exiled from myself. I stand before you adrift in the universe. I was one person and now I am another, one possessed of intolerable, ineradicable facts.*

"Is that so? How interesting. What are you going to order? I'm deciding between the sea bass and the salade niçoise."

And yet it isn't a foregone conclusion that despair is a rarefied state, a torture meted out only to the truly sensitive (poor dears) and arcane to everyone else. In fact, the troubling silence I received might have been caused by something very much like the opposite: not confusion but recognition. Not disinterest but revulsion. Despair *is* arcane in that it is wily, powerful, and paradoxical. It is the farthest thing from arcane in that it deals in universal problems: belief, desire, death, decay, impermanence, solitude, uncertainty, one's place in the universe, the search and need for meaning, the possibility that there is none to be found. The person in despair embodies these problems. He is their representative, like it or not. Usually it is the latter, and for good reason. Who wants to be knocked in the jaw by Ultimate Concerns in the middle of the work day, or at a café downtown? Who wants to be reminded that life can suddenly snap and an existential monsoon rush in? Who wants to sit in the shadow of the logic of suicide? It is unnerving to be the despairer's friend. It is like being on a cancer ward. You might worry that you too will fall. As you very well might.

Probably, though, you figure you'll be fine. After all, you are resilient. You are strong. You live a healthy lifestyle. You don't let yourself get preoccupied by dark abstract thoughts. You chose the right mate. You exercise regularly. You meditate. The despairer had some bad luck, it's true, but he also . . . slipped. He allowed himself to get tangled up and self-involved. Morbid. It isn't just that he is feeling despair, which would be bad enough. It's that he gave in to despair. He "succumbed," as we say. He made a bad choice.

This judgment, too, I thought I saw in the faces of those I confided in—those people who love me. I thought I saw them disappointed in me. Stonily disapproving. Was this paranoia? I'm sure they would deny it all. Or was it that I judged myself for my despair, and that my own judgment radiated outward? That my despair was ringed by shame. That I believed my despair *should* be ringed by shame. As I still sometimes do.

How I hate to confess it. My goal with the negative emotions is to arrive at a place of moral neutrality. No judgments, only feelings and whatever it is they are trying to say. It is a project of self-defense as much or more as it is a studied position. I already feel plenty bad. The last thing I want is to feel bad about feeling bad. Why compound the distress? Why fold it in on itself?

But despair—I can't shake it—is a special case. Something about it cries out for censure. Is it the danger it poses? Despair paralyzes. It annihilates movement. Everyone is angry. Everyone is sad. Everyone is bored. The world turns. Everyone despairs: The world seizes to a stop. Or worse: explodes into nihilism. If nothing has meaning, everything is allowed. Meaning is the intangible substance that directs and limits our actions. It is like gravity; it impels connection. The despairer, like the sociopath or the narcissist, can't connect, not to the self he once thought he knew and not to others. He may try, frantically. Floating in space, he flails for any foothold, any certainty. Anything. When he can't find anything that is solid, he has license to act any way he chooses, for nothing matters. Despair can lead to desperation and violence, demon children. Mass shootings, some criminologists argue, are at their core crimes of despair.

Or is it that despair feels like, or is, a dire personal challenge—a test of one's mettle? Despair says, "The juice doesn't seem worth the squeeze. What's the point?" The question sounds rhetorical, but you must answer it. Not to answer the question is to give in to the despair. It is a passive form of agreement, and so, alas, a kind of cowardice. A limp whine. ("Something has broken inside me!") Active agreement is, of course, suicide, and will be evaluated, like homicide, according to its merits.

And disagreement? The restoration or rebirth of meaning? Well, that's the test. That's the riddle. Despair is like a Zen koan. If the ground beneath you has disappeared, how do you walk?

•

If I were a believing Christian, as opposed to an agnostic Jew, I suspect I would have less trouble answering the riddle of despair. I would have a venerable tradition of advice, parables, and admonitions to guide me, and a clear goal—submission to the glory and will of God—at which to aim my efforts. Yet while I don't believe in a deity, and while I have nothing particular to submit myself *to*, I find myself drawn again and again to the Christian tradition and its visions of renewal.

When it comes to despair and Christianity, "visions of renewal" may seem a dubious phrase. In *The New York Times*, in 1993, the novelist Joyce Carol Oates described Christianity's view of despair as "the conviction that one is damned absolutely, thus a repudiation of the Christian Saviour and a challenge to God's infinite capacity for forgiveness." To indulge in hopelessness is deliberately to reject the divine promise of redemption, which makes it "the sole sin that cannot be forgiven." But this is misleading. Christianity has no single view of despair. What it has is a tradition that characterizes despair as the endpoint of a far more roundly denounced sin against God. This sin—what Gregory the Great called "the queen of all vices" and Thomas Aquinas called "the most grievous of sins"—is pride.

For the nonbeliever, especially in our therapeutic day and age, pride can feel like an unmitigated virtue, a sign that all is going right. You have reached a state of healthy and appropriate self-respect; you stand tall, with dignity and strength. Your children are behaving in a way you approve of and that reflects well on you; you beam with satisfaction and pleasure. "Look at what I did. Look at what I made. Look at who I am." For the Christian, however, and especially for the traditional Christian, pride is nothing less than a grotesque distortion in the orientation of a soul. It is the sin that caused our expulsion from Eden, the belief that we deserve to have the same knowledge as God. It is the central quality and fateful error of Satan, whom Thomas More referred to as that "proud spirit"—an angel who misunderstood himself to be equal to God. Pride is a twisted self-love and a trapdoor into damnation. The great eighteenth-century preacher Jonathan Edwards called it "the chief inlet of smoke from the bottomless pit, to darken the mind and mislead the judgment." Pride, C. S. Lewis wrote, is "the chief cause of misery in every nation and every family since the world began . . . [a] spiritual cancer: it eats up the very possibility of love, or contentment, or even common sense." In short, pride makes you think that you are what matters most. You are the center of concern: your qualities, your needs, your desires, your achievements. *You you you you you.* There is a wonderful phrase from Martin Luther's *Commentary on Romans* (1515–16) in which he describes the sinner as *homo incurvatus in se ipsum*: a person curved into himself. This is pride. This is the radical egotism of pride.

It isn't difficult to see the link between pride and despair. They are the positive and negative poles of the same impulse. Pride is a successful self-love. It is self-involvement unchallenged and delighted with itself. Despair is pride's queasy aftermath. It is the crisis of conscience. Pride believes that the self is the ultimate source of power, meaning, and creativity. Despair is what happens when this worldview falters and disintegrates, as it almost inevitably will. Pride mutates into despair by way of self-pity. *I thought I had the answers. I thought I knew.* But no. You didn't. Poor sap, you didn't. Your confidence was a sham, your resources insufficient. So . . . what now? Two choices. You could walk through the fire. You could molt. Recast yourself. But this would mean relinquishing not only your pride but (much harder to do) your habit of certainty. Your desire to know. To retain this, you make the second choice. You moan in perpetuity. You proclaim your devastation and disappointment—your brokenness. You curve inward. Despair arises, writes Thomas Merton, "when a man deliberately turns his back on all help from anyone else in order to taste the rotten luxury of knowing himself to be lost."

As a solution to despair, this makes a kind of paradoxical sense. Despair feels like a trap from which you must urgently escape. When you discover that you can't easily escape, you fall back on the solution that life itself is a trap. The solution is that there is no solution! Eureka! I give up! In this way, the certainty of despair provides a perverse solace for the pain of despair, as well as an excuse for the bummer of a person you know you have become. *Before I despaired*, you tell yourself, *I was deluded. Now I am awake. Now I can see that life is meaningless and hopeless.* Your arrogance reverberates through your despair. Listen! You can hear it like a rattle in a cough. *See how smart I am?* it says. *See how awake I am to the facts? I am miserable, but I am right.*

This is, of course, a seriously awkward position to be in. It means that in order to cope with your despair you have to commit fully to your despair. You have to continually stoke your belief in the absence of belief, which is your only remaining certainty. This is a full-time job. It requires great vigilance to stay broken. When you slip and feel good for a moment—when you enjoy five minutes of equanimity while playing Uno with your daughter, or find yourself lost in meaningful conversation with a friend—you must catch yourself and return swiftly to what Farber calls the "dismal certainty" of your despair. You must continually feed the meter of your self-pity and absolutism or else face the prospect of real, uncertain change, which feels utterly beyond you.

In other words, you must not be limber. You must be immovably pained. In the Middle Ages, Christianity had a ready avatar for the rigidity of despair. You can see it depicted in cathedrals across Europe, and in illuminated manuscripts: Judas Iscariot, the great betrayer of Jesus, trading his master's life for thirty pieces of silver—then dangling by his neck from a tree. Judas is the only figure in the Christian Bible, and in fact the whole Christian pantheon, to commit suicide. Medieval literature and iconography associated him closely with despair. What Judas despaired of was his own soul. He knew that what he had done was wrong. He repented. He even tried to give the money back. But he could not move from repentance to redemption. He could not budge from his belief in his own immorality. And so, in the clipped phrase of the Gospels, "he went and hanged himself."

What is the meaning of Judas's downfall? What brought him to iniquity and spiritual ruin? You could say, with many Christians over the centuries, that he was ruined by his treachery. You can't rat out the son of God and escape punishment. There is a grave price to be paid for betrayal. But Peter also betrayed Jesus, denying him three times, and also repented. And the next we see him he is off to visit the resurrected Christ—no harm, no foul—as chief of the disciples. You could say, with Oates and others, that Judas was damned by false belief. By refusing to accept that he was worthy of redemption, he disqualified himself from redemption. He was locked out of the Kingdom of God because he was convinced that he deserved to be locked out.

I am no theologian. But I object to a strand of illogic, a spiritual absurdity, in this argument. It indicts Judas for what he believed in life, prior to his suicide. He is an apostate. Damn him. In the Middle Ages, while Judas was often depicted as the personification of despair, Christ was depicted as the personification of hope—of infinite forgiveness and universal salvation. *Universal* salvation. The essence of gospel Christianity, as I understand it, is that there is no one in existence who is not worthy of redemption. If this is true then even Judas, despite his disbelief in his own worthiness, amply meets the criteria. So long as he lives, there is a chance for him to return to the fold. So long as he chooses to think and feel and breathe air, he is choosing to live in a world in which his beliefs and actions do not condemn him.

To return to my own, secular field: The "dismal certainty" of despair can be consummated in self-annihilation—it can be locked into place once and for all—but until that terrible culminating moment, the absolutism of despair remains notional and incomplete. Living itself is an act of hope. If you continue to live, your despair by definition cannot be complete. Beautifully, a small bright atom of hope, a pinprick of possibility, resides always within the black oleaginous mass of despair.

I say beautifully, but it can be a torture, this pinprick. It is perhaps the true essence of the torment of despair, to sense beneath the avalanche of your pain a splinter of light. A distant chance of return. To feel it yet not be able to reach it. Nothing so effectively increases the signal of pain as the unfulfilled promise of pain's relief. A person might do anything to escape that feeling. A person might consign himself to Hell itself, just to close the loop. To confirm, once and for all, the darkness, the certainty of it.

•

What if Judas had not tied that noose and hanged himself from that tree, becoming, in that instant, the very figure of despair? What if he had managed somehow, in his great shame and agony, to hold on? Would that splinter of light have brightened and spread? Would redemption have come? What is the path from despair to renewal?

In his own essay on despair, Leslie Farber quotes approvingly from T. S. Eliot's poem "East Coker."

> *I said to my soul, be still, and wait without hope*
> *For hope would be hope for the wrong thing; wait without love*
> *For love would be love of the wrong thing; there is yet faith*
> *But the faith and the love and the hope are all in the waiting.*
> *Wait without thought, for you are not ready for thought:*
> *So the darkness shall be the light, and the stillness the dancing.*

There happens to be a prescription in here, though it is impossible to follow it with any fidelity or confidence. It is, in fact, a prescription against confidence. It is a prescription against prescriptions. What Eliot knew is what Merton knew, and Farber, and much of the Christian tradition with its tales of souls lost and then found, blind and then sighted, grace abounding to the greatest of sinners. What he knew was that despair is a disease that can't be cured on its own terms, with its own wild energies. Despair is frantic for certainty, when what it needs is a rapprochement with uncertainty. Despair is deranged in its search for equanimity, and so finds only more derangement.

Yet incredibly, there is this sacred and consoling fact: People do rise up from despair. People do find ways out that do not involve a razor blade, a bottle of pills, or a gun—or, as much to the point here, a conversion experience. People do crawl their way through. The darkness sometimes becomes light.

I am no expert on renewal. I am no model. For one thing, my despair has not been "cured." It still returns periodically, like a bout of madness, making me quake with self-pitying need. During these times, I again daydream of death. I again seek relief in the thought of extinction—not of myself but of the intolerable dilemma of myself. I slide back into my own fetid bath.

And anyway, it may very well be, as I suspect, that there is no such thing as a model when it comes to the emergence from despair. The emotion is a paradox: a loss of hope in the possibility of hope that yet contains hope within it. And there is no solving a paradox, or at least there is no one solution. There is only attending to the paradox with as much humility as one can manage in the moments one can manage it. So: Where is your splinter of light? Where does it lead *you?* Go there, expect nothing. See what you receive.

•

My own light led me, purblind and reeling, to a tree. This tree—there was nothing special about it—stood at the top of a small hill between a bridle path and a baseball diamond near the southwest corner of Prospect Park, in Brooklyn. There was, I repeat, nothing special about this tree, except that somehow it was the tool that cracked open the space that let in the breeze that carried me back to life.

In my desperation, I had tried many solutions before I found that tree. Some of these "solutions" were mere anesthetics. I drank too much. I slept around. I watched a lot of TV on my computer. I slept. Some more promising solutions, such as the comfort of friendship, my despair itself sabotaged. It wasn't only that I couldn't succeed in getting my friends to acknowledge my "brokenness." It was that my conviction that I was broken set me at an impossible remove from them. It was like trying to hug through a sheet of glass. I clamored for my friends' love, attention, and consolation. At the same time, I envied and feared my friends. I envied them those exact qualities of life—solidity, continuity, connection, casual movement through the world—from which I believed myself to be terminally estranged. And I feared that they would succeed in seeing what I obsessively invited them to see: the ugliness and weakness of my despairing state.

Meanwhile, out of long habit, I read. I read greedily, like a pig at a trough, grateful (since I could no longer write) for the vicarious creative warmth the books provided, and grateful as well for any resonant wisdom, even if that wisdom resounded as if from a great distance, as in Ecclesiastes: "The fool foldeth his hands together, and eateth his own flesh." I found myself returning to the poet George Oppen, who warned of "The unearthly bonds / Of the singular / Which is the bright light of shipwreck." I found myself returning to Emerson, who declared that "In the presence of nature a wild delight runs through the man, in spite of real sorrows." And I read Thoreau: "I delight to come to my bearings." I read so much Thoreau. I could not take notes quickly enough. Has there ever been a writer less prone to despair than Henry David Thoreau? His gladness is monumental. His rapture for facts. His surety. His patience. His curiosity, passion, and humility.

"Bibliotherapy" is the dull term with which psychology describes the use of books to improve mental health. I suppose that's what this was, though the choice of texts was impulsive and largely fortuitous, and any self-awareness I achieved was of an unflattering sort. What these books offered me was not practical guidance or emotional uplift but rather points of startling contrast with my own funereal outlook. Reading them, I grew more and more conscious of the extent to which I had become curved into myself. "You can always see a face in the fire," writes Thoreau. But I could see no face, since I could not even see the fire. I could see nothing but myself. The upright spirit of these authors—the odor of woodsmoke, moss, and pine needles—was like a tap on my hunched shoulders. *Remember this? Remember reality?* I did, dimly, and with some resentment. But I did.

Out of this, I devised my own practical guidance. Gingerly, skeptically, I lifted my head and cast around for something external on which to fix my palsied attention. I was in search of something whose relationship to time was different from my own, something reliable and alive and slow. I was living, uncomfortably, in despairing time. I needed to find a way to live, again, in seasonal time. I needed a discipline of engagement.

I decided, therefore, to study a tree. What better? I decided that I would track a tree, day to day, month to month, through all its subtle changes, its flourishing, its senescence, its dormancy, its flourishing again. I would take notes, as if the tree itself were a book. I would make sketches. I would learn the parts of the tree's anatomy, acquainting myself with leaf scar, petiole, lenticel, and bract. I would do these things and in doing them I would, if I stuck with it, adjust and straighten my mental posture. I would restore my senses.

I put this plan into motion on a Wednesday afternoon. My daughter was just getting out of school, but it was her mother's day on the schedule and I was free to do as I pleased. The grass in the park was wet, and in my jacket pocket I carried a notebook, a pen, and a tree identification guide, a single illustrated sheet folded into quarters, from the website of the New York City Department of Parks and Recreation.

I spotted the tree while crossing the ball fields. I must have seen it many times before, but never with a purpose. It seemed enormous, a looming, spreading thing on the hill.

Right away I appreciated its bark. Its bark was thick and fibrous and had deep, rugged furrows. I plucked a leaf from a low branch. It was dark green on top and pale green beneath. I chewed on a stem, as I had read to do somewhere. It tasted like a tree stem. I looked down at the guide, then up at the tree, then down at the guide, then up at the tree, then down at the guide. I determined the species—littleleaf linden—which was a small triumph, for I had never identified a tree before. Then I sat down on a large root and rested.

That was it. That was all. The work of an afternoon. High in the linden's branches a robin was making a racket. Its breast looked almost purple from where I sat, directly beneath it. In the moment, I realize now, neither the metaphorical aptness nor the danger of sitting directly beneath a bird in a tree occurred to me.

•

We call it a depression. When my friends and family and I talk about that time in my life, we say that I went through a period of depression. This is shorthand. It is the parlance of the day. The word "depression" makes despair more explicable. It medicalizes it. It strips it of its existential and spiritual components so that it can be passed safely from hand to hand. It turns a verb, "to despair," into a noun: a syndrome.

When I became a therapist, my mother told me that my experience of depression would broaden my clinical effectiveness. Having been depressed, I would be better able to spot, understand, and treat depression in others. She herself, she said, did not know depression. I did. My pain, she assured me, would be put to valuable use.

This is probably true. All experience can be metabolized into wisdom. All experience can be enlisted in the cause of empathy.

Especially pain. It was comforting to be told this. It bolstered my confidence when, as a trainee, I had reason to feel unprepared and uncertain. Nevertheless, when I blink and think of that time in terms of despair rather than depression—when I remind myself of the true lineaments of my distress—I become leery of that comfort and of that confidence. I become leery of all comfort and all confidence. I remember, from the marrow out, the frantic unknowing, the grasping estrangement, the freezing, the fleeing, the prideful and stubborn self-isolation.

And I remember that linden, that one tree out of the world's three trillion that I turned to, more or less at random, to slow the flat spin of my blackout descent—to reassert and maintain the rules, however tangled and befuddling they may be, of everyday emotional gravity.

If you are lucky in love, as I have been, you will find yourself with a person able simultaneously to expose and to honor your cherished self-deceptions. At the time that I met Emily, not long after I met that linden, and in the very same park, I cherished the belief that I had found in myself a deep, regenerative passion for the study of trees. In those early months of our relationship, I accumulated a small library on the subject: books on the history of trees in general and the history of trees in the human imagination; illustrated guides to the trees of New York City and the continental United States; manuals for identifying trees by the shape and structure of their leaves; a didactic yet strangely resonant book titled *1001 Questions Answered About Trees* ("What can be done to wake up dormant seeds?" "How do branches 'marry' and grow together?"). It didn't take Emily long to notice that I seemed more inclined to buy books about trees than to read them, and that on our long walks around the city I was able to recall the names of only two or three common species, additional facts about which I could recite practically none. As for my beloved linden (*Tilia cordata*), my year-long "discipline of engagement" lasted less than a month, after which I mostly admired it, wistfully, from afar. Before long my library included a gift from Emily—a coffee-table book called *Remarkable Trees of the World*. The inscription read:

> To my darling,
> Who insists he loves trees.
> xxx
> Emily

This was of course teasing, not mockery, the difference between the two being, I think, that one aims to alienate a quality or experience from its claimant—to hammer a wedge between them—and one doesn't. What Emily seems to have understood long before I did, or could, was that my purported fascination with trees was at once comically false and completely serious. It was arbitrary in subject but profound in intention. It was a blind launch out of a polluted atmosphere, a first, desperate thrust toward self-renewal, and so something to be approached with tenderness and respect, though not solemnity.

There is a poem by Theodore Roethke, a famous and oblique poem, that opens, "In a dark time, the eye begins to see." My experience has been different. In a dark time, it has been my experience, the eye doesn't begin to see, it begins to *try* to see. The effort, grasping and absurd, is the thing, the vital and beautiful thing. Distress becomes a crisis not when it reaches a certain level but when one realizes that all the old methods for coping with distress, all the familiar, trusted instruments, have stopped working. Here is a nightmare, and here is a challenge. Here is an abyss, and here is a gauntlet. Here is a need. You have come to understand less, radically less, than you thought you did. In your new and vast ignorance, your only hope is the hope you coax into being. Do not worry too much about what you choose. Only choose. Motion can beget motion. Will can beget will. Find your toehold in the rock, and pray that a mountain forms behind it.

·

I remember that tree. I try to remember it. It was all so long ago. I have three children now, a second marriage that has already outlasted the first, another career. I have what sometimes feels, in a way that is both indisputable and illusory, to be an entirely different consciousness: a different mind. How limber we have to be, in our growing. How attentive to reality, how alert to the shifting, fragmented, uncertain facts of ourselves.

It might have been anything. It might have been a rock or a building. It might have been a foreign country or a language. The New York Knicks. Particle physics. The Babylonian Talmud. Free jazz. Clouds. In time it would again be my friends, a woman, my children, my patients, my work, my own small and valuable life. But it started as a tree on a hill in a park across the street from my apartment. These are the details and they matter. Something had, in fact, broken inside me, and it was this: the belief that the details matter and the desire to know them.

We have, if we continue on, many births, none of them easy. We live our lives until they don't seem to work anymore, or until the conditions shift around us. We go to sleep smiling and wake up with sand in our nostrils, drifts in the bed, dread in our heart. We hurry to the window. Did someone move the house? Has there been an accident? What's the story here? We reach for a broom and sweep ourselves dizzy.

I was curved inward. I foldeth my hands together and eateth my own flesh. Where was my splinter of light? Where were my delightful bearings?

Once, at the base of the linden tree, in deep shade, I found a squirrel rotting and collapsing. Something had eaten its eyes. With a stick I probed its visible spine, the elliptical bend of its ribs. How good it would be, I thought, to take it home and boil off its remaining flesh, mount its skeleton on a base, and keep it with me forever. How good and useful. But I left it where it was, and the next day it was gone.

I wish now that I had taken it. I wish I had that skeleton beside me now, a memento of a time of displacement and disbelief, of time and mind clotted and confused. But I remember it well enough. I remember its curved gray claws, its dull patchwork tail, its blank and ghoulish face. I remember sitting on a root and watching it, wanting to see the decay itself, the slow and reliable movement of the decay. I remember, I feel, the root against my thighs. I feel the shade and hear the bird in the branches, singing.

"Nice try," it sings. "Nice try. Keep trying. Keep trying."

ACKNOWLEDGMENTS

It is customary on an acknowledgments page to save your spouse for last, to underscore the point that no one in the world has been more vital to the book's composition. But why wait? Emily Bobrow, my wife, is the first *and* last person to thank. Without her love, humor, patience, honesty, critical acumen, and encouragement, this book would not exist. Emily made everything possible. She said what needed to be said, read what needed to be read, and brought meaning to my days. My gratitude to her is boundless.

When I started this book, I expected it would be finished in a few years. For various reasons (some of them alluded to in the text), it took longer than that. At Simon & Schuster, Priscilla Painton gave me all the time I needed and along the way evinced only kindness and trust. I am immensely grateful for her support and friendship. Ian Straus, my wonderful editor, shepherded the book through in a spirit of generosity and equanimity that means the world to me. It was a gift to be able to work with him.

Melanie Jackson, my brilliant agent, was a guardian angel throughout the process, as she has been since the beginning of my career. Two decades ago, she took a chance on a young and inexperienced writer, and she hasn't wavered since. I am deeply, joyfully indebted to her.

Many friends kept me going when I didn't think I could, or didn't want to. Special thanks to Tanya Goldsmith, Peter Terzian, Daniel Torday, Lindsay Goldwert, Peter Mendelsund, James Marcus, Benjamin Kunkel, Tyler Maroney, Josh Bobrow, Motti Salzberg, Imari Hardon, Damise Vaughn, and Adam Twente. Stephen Koch was a source of almost daily support, always there to listen and offer his guidance. Michael Feinberg, Marco Roth, Kate Bolick, Oliver Munday, and Alexander Jusdanis each offered invaluable moral support and critical input, reading the manuscript at different points and successfully talking me down from numerous high ledges. Double shout-outs to Oliver for designing the beautiful cover, and to Stephen for permitting the use of Peter Hujar's exquisite photograph.

Several scholars graciously offered their time and knowledge to me when I contacted them for help. I'd like to thank Susan Matt, Michael Lewis, Patricia DeYoung, Tom Gilovich, Lisa Feldman Barrett, and Andreas Elpidorou for their generosity. As Chapter Two suggests, Lisa's work was of great importance to me, as was her willingness to walk me through the finer points of the scientific research on emotions. Andreas sent me reams of material and encouraged me as I developed my argument on boredom.

Many thanks to the editor Jonathan Cox for crucial guidance on the book's structure.

At a final stage in the writing of this book, when I needed it most, I was fortunate to receive two much-needed residencies. My immense gratitude goes out to the incomparable staff at MacDowell—one of this country's great institutions—as it does to the eccentric founder and proprietor of the Clipper Ship Residency, of which I have the honor of being the first and, so far, only resident.

It is hard to overstate what a privilege it is day after day to work with my patients, from whom I gain insight into the workings of our emotions that far exceeds anything I could learn from books. Their trust, honesty, and strength are continual sources of inspiration to me.

As for my family, I could not be more fortunate. My brothers, David Smith and Scott Smith, buoyed me throughout with their love and humor. My mother, Marilyn Smith, cheered me on, tolerated my bad moods, helped with the kids, and just generally acted as a model of empathy, resilience, humanity, and forgiveness to which I can only aspire. My in-laws, Philip Bobrow and Faith Bobrow, have been extraordinarily generous and loving, as well as tolerant whenever I had to slip away for a spell to work. And my children, my beloved children—well, they supplied me with every emotion, negative and positive, that I needed to write this book. I am grateful to them for all of it.

Finally, my thanks to Emily. My love. My life.

SELECTED BIBLIOGRAPHY

The literature on emotions is immense. It spans numerous disciplines, including, but not limited to, psychology, psychiatry, philosophy, anthropology, sociology, and evolutionary biology. I make this statement, obvious though it may be, to underscore that what follows is by necessity limited and idiosyncratic. I began this book with no agenda greater than the impulse to better understand—and, in my way, to defend the legitimacy of—those negative emotions we all harbor and must live our lives alongside. My own patients know that the only human quality for which I am comfortable proselytizing is curiosity, and curiosity is by nature open, exploratory, and perplexed—which is to say, willing to be perplexed.

I didn't always succeed on the willingness front, but curiosity was the general spirit in which I chose—or, more accurately, found—the sources for this book. Whenever I reached for some illusory expertise or comprehensiveness was invariably when I found myself aggravated and unhappy. I often had to remind myself to destroy the map and enjoy the appropriateness of being lost. I often had to summon my many memories, all of them sweet, of wandering in the stacks of libraries and bookstores, just seeing what, among the mass of possibilities, happened to capture my attention.

This bibliography consists of books, essays, papers, and articles that captured my attention, and that I found useful in getting at least a little closer to the mystery of our emotional selves. I should say *particularly* useful, because I consulted many other sources that I chose not to include here, either because they did not align with my specific interests and temperament, or because they did not have a notable influence on the finished work.

I have arranged what follows according to chapter, beginning with my condensed exploration of the morality of emotions in Chapter Two. The reader should bear in mind, however, that there has been considerable cross-pollination between chapters. A book that appears by virtue of its generality under the heading "Chapter Three: What Is an Emotion?"—Robert Solomon's *Not Passion's Slave*, for example—may have played an equally important role in informing and bringing to fruition a chapter on a specific emotion such as envy. And a source that was crucial to my understanding of a specific emotion may have helped me to better understand the assumptions and judgments we make about negative emotions in general. In short, the boundaries established here are, like the boundaries between our lived emotions, more porous than they may appear.

An asterisk placed before a source denotes my view of it as particularly authoritative, articulate, or helpful.

Chapter Two: The Morality of Emotions

Alighieri, Dante. *Purgatorio*. Translated by Allen Mandelbaum. New York: Bantam Books, 1984.

Aristotle. *Introduction to Aristotle*. Edited by Richard McKeon. New York: Modern Library, 1947.

Aurelius, Marcus. *Meditations*. Translated by Martin Hammond. Introduction by Diskin Clay. London: Penguin Classics, 2006.

Clarke, Kevin M., ed. *The Seven Deadly Sins: Sayings of the Fathers of the Church*. Foreword by Mike Aquilina. Washington, D.C.: The Catholic University of America Press, 2018.

*Dixon, Thomas. "'Emotion': The History of a Keyword in Crisis." *Emotion Review* 4, no. 4 (October 2012): 338–344.

Epictetus. *Discourses, Fragments, Handbook*. Translated and edited by Robin Hard. Oxford: Oxford University Press, 2014.

*Irvine, William Braxton. *A Guide to the Good Life: The Ancient Art of Stoic Joy*. Oxford: Oxford University Press, 2009.
Kagan, Jerome. *What Is an Emotion?* New Haven: Yale University Press, 2007.
Kristjánsson, Kristján. "On the Very Idea of 'Negative Emotions.'" *Journal for the Theory of Social Behaviour* 33, no. 4 (2003): 351–364.
———. *Virtues and Vices in Positive Psychology: A Philosophical Critique*. Cambridge: Cambridge University Press, 2013.
Orloff, Judith. *Emotional Freedom: Liberate Yourself from Negative Emotions and Transform Your Life*. New York: Harmony Books, 2009.
Seneca. *Dialogues and Essays*. Translated and edited by John Davie. Introduction and notes by Tobias Reinhardt. Oxford: Oxford University Press, 2007.
Solomon, Robert C., and Lori D. Stone. "On 'Positive' and 'Negative' Emotions." *Journal for the Theory of Social Behaviour* 32, no. 4 (2002): 417–435.
*Sorabji, Richard. *Emotion and Peace of Mind: From Stoic Agitation to Christian Temptation*. Oxford: Oxford University Press, 2000.
Wagner, Dylan D., and Todd F. Heatherton. "Emotion and Self-Regulation Failure." In *Handbook of Emotion Regulation*, 2nd ed., edited by James J. Gross, 613–628. New York: The Guilford Press, 2015.

Chapter Three: What Is an Emotion?

Barrett, Lisa Feldman. "Are Emotions Natural Kinds?" *Perspectives on Psychological Science* 1, no. 1 (2006): 28–58.
*———. *How Emotions Are Made: The Secret Life of the Brain*. Boston: Houghton Mifflin Harcourt, 2017.
———. *Seven and a Half Lessons About the Brain*. Boston: Houghton Mifflin Harcourt, 2020.
———. "Variety is the Spice of Life: A Psychological Construction Approach to Understanding Variability in Emotion." *Cognition and Emotion* 23, no. 7 (2009): 1284–1306.
Barrett, Lisa Feldman, and Tsiona Lida. "Constructionist Theories of Emotions in Psychology and Neuroscience." In *Emotion Theory: The Routledge Comprehensive Guide, Volume I: History, Contemporary Theories, and Key Elements*, edited by Andrea Scarantino, 350–387. London: Routledge, 2025.
Beck, Julie. "Hard Feelings: Science's Struggle to Define Emotions." *The Atlantic*, February 24, 2015.
Briggs, Jean L. *Never in Anger: Portrait of an Eskimo Family*. Cambridge, MA: Harvard University Press, 1970.
*Calhoun, Cheshire, and Robert C. Solomon, eds. *What Is an Emotion?: Classic Readings in Philosophical Psychology*. New York: Oxford University Press, 1984.
Cornelius, Randolph R. *The Science of Emotion: Research and Tradition in the Psychology of Emotion*. Upper Saddle River, NJ: Prentice Hall, 1996.
Danziger, Kurt. *Naming the Mind: How Psychology Found Its Language*. London: SAGE Publications, 1997.
Darwin, Charles. "A Biographical Sketch of an Infant." *Mind* 2, no. 6 (July 1877): 285–294.
———. *The Expression of the Emotions in Man and Animals*. Edited by Paul Ekman. Oxford: Oxford University Press, 1998.

*Dixon, Thomas. *The History of Emotions: A Very Short Introduction*. Oxford: Oxford University Press, 2023.

Ekman, Paul. "An Argument for Basic Emotions." *Cognition and Emotion* 6, no. 3-4 (1992): 169-200.

———. "Basic Emotions." In *Handbook of Cognition and Emotion*, edited by Tim Dalgleish and Mick J. Power, 45-60. Chichester, UK: John Wiley & Sons, 1999.

Ekman, Paul, and Daniel Cordaro. "What Is Meant by Calling Emotions Basic." *Emotion Review* 3, no. 4 (2011): 364-370.

Fox, Andrew S., Regina C. Lapate, Alexander J. Shackman, and Richard J. Davidson, eds. *The Nature of Emotion: Fundamental Questions*. 2nd ed. Oxford: Oxford University Press, 2018.

Geertz, Clifford. "The Growth of Culture and the Evolution of Mind." In *The Interpretation of Cultures: Selected Essays*, 55-83. New York: Basic Books, 1973.

Gendron, Maria. "Defining Emotion: A Brief History." *Emotion Review* 2, no. 4 (October 2010): 371-372.

*Graver, Margaret. *Stoicism and Emotion*. Chicago: University of Chicago Press, 2007.

Gross, Daniel M. "Defending the Humanities with Charles Darwin's *The Expression of the Emotions in Man and Animals* (1872)." *Critical Inquiry* 37, no. 1 (Autumn 2010): 1-31.

Izard, Carroll E. "The Many Meanings/Aspects of Emotion: Definitions, Functions, Activation, and Regulation." *Emotion Review* 2, no. 4 (October 2010): 363-370.

*James, William. "What Is an Emotion?" *Mind* 9, no. 34 (July 1884): 188-205.

*Johnson, Gregory. "Theories of Emotion." *Internet Encyclopedia of Philosophy*. Accessed April 28, 2025. https://iep.utm.edu/theories-of-emotion/.

*Keltner, Dacher, Keith Oatley, and Jennifer M. Jenkins. *Understanding Emotions*. 3rd ed. Hoboken, NJ: John Wiley & Sons, 2013.

Sabini, John, and Maury Silver. "Ekman's Basic Emotions: Why Not Love and Jealousy?" *Cognition and Emotion* 19, no. 5 (2005): 693-712.

Scarantino, Andrea, and Ronald de Sousa. "Emotion." In *The Stanford Encyclopedia of Philosophy*, edited by Edward N. Zalta, Summer 2021 Edition. https://plato.stanford.edu/archives/sum2021/entries/emotion/.

Schmitter, Amy M. "17th and 18th Century Theories of Emotions." In *The Stanford Encyclopedia of Philosophy*, edited by Edward N. Zalta, Summer 2021 Edition. https://plato.stanford.edu/entries/emotions-17th18th/.

Smith, Tiffany Watt. *The Book of Human Emotions*. New York: Little, Brown and Company, 2015.

Solomon, Robert C. *Not Passion's Slave: Emotions and Choice*. New York: Oxford University Press, 2003.

———. *The Passions: Emotions and the Meaning of Life*. Indianapolis: Hackett Publishing Company, 1993.

Chapter Four: Annoyance

Beheshti, Mohammad Hossein, Roohalah Hajizadeh, Maryam Borhani Jebeli, Ali Tajpoor, Ghasem Zia, and Niloofar Damyar. "The Role of Individual and Personality Traits in Noise Annoyance." *Annals of Medical and Health Sciences Research* 8, no. 3 (2018): 133-138.

SELECTED BIBLIOGRAPHY 223

Beutel, Manfred E., Christoph Jünger, Eva-Maria Klein, Petra Wild, Karl Lackner, Maria Blettner, and Elmar Brähler. "Noise Annoyance Is Associated with Depression and Anxiety in the General Population—The Contribution of Aircraft Noise." *PLOS One* 11, no. 5 (2016): e0155357.

Chess, Stella, and Alexander Thomas. *Temperament and Development*. New York: Brunner/Mazel, 1977.

Frymer-Kensky, Tikva. "The Atrahasis Epic and Its Significance for Our Understanding of Genesis 1–9." *The Biblical Archaeologist* 40, no. 4 (1977): 147–155.

Guski, Rainer, Ute Felscher-Suhr, and Rolf Schuemer. "The Concept of Noise Annoyance: How International Experts See It." *Journal of Sound and Vibration* 223, no. 4 (1999): 513–527.

Jarosińska, Dorota, Marie-Ève Héroux, Poonam Wilkhu, James Creswick, Jos Verbeek, Jördis Wothge, and Elizabet Paunović. "Development of the WHO Environmental Noise Guidelines for the European Region: An Introduction." *International Journal of Environmental Research and Public Health* 15, no. 4 (2018): 813.

*Kagan, Jerome. *Galen's Prophecy: Temperament in Human Nature*. Boulder, CO: Westview Press, 1997.

Lindvall, Thomas, and Edward P. Radford. "Measurement of Annoyance Due to Exposure to Environmental Factors." *Environmental Research* 6 (1973): 1–36.

Okokon, Enembe O., Tarja Yli-Tuomi, Anu W. Turunen, Pekka Tiittanen, Jukka Juutilainen, and Timo Lanki. "Traffic Noise, Noise Annoyance and Psychotropic Medication Use." *Environment International* 119 (July 2018): 287–294.

Palca, Joe, and Flora Lichtman. *Annoying: The Science of What Bugs Us*. Hoboken, NJ: John Wiley & Sons, 2011.

Paunović, Katarina, Branko Jakovljević, and Goran Belojević. "Predictors of Noise Annoyance in Noisy and Quiet Urban Streets." *Science of the Total Environment* 407, no. 12 (2009): 3707–3711.

*Pieslak, Jonathan. "Cranking Up the Volume: Music as a Tool of Torture." *Global Dialogue* 12, no. 1 (Winter/Spring 2010): 1–11.

Plutchik, Robert. "The Nature of Emotions." *American Scientist* 89, no. 4 (2001): 344–350.

Robin, Monique, Annie Matheau-Police, and Caroline Couty. "Development of a Scale of Perceived Environmental Annoyances in Urban Settings." *Journal of Environmental Psychology* 27, no. 1 (2007): 55–68.

*Ross, Alex. "The Sound of Hate." *The New Yorker*, July 4, 2016.

Schnell, Izhak, Oded Potchter, Yaakov Yaakov, Yoram Epstein, Shmuel Brener, and Haim Hermesh. "Urban Daily Life Routines and Human Exposure to Environmental Discomfort." *Environmental Monitoring and Assessment* 184, no. 7 (2012): 4575–4590.

World Health Organization. *Burden of Disease from Environmental Noise: Quantification of Healthy Life Years Lost in Europe*. Copenhagen: WHO Regional Office for Europe, 2011.

Chapter Five: Shame

Broucek, Francis J. *Shame and the Self*. New York: The Guilford Press, 1991.
*DeYoung, Patricia A. *Understanding and Treating Chronic Shame: Healing Right Brain Relational Trauma*. 2nd ed. New York: Routledge, 2021.
Gilbert, Paul, and Bernice Andrews, eds. *Shame: Interpersonal Behavior, Psychopathology, and Culture*. New York: Oxford University Press, 1998.
Gilbert, Paul, J. Pehl, and S. Allan. "The Phenomenology of Shame and Guilt: An Empirical Investigation." *British Journal of Medical Psychology* 67, no. 1 (1994): 23–36.
Hatfield, Elaine, John T. Cacioppo, and Richard L. Rapson. "Emotional Contagion." *Current Directions in Psychological Science* 2, no. 3 (June 1993): 96–100.
Hatfield, Elaine, Richard L. Rapson, and Yen-Chi L. Le. "Emotional Contagion and Empathy." In *The Social Neuroscience of Empathy*, edited by Jean Decety and William Ickes, 19–30. Cambridge, MA: MIT Press, 2009.
*Kagan, Robert. "Shame." *The Atlantic Monthly*, February 1992.
Kaufman, Gershen. *The Psychology of Shame: Theory and Treatment of Shame-Based Syndromes*. 2nd ed. New York: Springer Publishing Company, 2004.
Kirby, James N., Olivia Grzazek, and Paul Gilbert. "The Role of Compassionate and Self-Image Goals in Predicting Psychological Controlling and Facilitative Parenting Styles." *Frontiers in Psychology* 10 (2019): 1041.
Kirby, James N., Michael J. Tellegen, and Stephen R. Steindl. "Human Evolution and Culture in Relationship to Shame in the Parenting Role: Implications for Psychology and Psychotherapy." *Psychology and Psychotherapy: Theory, Research and Practice* 92, no. 2 (2019): 238–260.
Lansky, Melvin R., and Andrew P. Morrison, eds. *The Widening Scope of Shame*. Hillsdale, NJ: The Analytic Press, 1998.
Lewis, Michael. "The Role of the Self in Shame." *Social Research: An International Quarterly* 70, no. 4 (2003): 1181–1204.
*———. *Shame: The Exposed Self*. New York: Free Press, 1992.
McGoldrick, Monica, and Randy Gerson. *Genograms in Family Assessment*. New York: W. W. Norton & Company, 1985.
Melville, Herman. *Billy Budd, Bartleby, and Other Stories*. Edited with an introduction by Peter M. Coviello. New York: Penguin Classics, 2016.
Mills, Rosemary S. L. "Taking Stock of the Developmental Literature on Shame." *Developmental Review* 25, no. 1 (2005): 26–63.
Mills, Rosemary S. L., Wendy S. Freeman, Ian P. Clara, Frank J. Elgar, Bobbi R. Walling, and Leanne Mak. "Parent Proneness to Shame and the Use of Psychological Control." *Journal of Child and Family Studies* 16, no. 3 (2007): 359–374.
Mojallal, Mahsa, Raluca M. Simons, and Jeffrey S. Simons. "Childhood Maltreatment and Adulthood Proneness to Shame and Guilt: The Mediating Role of Maladaptive Schemas." *Motivation and Emotion* 45, no. 2 (2021): 197–210.
Morrison, Andrew P. *The Culture of Shame*. Northvale, NJ: Jason Aronson, 1998.
———. *Shame: The Underside of Narcissism*. Hillsdale, NJ: The Analytic Press, 1989.
*Nathanson, Donald L., ed. *The Many Faces of Shame*. New York: The Guilford Press, 1987.

———. *Shame and Pride: Affect, Sex, and the Birth of the Self*. New York: W. W. Norton & Company, 1992.
Parkinson, Brian. "Interpersonal Emotion Transfer: Contagion and Social Appraisal." *Social and Personality Psychology Compass* 5, no. 7 (2011): 428–439.
Smith, Daniel B. *Muses, Madmen, and Prophets: Hearing Voices and the Borders of Sanity*. New York: Penguin Books, 2007.
Stearns, Peter N. *Shame: A Brief History*. Urbana: University of Illinois Press, 2017.
Tangney, June Price, Patricia Wagner, and Richard Gramzow. "Proneness to Shame, Proneness to Guilt, and Psychopathology." *Journal of Abnormal Psychology* 101, no. 3 (1992): 469–478.
Teyber, Edward, Faith H. McClure, and Robert Weathers. "Shame in Families: Transmission Across Generations." In *Shame in the Therapy Hour*, edited by Ronda L. Dearing and June Price Tangney, 127–144. Washington, D.C.: American Psychological Association, 2011.
Tronick, Ed. *The Neurobehavioral and Social-Emotional Development of Infants and Children*. New York: W. W. Norton & Company, 2007.
Tronick, Ed, and Marjorie Beeghly. "Infants' Meaning-Making and the Development of Mental Health Problems." *American Psychologist* 66, no. 2 (2011): 107–119.
Tronick, Ed, and Claudia M. Gold. *The Power of Discord: Why the Ups and Downs of Relationships Are the Secret to Building Intimacy, Resilience, and Trust*. New York: Little, Brown Spark, 2020.
Welten, Stephanie C. M., Marcel Zeelenberg, and Seger M. Breugelmans. "Vicarious Shame." *Cognition and Emotion* 26, no. 5 (2012): 836–846.
Wurmser, Leon. *The Mask of Shame*. Baltimore: Johns Hopkins University Press, 1981.

Chapter Six: Envy

Archer, Alfred, Alan Thomas, and Bart Engelen. "The Politics of Envy: Outlaw Emotions in Capitalist Societies." In *The Moral Psychology of Envy*, edited by Sara Protasi, 181–197. Lanham, MD: Rowman & Littlefield, 2022.
Bacon, Francis. "Of Envy." In *The Essays*, edited by John Pitcher, 79–81. Harmondsworth: Penguin Classics, 1985.
Byatt, A. S. "Envy: The Sin of Nations and Families," *The New York Times*, July 18, 1993.
*D'Arms, Justin. "Envy." In *The Stanford Encyclopedia of Philosophy*, edited by Edward N. Zalta, Spring 2017 Edition. https://plato.stanford.edu/archives/spr2017/entries/envy/.
Epstein, Joseph. *Envy*. New York: Oxford University Press, 2003.
*Farber, Leslie H. "Faces of Envy." In *The Ways of the Will: Selected Essays*, edited by Robert Boyers and Anne Farber, 233–245. Expanded ed. New York: Basic Books, 2000.
*Foster, George M. "The Anatomy of Envy: A Study in Symbolic Behavior." *Current Anthropology* 13, no. 2 (April 1972): 165–202.
———. *Tzintzuntzan: Mexican Peasants in a Changing World*. Boston: Little, Brown and Company, 1967.
Girard, René. *All Desire Is a Desire for Being*. Edited and introduced by Cynthia L. Haven. London: Penguin Classics, 2023.

———. *A Theatre of Envy: William Shakespeare*. Oxford: Oxford University Press, 1991.
Harrison, Robert Pogue. "The Prophet of Envy." *The New York Review of Books*, December 20, 2018.
Lanchester, John. "You Are the Product." *London Review of Books* 39, no. 16 (August 17, 2017): 3–10.
*Matt, Susan J. *Keeping Up with the Joneses: Envy in American Consumer Society, 1890–1930*. Philadelphia: University of Pennsylvania Press, 2003.
Meier, Adrian, and Benjamin K. Johnson. "Social Comparison and Envy on Social Media: A Critical Review." *Current Opinion in Psychology* 45 (June 2022): 101302.
Miceli, Maria, and Cristiano Castelfranchi. "The Envious Mind." *Cognition and Emotion* 21, no. 3 (2007): 449–479.
Pera, Aurel. "Psychopathological Processes Involved in Social Comparison, Depression, and Envy on Facebook." *Frontiers in Psychology* 9 (2018): 22.
Protasi, Sara. "Varieties of Envy." *Philosophical Psychology* 29, no. 4 (2016): 535–549.
Ramachandran, Vilayanur S., and Baland Jalal. "The Evolutionary Psychology of Envy and Jealousy." *Frontiers in Psychology* 8 (2017): 1619.
Schoeck, Helmut. *Envy: A Theory of Social Behaviour*. New York: Harcourt, Brace & World, 1969.
Smith, R. H. "Envy and Its Transmutations." In *The Social Life of Emotions*, edited by L. Z. Tiedens & C. W. Leach, 43–63. Cambridge: Cambridge University Press, 2004.
Tandoc, Edson C., Jr., Patrick Ferrucci, and Margaret Duffy. "Facebook Use, Envy, and Depression among College Students: Is Facebooking Depressing?" *Computers in Human Behavior* 43 (February 2015): 139–146.
Veblen, Thorstein. *The Theory of the Leisure Class*. Edited by Martha Banta. Oxford World's Classics. Oxford: Oxford University Press, 2009.
Verduyn, Philippe, Nino Gugushvili, Karlijn Massar, Karin Täht, and Ethan Kross. "Social Comparison on Social Networking Sites." *Current Opinion in Psychology* 36 (December 2020): 32–37.
Walters, Jordan David Thomas. "The Aptness of Envy." *American Journal of Political Science* 69, no. 1 (2025): 330–340.

Chapter Seven: Boredom

Barbalet, J. M. "Boredom and Social Meaning." *The British Journal of Sociology* 50, no. 4 (December 1999): 631–646.
*Brodsky, Joseph. "In Praise of Boredom." In *On Grief and Reason: Essays*, 377–384. New York: Farrar, Straus and Giroux, 1995.
Chin, Alycia, Amanda Markey, Saurabh Bhargava, Karim S. Kassam, and George Loewenstein. "Bored in the USA: Experience Sampling and Boredom in Everyday Life." *Emotion* 17, no. 2 (2017): 359–368.
Eastwood, John, Alexandra Frischen, Mark Fenske, and Daniel Smilek. "The Unengaged Mind: Defining Boredom in Terms of Attention." *Perspectives on Psychological Science* 7, no. 5 (2012): 482–95.
*Elpidorou, Andreas. "The Bored Mind is a Guiding Mind: Toward a Regulatory

Theory of Boredom." *Phenomenology and the Cognitive Sciences* 17, no. 3 (2018): 455–84.
———. "Boredom in Art." *Behavioral and Brain Sciences* 40 (2017): e359.
———. "Boredom's Push." *OUPblog*. Oxford University Press, September 16, 2017. https://blog.oup.com/2017/09/boredoms-push/.
*———. "The Bright Side of Boredom." *Frontiers in Psychology* 5 (2014): 1245.
———. "The Good of Boredom." *Philosophical Psychology* 31, no. 3 (2018): 323–351.
———. "Is Boredom One or Many? A Functional Solution to the Problem of Heterogeneity." *Mind & Language* 36, no. 3 (2021): 491–511.
———. "Neglected Emotions." *The Monist* 103, no. 2 (2020): 135–146.
*———. *Propelled: How Boredom, Frustration, and Anticipation Lead Us to the Good Life*. New York: Oxford University Press, 2020.
Fernandez, Luke, and Susan J. Matt. *Bored, Lonely, Angry, Stupid: Changing Feelings About Technology, from the Telegraph to Twitter*. Cambridge, MA: Harvard University Press, 2019.
Gary, Kevin Hood. "The Problem of Boredom." In *Why Boredom Matters: Education, Leisure, and the Quest for a Meaningful Life*, 21–46. Cambridge: Cambridge University Press, 2022.
Kierkegaard, Søren. "Crop Rotation: An Attempt at a Theory of Social Prudence." In *Either/Or: A Fragment of Life*, translated by Alastair Hannay, 127–139. London: Penguin Classics, 1992.
Moller, Dan. "The Boring." *Journal of Aesthetics and Art Criticism* 72, no. 2 (2014): 181–191.
Moravia, Alberto. *Boredom*. Translated by Angus Davidson. Introduction by William Weaver. New York: New York Review Books, 2004.
*Phillips, Adam. "On Being Bored." In *On Kissing, Tickling, and Being Bored: Psychoanalytic Essays on the Unexamined Life*, 71–80. Cambridge, MA: Harvard University Press, 1993.
Raposa, Michael L. *Boredom and the Religious Imagination*. Charlottesville: University Press of Virginia, 1999.
Svendsen, Lars. *A Philosophy of Boredom*. Translated by John Irons. London: Reaktion Books, 2005.
Talbot, Margaret. "What Does Boredom Do to Us—and for Us?" *The New Yorker*, August 20, 2020.
*Toohey, Peter. *Boredom: A Lively History*. New Haven: Yale University Press, 2011.
Westgate, Erin C., and Timothy D. Wilson. "Boring Thoughts and Bored Minds: The MAC Model of Boredom and Cognitive Engagement." *Psychological Review* 125, no. 5 (2018): 689–713.
Wilson, Timothy D., David A. Reinhard, Erin C. Westgate, Daniel T. Gilbert, Nicole Ellerbeck, Cheryl Hahn, Casey L. Brown, and Adi Shaked. "Just Think: The Challenges of the Disengaged Mind." *Science* 345, no. 6192 (July 4, 2014): 75–77.

Chapter Eight: Regret

Bleichrodt, Han, and Peter P. Wakker. "Regret Theory: A Bold Alternative to the Alternatives." *Economic Journal* 125, no. 583 (2015): 493–532.

Davidai, Shai, and Thomas Gilovich. "The Ideal Road Not Taken: The Self-Discrepancies Involved in People's Most Enduring Regrets." *Emotion* 18, no. 3 (2018): 439–452.

Gilbert, Daniel T., Carey K. Morewedge, Jane L. Risen, and Timothy D. Wilson. "Looking Forward to Looking Backward: The Misprediction of Regret." *Psychological Science* 15, no. 5 (2004): 346–350.

Gilovich, Thomas, and Victoria Husted Medvec. "The Experience of Regret: What, When, and Why." *Psychological Review* 102, no. 2 (1995): 379–395.

———. "The Temporal Pattern to the Experience of Regret." *Journal of Personality and Social Psychology* 67, no. 3 (1994): 357–365.

Gilovich, Thomas, Victoria Husted Medvec, and Daniel Kahneman. "Varieties of Regret: A Debate and Partial Resolution." *Psychological Review* 105, no. 3 (1998): 602–605.

Gilovich, Thomas, Ranxiao Frances Wang, Dennis Regan, and Sadafumi Nishina. "Regrets of Action and Inaction Across Cultures." *Journal of Cross-Cultural Psychology* 34, no. 1 (2003): 61–71.

Kahneman, Daniel. *Thinking, Fast and Slow*. New York: Farrar, Straus and Giroux, 2011.

Kahneman, Daniel, and Dale T. Miller. "Norm Theory: Comparing Reality to Its Alternatives." *Psychological Review* 93, no. 2 (1986): 136–153.

Kierkegaard, Søren. "Diapsalmata." In *Either/Or: A Fragment of Life*, translated by Alastair Hannay, 127–139. London: Penguin Classics, 1992.

Landman, Janet. "Regret: A Theoretical and Conceptual Analysis." *Journal for the Theory of Social Behaviour* 17, no. 2 (1987): 135–160.

———. *Regret: The Persistence of the Possible*. New York: Oxford University Press, 1993.

Price, Carolyn. "The Many Flavours of Regret." *The Monist* 103, no. 2 (2020): 147–162.

Price, Carolyn, and Thomas Dixon. "Regrets, Hot and Cold." *The History of Emotions Blog*, June 9, 2017. https://emotionsblog.history.qmul.ac.uk/2017/06/regrets-hot-and-cold/.

Thoreau, Henry David. *Walden: A Fully Annotated Edition*. Edited by Jeffrey S. Cramer. New Haven: Yale University Press, 2004.

Wroe, Ann. *Orpheus: The Song of Life*. New York: Overlook Press, 2012.

Zeelenberg, Marcel. "The Science of Regret." TEDx Talks, YouTube. Posted September 27, 2016. https://www.youtube.com/watch?v=ZPCV3Oe1fYw.

———."The Use of Crying Over Spilled Milk: A Note on the Rationality and Functionality of Regret." *Philosophical Psychology* 12, no. 3 (1999): 325–340.

Zeelenberg, Marcel, and Rik Pieters. "A Theory of Regret Regulation 1.0." *Journal of Consumer Psychology* 17, no. 1 (2007): 3–18.

Chapter Nine: Despair

Barasch, Moshe. "Despair in the Medieval Imagination." *Social Research* 66, no. 2 (1999): 565–576.

Beary, Alina. "Humility and Despair." *Journal of Psychology and Christianity* 40, no. 3 (2021): 267–271.

Bürgy, Martin. "Phenomenological Investigation of Despair." *Psychopathology* 41 (2008): 147–156.

*Farber, Leslie H. "Despair and the Life of Suicide." In *The Ways of the Will: Selected Essays*, edited by Robert Boyers and Anne Farber, 133–156. Expanded ed. New York: Basic Books, 2000.

*———. "The Therapeutic Despair." *Psychiatry: Interpersonal and Biological Processes* 21, no. 1 (1958): 7–20.

Fletcher, Angus. "The Place of Despair and Hope." *Social Research* 66, no. 2 (1999): 565–576.

Hagen, Edward H. "Evolutionary Theories of Depression: A Critical Review." *The Canadian Journal of Psychiatry* 56, no. 12 (2011): 716–726.

Merton, Thomas. *Seeds of Contemplation*. New York: New Directions, 1949.

Oates, Joyce Carol. "Despair: The One Unforgivable Sin." *The New York Times*, July 25, 1993.

Pecchenino, Rowena A. "Have We Cause for Despair?" *Journal of Behavioral and Experimental Economics* 58 (2015): 56–62.

Shanahan, Lilly, and William E. Copeland. "Psychiatry and Deaths of Despair." *JAMA Psychiatry* 78, no. 7 (2021): 695–696.

Shanahan, Lilly, Sherika N. Hill, Lauren M. Gaydosh, Annekatrin Steinhoff, E. Jane Costello, Kenneth A. Dodge, Kathleen Mullan Harris, and William E. Copeland. "Does Despair Really Kill? A Roadmap for an Evidence-Based Answer." *American Journal of Public Health* 109, no. 6 (2019): 854–858.

Steinbock, Anthony J. "The Phenomenology of Despair." *International Journal of Philosophical Studies* 15, no. 3 (2007): 435–451.

Williams, Mark, Melanie Fennell, Thorsten Barnhofer, Rebecca Crane, and Sarah Silverton. "The Origins of Despair: An Evolutionary Perspective." In *Mindfulness-Based Cognitive Therapy with People at Risk of Suicide*, 11–30. New York: The Guilford Press, 2015.

INDEX

abandonment, 100. *See also* withdrawal
Abbott and Costello, 63
Abu Ghraib, 71
acceptance, 64
acedia, 24, 25, 153, 154
Achilles, 66
Adler, Alfred, 123
Adler, Felix, 117–18
advertisements, 122–23
affection(s), 26, 198–99
aging, 15–17
Alighieri, Dante, 24–26
anger, 24, 40, 42, 44, 48, 49, 50, 85, 148
   annoyance as diluted form of, 65
   as basic emotion, 64
   as "capital" sin, 24
   culture and, 30–33, 51, 52–53, 114–15
   gender and, 115
   interference of, 27
   manifestations of, 45–46
   parenthood and, 115
   retribution and, 66
   Stoics and, 139
   Utku and, 30–33, 51, 52–53
   wisdom of, 165–66
"animal spirits," 35
annoyance, 6–7, 13, 52, 57–81
   as aversion, 65
   comedy and, 63–64
   control and, 71
   as diluted form of anger, 65
   as father of invention, 76–77
   as frustration, 65
   gradations of, 63
   hearing and, 69
   humor of, 63
   insulation from, 77
   permanent, 62
   "petty," 63
   seriousness of, 65–66
   taste and, 71
   togetherness and, 67
   ubiquity of, 67
anticipation, 65
anxiety, 62, 86, 103, 124, 163, 167, 180, 181, 195, 198
   "eco-anxiety," 189
   fatherhood and, 53
   neighbors and, 57–59
   relocation and, 59–60
Apocalypse Now, 72
Apple, Fiona, 20–21
Aristophanes, 63
Aristotle, 22, 23, 64, 66, 95
Atrahasis Epic, 78
attachment, 97–98
Aurelius, Marcus, 23–24, 81

aversion, 65, 115
avoidance, 93
awumbuk, 50–51

babies
   crying, 71
   facial expressions and, 44–46
Baining people, 50–51
Barnes, Julian, 99
Barrett, Lisa Feldman, 43, 46, 48–49, 50
Basic Emotion Theory, 40–48
Beckett, Samuel, 179
behaviorism, 38–40
Berkshire Hathaway, 124–25
Bernays, Edward, 122–23
bibliotherapy, 208–9
biology, 25–26, 51
Book of Rites, 64
boredom, 13, 137–60, 194
   in children's literature, 145–46
   creativity and, 152–53
   danger of, 150–51
   desire to escape, 149
   as emotional instrument, 150
   meaning and, 155–56
   moral stigma of, 144–47
   redemptive power of, 151–52
   repetition and, 154–55
   shame and, 151
   as voice with which time speaks to us, 155
   writing and, 152
Boredom Studies, 149
Bosch, Hieronymus, 4–5, 9, 24
brain, as predictor of events rather than responder, 47–48. *See also* neuroscience
Branch Davidian compound, Waco, Texas, 70–71
Briggs, Jean, 31–33, 42, 51–53
Brodsky, Joseph, 154–55
Brown, Margaret Wise, 145
Buffett, Warren, 124

Burton, Robert, 4, 9
Bush administration, 71

Cagney, James, 70
Cain and Abel, story of, 116–17
"capital" sins, 24
Carle, Eric, 145
Carroll, Lewis, 145, 146
Cassian, John, 24
Catechism of the Catholic Church, 25
Catholic Church, 24
Cervantes, Miguel, 125
Chaplin, Charlie, 64
Chaucer, Geoffrey, 24, 153
Chess, Stella, 74
Chick Webb and His Orchestra, 70
children's literature, 145–46
Christianity, 143–44, 201–3
   early, 23–24
   in Middle Ages, 204–5
Church Fathers, 23–24
CIA black sites, 71
city life, 57–62, 67–68. *See also* New York City
climate change, 189–90
coercion, psychological, 71
cognitivism, 34
comedy, 63
command hallucinations, 84
comparison, 120–21
compassion, 83, 113. *See also* empathy
compulsion, regret and, 182–83
"conceptual acts," 48–50
Confucianism, 64
consumerism, 118–24, 128–30
consumers, emotional manipulation of, 121–24, 128–29
contempt, 14, 64
context, 51–54, 115
control, 71
creativity, 151, 152–53
criticism, propensity for, 12–13
culture
   anger and, 114–15

cultural relativism, 40
  negative emotions and, 112, 114

Darwin, Charles, 37–38, 40
  The Descent of Man, 38
  The Expression of the Emotions in Man and Animals, 38, 43
  On the Origin of Species, 38
Darwin, William Erasmus, 37–38
Darwinian universalism, 38–40
deception, 102
delight, 48
delusion, 60, 77
Dennis the Menace, 66–67
depression, 103, 124, 129, 210
Descartes, René, 35
desire(s), 26, 48, 119. *See also* envy; longing
  consumerism and, 121, 122, 123, 125–26, 128–29, 133
  mimetic, 127–28
despair, 79, 100, 187–214
  Christianity and, 201–3
  "dismal certainty" of, 205
  "eco-despair," 189
  etymology of, 194
  meaning and, 201
  pride and, 203
  shame and, 200
  solution to, 203–4
  torment of, 206
Dia Beacon, 6, 7
Dickinson, Emily, 165
Dillard, Annie, 152–53
Dionysus, 63
disappointment, 148
discomfort, 79
disgust, 36, 40, 64, 178–79
displacement, 123
"display rules," 41, 44–46
dissatisfaction, 121–22, 124–25, 182
distraction, 151
distress, 81, 87, 89, 171, 172, 183, 184
diversion, 91

divorce, 15, 19, 62, 142, 157
  despair and, 187–89
  as emotional explosion, 10–12
  trauma of, 188, 194–95
Dixon, Thomas, 26
Dostoevsky, Fyodor, 149
dread, 48, 193, 197, 213
Duvall, Robert, 72
dying, 82–83

Ecclesiastes, 208
Eden, expulsion from, 202
Edwards, Jonathan, 202
Einstein, Albert, 74
Ekman, Paul, 39–43, 64
Eliot, T. S.
  "East Coker," 206
  The Waste Land, 13
Elpidorou, Andreas, 150, 151, 152
"emotion paradox," 46
"emotional communities," 112–14
"emotional contagion," 95–97
"emotional escalation," 9, 10
emotional expression, 37–38, 39, 40–41, 43–44. *See also* facial expressions
"emotional regime," 118
emotional surveillance, 143
emotional vulnerability, 143
emotions, 6–8, 178–79. *See also specific emotions*
  ascription of meaning to, 42
  biographies of, 115
  as bridge between perceptions and bodily response, 35–36
  concepts of, 48–51
  context and, 51–54, 115
  defining, 30–54
  "evil," 24
  evolution and, 38–40
  inevitable, 175
  manipulation of, 121–24, 128–29
  morality of, 22–29
  mystery of, 34–35

emotions (*cont.*)
  negative, 22–24, 27–29, 34, 62, 74, 79–81, 112, 115, 148, 163–64, 166, 200 (*see also specific emotions*)
  as perceptions, 35
  physiology of, 25–26, 36, 37, 39, 45–47, 51
  polarity of, 194, 203
  positive, 22, 27–28 (*see also specific emotions*)
  as sins, 24, 202
  suppression of, 42, 73
  targets of, 97
  "triggered by changes," 177
  turbulence of, 9–10, 18, 32–33
  use of the term, 26
empathy, 83, 89, 96, 113, 144, 210
engagement, 28, 144, 151, 194, 209, 211
enlightenment, 156
Enlil, 78
envy, 13, 22–23, 24, 25, 48, 49, 105–33
  as chronic condition, 121
  cluelessness and, 128–29
  consumerism and, 118–24
  etymology of, 116
  fear of, 111, 131
  as motivation, 118–20, 122–24, 128–29
  redefinition of, 118–21
  secrecy and, 119, 131
  self-defense and, 131–32
  social media and, 126–27
  Stoics and, 139
Epictetus, 81
etiquette, 68
evolution, theory of, 37–38, 39
experience, 210
external mediation, 125–26
extroversion, 74
Eysenck, Hans, 74

facial expressions
  babies and, 44–46
  Basic Emotion Theory and, 40–44
  context and, 44–45
Farber, Leslie, 196–97, 206
fascination, 197
fatherhood, 14–15, 53, 137–42, 157–60
FBI, 70–71
fear, 73, 167
  as basic emotion, 64
  Basic Emotion Theory and, 47
  of envy, 111, 131
  facial expressions and, 40, 44
  interference of, 27
  physiological response and, 36, 39
Fenichel, Otto, 90–91
Filipinos, 50
flow state, 149
Foreign Correspondent, 70
forgiveness, 90
Foster, George, 109–11, 119
  "The Anatomy of Envy," 131
  Tzintzuntzan, 109–11
Franklin, Benjamin, 22
Freud, Sigmund, 122–23, 164
Fridlund, Alan, 34
Frost, Robert, 155
frustration, 65, 85, 151

Galás, Diamanda, 70
Geertz, Clifford, 50
generosity, 132
genetics, 73
Genn, Rachel, 182
genograms, 99–100
ghosting, 93. *See also* withdrawal
gigil, 50
Gilovich, Thomas, 179, 180–81
Girard, René, 125–28
giving, joy of, 132
"global attributions," 91
gratification, 151
gratitude, 132–33, 166
Great Recession, 57, 61–62

greed, 24
Greek Orthodox Church, 186
Greeks, ancient, 35, 63, 80–81. *See also* specific figures
Greene, Graham, 5
Gregory the Great, Pope, 24, 202
grief, 48, 198
Grisham, C. J., 71–72
Gross, James, 65
Guantanamo Bay, 71
guilt, 148, 151, 164, 165, 168

Handbook of Emotion Regulation, 28–29
happiness, 40, 64
Harrison, Robert Pogue, 128
Hassinger, Maren, 7–8
hatred, 194
hearing, annoyance and, 69, 70–72
heavy metal, 71
Heizer, Michael, 8
Hitchcock, Alfred, 70
Hitler, Adolf, 64
homesickness, 100, 167
Hoover, Herbert, 121
Hughes, Ray Osgood, 118
Hume, David, 25
humility, 207
humoral theory, 74

identity, lost, 188
Ifaluk, 51
ihuma, 31–33, 42, 53
"Image of Limited Good," 110–11, 119
imagination, misuse of, 183–84
Imitatio, 128. *See also* mimetic desire
In Character: Actors Acting, 43
inaction, regret of, 180–81
infants, temperaments of, 74
"inferiority complex," 123

"internal mediation," 126–27
intimacy, 83, 84, 102
Inuit, 30–33, 51, 53
IRA, 69
Iraq, invasion of, 71
irritability, 63, 79–80, 81
irritation, 13, 65, 70–72, 79–80, 81, 85. *See also* annoyance
Israel, 71
Izard, Carroll, 34

Jackson, Michael, 71
James, William, 35–37
Jesus, 204–5
Johnson, Nora, 140
joy, 64, 132. *See also* happiness
Judaism, 201
Judas Iscariot, 204–5
judgment, neutralization of, 19–21
Juster, Norton, *The Phantom Tollbooth*, 145, 146

Kagan, Jerome, 26–27
Kahneman, Daniel, 177–79
Kazantzakis, Nikos, *The Last Temptation*, 186
Kettering, Charles, 121
Kierkegaard, Søren, 150–51, 174–75, 185
kizginlik, 50

Landau, Martin, 43, 44
Landman, Janet, 170–71, 172–74, 178
Le Bon, Gustave, 95–96
Leo, Melissa, 44
Lewin, Kurt, 180–81
Lewis, C. S., 202
Lewis, Helen Block, 93
Lichtman, Flora, 65

literature, 12–13. *See also specific authors*
living standards, 124–25
loathing, 100, 193
longing, 48, 109
Lorde, Audre, 165
love, 137–38, 140, 165, 194, 211
lusts, 26
Luther, Martin, 202, 203

Madison, Oscar, 63–64
malaise, 154–55
Marines, 72
Marx, Harpo, 63
Matt, Susan, 119, 119–20, 123
Mead, Margaret, 39, 40
meaning, 196–97
  ascribed to emotions, 42
  boredom and, 155–56
  despair and, 201
meaninglessness, 196–97
Medvec, Victoria Husted, 179, 180–81
Melville, Herman, 118
memories, 48, 93, 100, 158, 165, 166, 168
mental health experts, 26
mental illness. *See also specific conditions*
  hidden, 98–99, 101
  shame and, 98–99
Merton, Thomas, 203, 206
Metallica, 71
Micronesia, 51
midlife crisis, 15
"mimetic crisis," 128–30
mimetic desire, 127–28
Mimetic Theory, 125–27
money, 119
morality of emotions, 22–29
Moravia, Alberto, 147–48
morbidity, 12–13
More, Thomas, 202

Mudvayne, 71
Munger, Charlie, 124–25, 126
music, 19–20, 70–72
Mussolini, Benito, 64

Napoleon Bonaparte, 76
narcissism, 91
Nathanson, Donald, 91
National Facility for the Regulation of Regret (NFRR), 182
nausea, 59, 69
negative emotions, 34, 62, 74, 79–81, 112, 200. *See also specific emotions*
  clinging to, 148
  cultural messages about, 115
  gratitude for, 166
  moral neutrality towards, 200
  morality and, 22–24, 200
  Positive Psychology and, 27–29
  respect for, 163–64
  wisdom of, 79
negativity, 12–13, 18–19
nervous system, 39, 42, 57, 60, 71, 96, 139
neuroscience, 47, 51
neuroticism, 74
New York City, living in, 57–62, 67–68, 72–73, 74–75, 78, 105–6, 167
The New York Times, 202
Nietzsche, Friedrich, 148
ningaq, 52, 53
noise, 69, 70–72, 74–76, 81
Noriega, Manuel, 70
Northern Ireland, 69
nostalgia, 48, 49, 158. *See also memories*
Nunavut, Canada, 30–33
NYPD, 72

Oates, Joyce Carol, 202, 205
Occupy Wall Street protesters, 72

One, Two, Three, 70
openness, 151
Oppen, George, 208
Orloff, Judith, 27
Orpheus and Eurydice, story of, 162–63, 185
Oscar the Grouch, 63
oversensitivity, 63

pain, 211
Palca, Joe, 65
Palestinians, 71
panic attacks, 103–4
Papua New Guinea, 50–51
passions, 26
perceptions, 35
"period of disorientation," 13
personality, vs. temperament, 74
pessimism, 12–13, 28, 124, 189
phenomenologists, 34
philosophers, 34
physiology, 25–26, 36, 37, 39, 45–47, 51
Pieslak, Jonathan, 69–70, 71
Pintupi, 51
Plutchik, Robert, 64–65
Ponticus, Evagrius, 24, 153
Portuguese, 50
"positional goods," 126
positive emotions, 22, 27–28. *See also specific emotions*
Positive Psychology, 27–28
prayer, 153
pride
    despair and, 202, 203
    parental, 139
    as sin, 24, 202
    Stoics and, 139
Prospect Theory, 177–79
psychologists, 26, 34
psychology, 22, 38–40, 45, 74
psychosis, 84–85, 103

psychotherapy, 17–18
public relations, 122–23

qiquq, 52

reading, 208–9
Reddy, William, 114
regret, 13, 48, 49, 161–86
    of action, 177, 178–79, 181
    "adaptive function" of, 166
    addictive element to, 183, 185
    compulsion and, 182–83
    as dialectic of suffering, 183
    distress and, 171, 172, 183, 184
    dual nature of, 177
    familiarity of, 181
    freshness of, 180–81
    hatred for, 184–85
    imagination and, 183–84
    of implication, 177
    of inaction, 177, 180–81
    as inevitable emotion, 175
    as instrument spotlighting mistakes, 172, 173
    leading to behavioral change, 169
    literature on, 168
    living without, 176–77
    as looking back, 182
    memory and, 165
    metastatization of, 180–81
    pain of, 183
    poor reputation of, 170
    purpose of, 167–68
    "regret-related disturbances," 182
    revisionist accounts of, 170–71
    as self-blame, 182
    self-corrective theory of, 169
    as stopgap measure, 168

regret (*cont.*)
    as warning signal, 168–69
    wisdom of, 168–69, 171, 176
remorse, 164–65, 168
renewal, 207
repetition, 154–55
repression, 73
"resentful longing," 109
resentment, 48, 109, 151
resignation, 73, 78
Richter, Gerhard, 7
Roethke, Theodore, 212
Rooney, Andy, 13
Rosenwein, Barbara, 112–14
Ross, Alex, 70
Russia, 50

sadness, 24, 40, 50, 64
satire, 64
saudade, 50
secrecy, 98–99, 131. *See also* shame
Seinfeld, 63
self-annihilation, 205
self-awareness, 132
self-blame, 172, 182
self-control, 31–33, 42, 52
self-deception, 211–12
self-defense, 131–32
self-exposure, risking, 102, 103
self-loathing, 100
self-love, 203
self-pity, 203
self-preservation, 73
self-reproach, 177
Seligman, Martin, 28
senses, hierarchy of, 69
Sesame Street, 63–64
seven deadly sins, 24
shame, 13, 60, 79, 82–104, 106, 198
    ambiguity and, 90
    atmospherics of, 95
    boredom and, 151
    causes of, 102
    causing, 94–95
    communicability of, 95–97
    deception and, 102
    despair and, 200
    diversion and, 91
    epidemiology of, 95
    etymology of, 91
    furtiveness and, 90
    inheritance of, 95–97, 102, 104
    mental illness and, 98–99, 101
    treatment of, 102
sins, emotions as, 24, 202
Smith, Adam, 95
Smith, David, 10, 74–75
Smith, Tiffany Watt, 50, 116
Smithson, Robert, 7
social constructionists, 34, 48, 50
social media, 126–28, 129
Socrates, 74
Solomon Robert, 26
"sonic irritation," 69–72, 74–76
"sops," 131
Spears, Britney, 71
Spenser, Edmund, 24
Spinoza, Baruch, 25, 157, 191
spite, 22–23
Steinberg, Saul, 152
Still Face study, 86–89
Stoics, 23, 80–81, 143
Stone, Lori, 26
suicidal ideation, 193–94, 200
suicide, 204–5
surprise, 40, 64, 65
sympathy, 97

taste, 71
teenagers, 72
temperament, 61, 63
    vs. personality, 74
    power of, 80–81
Theory of Constructed Emotion, 46–47, 48

Thiel, Peter, 127–28, 129
Thomas, Alexander, 74
Thomas Aquinas, 24, 202
Thoreau, Henry David, 161–62, 208, 209
Throbbing Gristle, 70
time, passage of, 15–17
tolerance, 72–73
Tompkins, Silvan, 96
torture, 69
trauma, 188, 198
trees, study of, 209–10, 211–12, 213–14
triangulated desire, 126–27
Tronick, Ed, 86–89
trust, 84
truth, gift of, 17
Turkey, 50
Tversky, Amos, 177–79
Tzintzuntzan, 109–11, 112, 116, 119

uluru, 52
uncertainty, 44, 180
U.S. Air Force, Survival, Evasion, Resistance, and Escape (SERE) program, 69–70
U.S. Army, 70

Utku (Utkuhikhalingmuit), 30–32, 42, 51–53

Veblen, Thorstein, 120–21
Victoria, 118

Wallace, David Foster, 155–56
War on Terror, 71
Warner Brothers cartoons, 63
Wheel of Emotions, 65
White, E. B., 60, 145
Winnicott, D. W., 98
wisdom, 168, 180, 198, 208
  of anger, 165–66
  of negative emotions, 79
  of regret, 168, 171, 176
  of remorse, 165
withdrawal, 86–89, 91–93
writing, 156–57, 189–93, 195, 198

Zappa, Frank, 71
Zeelenberg, Marcel, 168, 169–71, 172–74, 178
Zuckerberg, Mark, 127–28, 129

ABOUT THE AUTHOR

Daniel Smith is a psychotherapist and *New York Times* bestselling author. His books include *Monkey Mind* and *Muses, Madmen, and Prophets*, and his essays, articles, and fiction have appeared in *The New Yorker, The New York Times Magazine, The Atlantic,* and *Harper's Magazine,* among other publications. He lives with his family in Brooklyn.